THE YOUNG TURKS

THE
YOUNG TURKS

THE COMMITTEE OF
UNION AND PROGRESS IN
TURKISH POLITICS
1908–1914

FEROZ AHMAD

OXFORD
AT THE CLARENDON PRESS
1969

Oxford University Press, Ely House, London, W. 1

GLASGOW NEW YORK TORONTO MELBOURNE WELLINGTON
CAPE TOWN SALISBURY IBADAN NAIROBI LUSAKA ADDIS ABABA
BOMBAY CALCUTTA MADRAS KARACHI LAHORE DACCA
KUALA LUMPUR SINGAPORE HONG KONG TOKYO

PRINTED IN GREAT BRITAIN

TO
MY MOTHER AND
FATHER

PREFACE

THIS book is a study of a political society called the Committee
of Union and Progress (*İttihad ve Terakki Cemiyeti*) between
the years 1908 and 1914. Because of the role it played in the
Young Turk revolution which forced Sultan Abdülhamid[1] to
restore the 1876 Constitution, the CUP emerged as the dominant
political group in the Ottoman Empire. But the Committee's
position did not remain unchallenged for long. Political forces
which had previously been obscured by the struggle against the
Palace came to the surface, and there began a period of political
activity, socio-economic change, and debate unequalled in the
history of modern Turkey.

This study endeavours to show that, though the Committee
emerged from the revolution as the most powerful single group,
its monopoly of political power was not automatically guaranteed.
Political and social conditions prevailing within and outside the
Empire forced the CUP to share power with such traditional
ruling groups as the bureaucratic élite, symbolized by the Sublime
Porte (*Babıâli*) and the army. Furthermore, the Committee was
not a monolithic political organization, and the internal divisions
prevented it from putting up a united front and assuming power.
It was only in 1913–14 that the Committee succeeded in resolving
the major internal conflicts and cleavages. In the six years under
review, the social and political attributes of the CUP were also
undergoing constant change. By 1914 the Committee had nar-
rowed down its affiliations and was in a position to establish the
so-called 'triumvirate' of Enver, Talât, and Cemal. These figures
were in themselves manifestations of factions in the CUP.

This book is based on a study which was accepted by the
University of London as a Ph.D. thesis. It has been thoroughly
revised and much new material has been added. The original
study was written under the guidance of Professor Bernard
Lewis, who not only supervised but always encouraged and
inspired. It is my very pleasant duty to express my thanks and

---

[1] A very brief sketch of most of the personalities encountered in the text is
given in the Biographical Appendix.

acknowledge my gratitude to him. The thesis was revised while I was Senior Reseach Fellow at the School of International Affairs, Columbia University, New York, during the year 1966–7. I should like to thank Dean Andrew Cordier and the School for their generous hospitality and for a most pleasant year. At Columbia it was my good fortune to work with Professor Dankwart A. Rustow, and the study owes much to his innumerable suggestions and vast store of knowledge. My grateful thanks are due to Professor Rustow for putting at my disposal both his time and his notes gathered over the years. I wish to thank Professor J. C. Hurewitz for reading my manuscript and making many helpful suggestions; and Professor Charles Issawi for valuable advice on technical matters. It is also my pleasure to acknowledge my debt to Dr. Mohammad Sadiq of Aligarh University, who was both a colleague and a friend while we researched in Turkey, and who helped my researches in a number of ways. Let me also express my thanks to the staffs of the Public Record Office, the library of the School of Oriental and African Studies, the Senate House Library (London); and the libraries of Belediye and Beyazıt (Istanbul). Finally, it remains for me to thank my wife without whose active help and good humour this book would never have been completed.

CONTENTS

ABBREVIATIONS

AA	*Aylık Ansiklopedi*
Bell.	*Belleten* (Journal of the Turkish Historical Society)
BD	*British Documents on the Origins of the War, 1898–1914* (eds. G. P. Gooch and Harold Temperley)
BSOAS	*Bulletin of the School of Oriental and African Studies*
CHJ	*Cambridge Historical Journal*
CR	*Contemporary Review*
DDF	*Documents Diplomatiques Français, 1871–1914* (ed. Ministère des Affaires Étrangères)
EI¹, EI²	*Encyclopaedia of Islam*, 1st and 2nd editions
FR	*Fortnightly Review*
GDD	*German Diplomatic Documents, 1871–1914* (ed. E. T. S. Dugdale)
İA	*İslâm Ansiklopedisi*
MEA	*Middle Eastern Affairs*
MEJ	*Middle East Journal*
MES	*Middle Eastern Studies*
NC	*The Nineteenth Century*
PRO	Public Record Office (London)
Res. Tar. Mec.	*Resimli Tarih Mecmuası*
RMM	*Revue du monde musulman*
Tar. Dün.	*Tarih Dünyası*
YT	*Yakın Tarihimiz*
WI	*Welt des Islams*

NOTES ON TRANSCRIPTION
PLACE-NAMES, AND DATES

In the following pages, the official modern Turkish orthography has been used for transcribing Turkish in the Latin script, except when quoting directly from foreign sources. Some notes on pronunciation based mainly on G. L. Lewis, *Teach Yourself Turkish*, 3rd ed. (1959), are given as an aid to readers unacquainted with Turkish.

c—*j* as in *jam*.

ç—*ch* as in *church*.

b, d as in English, though at the end of a syllable they are usually pronounced and sometimes written p, t (e.g. Recep, Ragıp, Cahit, and Cavit for Receb, Ragıb, Cahid, and Cavid). All are correct and therefore the reader will come across both versions in the text.

ğ—soft g lengthens the preceding vowel.

ı—something like *u* in *radium*.

ö—French *eu* as in *deux* or *seul*.

ş—*sh* as in *shut*.

ü—French *u* as in *lumière*.

Modern Turkish place-names have been used in the text; thus Istanbul and not Constantinople, Edirne and not Adrianople, again, except when quoting. The term 'Ottoman' has usually been confined to official usage: e.g. 'Ottoman Government', 'Ottoman army'. The terms Turkey, Turkish, Turks were used whenever they seemed more suitable for conveying the intended meaning.

In the Ottoman Empire at this period four different calendars were in use. There was the *Hicri*, the Turkish Solar *Hicri*, the Julian, and the Gregorian. I have standardized the dates using the Gregorian calendar, with few exceptions.

I

THE ANTECEDENTS OF THE
REVOLUTION OF 1908

EARLY in February 1908 a student at the Salonika Law School wrote to a relative in Manastır that he had been asked by his friends at the School to join a secret society. The membership of this society would involve the swearing of a sacred oath and the acceptance of prohibited literature. The relative, a minor judicial functionary, submitted the letter to the authorities who investigated the matter. Their inquiry led to the arrest of some ten law students and about the same number of junior officers from the Third Army Corps stationed at Salonika. They were carefully interrogated, and a long and thorough investigation followed. After some weeks most of the detainees were released, though Nâzım Bey, chief of the military police in Salonika and the officer who conducted the inquiry, detained one or two of the junior officers.[1]

The failure of the authorities to unearth the secret society is proof of the stringent precautions taken by the Committee of Union and Progress in the initiation of its new members. It also reveals the power the Committee had acquired among some of the higher officials in Macedonia, many of whom are said to have co-operated to quash Nâzım Bey's inquiry. It is no coincidence that Manyasizâde Refik, an active and influential Unionist and Minister of Justice in Kâmil Paşa's Cabinet, was one of the principle lecturers at the Law School, while Azmi Bey, the Director of the School, and Hacı Âdil Bey, a lecturer and director at the Customs House, were both members of the CUP. The lenient treatment of the law students may be attributed to the influence of these men.

[1] Annual Report, 1908, enclosure in Sir Gerard Lowther to Sir Edward Grey, no. 105 con., Pera, 17 Feb. 1909, F.O. 371/768/7053. Because of its secret nature this incident does not seem to have found a place in any Turkish source. Yet it may explain why there was an attempt to assassinate Nâzım Bey soon after. See below, p. 2.

In May 1908 the Committee of Union and Progress considered coming out into the open and taking charge of the situation in Macedonia. They held a meeting in Salonika and decided that they should reveal to the Great Powers the existence and influence of their society. The Powers should be told that the Committee alone could bring peace to Macedonia and therefore Europe should abandon its futile schemes of reform. The Unionists drew up a manifesto and sent it to the consuls of the Powers.[1] There was no reponse from the Powers; they could hardly acknowledge the manifesto of an illegal secret organization whose strength they did not know. But it seems that the Committee had decided on positive action, so that when the insurrection broke out in July the Committee was in a position to direct it.[2]

The immediate and short-term motive for the revolutionary outbreaks of June–July 1908 seems to have been self-preservation. The Committee, alarmed at the success of Abdülhamid's espionage network, decided to take swift and drastic measures against agents of the Palace in Macedonia. Failure to silence them could mean the destruction of the entire secret organization. Colonel Nâzım, who had conducted the February inquiry and made his report to the Palace, was the first agent on the list for assassination. On 11 June, Nâzım Bey was shot and wounded but could leave for Istanbul next day.[3]

The attempt on Nâzım Bey's life coincided with the meeting of Edward VII and Nicholas II at Reval. They discussed Anglo–Russian relations and agreed on a joint initiative to introduce far-reaching reform in order to end the anarchy prevailing in Macedonia. But no reform scheme was drawn up.[4] In the Ottoman

---

[1] Consul-General Lamb to Grey, T. P., Salonica, 23 July 1908, F.O. 371/544/25634; Ali Cevat, *İkinci Meşrutiyetin İlânı ve Otuzbir Mart Hadisesi* (1960),158, and E. F. Knight, *The Awakening of Turkey* (1909), 130.

[2] Accounts written after the event state that the Committee had decided to stage a coup. See Knight, op. cit. 133; Annual Report, 1908; C. R. Buxton, *Turkey in Revolution* (1909), 53–4; Sir Edwin Pears, *Forty Years in Constantinople* (1916), 287.

[3] Halil Menteşe, 'Eski Meclisi Mebusan Reisi Halil Menteşenin Hatıraları', *Cumhuriyet*, 17 Oct. 1946; İsmail Hami Danişmend, *İzahlı Osmanlı Tarihi Kronolojisi*, iv, 2nd ed. (1961), 361; A. Sarrou, *La Jeune Turquie et la révolution* (1912), 16–17; E. E. Ramsaur, *The Young Turks: Prelude to the Revolution of 1908* (1957), 132–3.

[4] C. P. Gooch and H. W. V. Temperley (eds.), *British Documents on the Origins of the War, 1898–1914*, v (1928), 232–46. Russian account of the Reval meeting in M. Isvolski to Count Benckendorff, ibid. 245–6. See also

Empire this meeting was interpreted as the prelude to Anglo–Russian collaboration and intervention in Macedonia. There was alarm and apprehension and Niyazi Bey, who initiated the insurrection in July, is reported to have had three sleepless nights after the Reval meeting.[1] Reval, then, provided a further reason for changing the government and introducing reform before the Powers did so. It gave a greater sense of urgency to the constitutionalists already stirred by the Sultan's repressive measures.

In Europe the Reval meeting was seen as the event which triggered off the revolution. This was because few people in Europe, indeed in Macedonia itself, were aware of the secret societies at work in the Empire. They noticed that the revolutionary outbursts coincided with the Reval meeting and concluded that the former was directly related to the latter.[2] But this was not the whole story though it has almost acquired the status of a 'historical fact'. M. Steeg, French delegate on the Macedonian Financial Commission, and someone who knew the situation wrote:

Je suis persuadé cependant, que la question des réformes n'était que secondaire, et que le mouvement visait essentiellement le régime hamidien, c'est-à-dire l'absolutisme et la corruption du Palais. La question des réformes macédoniennes n'est certainement pas au premier des préoccupations des membres du comité.[3]

In the same way Europe thought that the constitutional movement was directed from Europe by Ottoman exiles with whom they were familiar. But nothing could have been further from the truth.[4] It is impossible to deny the psychological significance of

A. W. Ward and C. P. Gooch (eds.) *The Cambridge History of British Foreign Policy, 1783–1919*, iii (1923), 399–401.

[1] Knight, op. cit. 153; Ward and Gooch, op. cit. 400; *WI*, vi (1961), 265–6; Danişmend, *Kronoloji*, iv. 360.

[2] Ibid. See also Goschen to Grey, no. 94 con., Vienna, 22 July 1908, F.O. 371/544/26021, especially enclosures from the Austrian and German press. Annual Report, 1908, 2–3 (op. cit., p. 1, n. 1).

[3] M. Steeg to M. George Louis, Uskub, 30 July 1908. Ministère des Affaires Étrangères, *Documents Diplomatiques Français, 1871–1914* (1950–6), 2ᵉ série, xi, no. 419, 719–22 (hereafter cited as *DDF*). See also General di Robilant's—the Italian commander of the *gendarmerie*—report on the internal situation and the CUP. Enclosure no. 3 in Barclay to Grey, no. 392 con., Therapia, 16 July 1908, F.O. 371/544/25303. See also Ramsaur, *Young Turks*, 134.

[4] Ali Haydar Midhat, *Hatıralarım* (1946), 189. Ramsaur, *Young Turks*, 129–30.

Reval on the reformers. But the origins of the insurrection must be sought elsewhere.

Nâzım Bey, who was shot in Salonika on 11 June, returned to Istanbul and submitted his findings to the Palace. After hearing Nâzım's report the Sultan ordered another commission of inquiry to be sent to Salonika, ostensibly to inspect the arsenals of the Third Army, in reality to unearth the secret societies.[1] Upon the arrival of Mahir Paşa's commission in Salonika events began to move with increased momentum. Esat Paşa, Commander-in-Chief of the Third Army, and Ali Rıza Paşa, his Chief of Staff, were recalled to Istanbul. They were held primarily responsible for the disaffection in the Third Army, and the Palace calculated that if they were replaced by new officers loyal to the Sultan, who would impose stricter discipline, the movement in the army would collapse.[2] İbrahim Paşa, who had been a reactionary earlier, replaced Esat Paşa. But now as commander of the Third Army he co-operated with the liberal Hilmi Paşa, Inspector-General of Macedonia. They made representations to the Palace to have the commission recalled, and early in July Mahir Paşa was summoned to the capital.[3] Some subordinate members of his commission were left behind, but they proved to be ineffective against the Committee's policy of terrorism.

Mahir Paşa had little success in uncovering the secret societies, and the organization of the CUP in Salonika remained intact. In Istanbul, however, he caused some confusion by denouncing Hilmi Paşa and other high officials in Macedonia of treasonable activities. He even accused the Grand Vezir Avlonyalı Ferid Paşa's son-in-law, Ali Paşa. He may well have been right but his reward for being so bold was exile to Bursa.[4]

In another part of Macedonia the Sultan's espionage met with greater success. The Palace agent in Manastır, the Military Chaplain (*alay müftüsü*) of the army units stationed there, succeeded in infiltrating the conspiratorial group led by Adjutant-Major Niyazi. Niyazi was already known to the secret police and had once been cited before a court-martial. But on account of a lack of evidence he had been acquitted, and against the advice of

[1] Ahmed Bedevî Kuran, *Osmanlı İmparatorluğunda İnkılâp Hareketleri ve Millî Mücadele* (1959), 466; Ramsaur, *Young Turks*, 134; Cevat, 158; Annual Report, 1908 (op. cit., p. 1, n. 1).

[2] Annual Report, 1908. These events not mentioned elsewhere.

[3] Ibid.   [4] Barclay to Grey, no. 392 (op. cit., p. 3 n. 3).

the *vali* of Manastır he had been allowed to return to his post at Resne. The mufti's discovery forced him to act before his group was broken up. He set about organizing his rebellion and called a secret meeting for 28 June. The mufti, who was returning to Istanbul to make his report, was shot and seriously wounded on 12 July.[1] The meeting that Niyazi had called for 28 June met at the house of a certain Hacı Ağa. At this meeting Niyazi announced his intention to proclaim open revolt against the Palace and to fight for the re-establishment of the constitution. The problem was discussed and the date for the insurrection was set for Friday 3 July.[2] When the meeting was over Niyazi sent Kemal Efendi to Manastır 'to apprise the central Committee in that town of Niyazi's plan and to obtain permission to carry it out. . . . Within two days Cemal returned . . . with the required permission from the central Committee and Niyazi made preparations for the fateful Friday.'[3] He informed other local conspiratorial units of his plan and gave them their instructions.[4]

On 3 July, while most of the officers of the garrison were away at Friday prayers, Niyazi and his men helped themselves to arms, ammunition, and the treasury chest and took to the hills. Niyazi took with him about 200 regular soldiers and about the same number of irregulars and civilians.[5] Among the civilians with

[1] Menteşe, *Cumhuriyet*, 17 Oct. 1946; Danişmend, *Kronoloji*, iv. 361; Vice-Consul Heathcote to Barclay, Monastir, 13 July 1908, enclosure in Barclay to Grey, no. 400 con., Therapia, 20 July 1908, F.O. 371/544/25649; Knight, op. cit. 151. Menteşe gives 7 July as the date of the abortive assassination, op. cit.

[2] Kuran, *Osmanlı*, 465; Menteşe, *Cumhuriyet*, 17 Oct. 1946; Knight, op. cit. 154.

[3] Knight, op. cit. 157; Ahmed Niyazi, *Hatırat-ı Niyazi* (1910), 236. At the 1908 CUP Congress, the Central Committee decided to continue serializing Niyazi's memoirs, prohibiting the publication of all others. See T. Z. Tunaya, *Türkiye'de Siyasî Partiler, 1859–1952* (1952), 207, clause 4. Though these memoirs are valuable as a source for this period their political bias must not be forgotten: to exaggerate the role of the Committee in the insurrection, and to make it appear as if the movement was directed at all times and through all stages by the CUP. This is also true of all other Unionist memoirs. The Committee was most conscious of history and even considered having an official history of the movement specially written. But, on account of the turbulent times this project never materialized. See Hüseyin Cahit Yalçın, *Talât Paşa* (1943), 8.

[4] İsmail Hakkı Uzunçarşılı, '1908 Yılında İkinci Meşrutiyetin Ne Suretle İlân Edildiğine dair Vesikalar', *Bell.* xx/77 (1956), 153–4.

[5] Niyazi, op. cit. 236; Uzunçarşılı, *Bell.* xx/77 (1956), 107–8; Danişmend, *Kronoloji*, iv. 361; Kuran, *Osmanlı*, 465 ff.; Military Attaché Surtees to Barclay,

Niyazi there was Hoca Cemal the Mayor of Resne, Tahsin Efendi the tax-inspector, and Tahir Bey the Police Commissioner.[1] The purpose of including civilians was to try to set up an administration which would be able to gather taxes and administer justice. Niyazi seemed to visualize a long-drawn-out struggle against the Palace.

On the day of his flight from Resne Niyazi issued certain manifestos to the authorities of the local towns as well as to *vali* of Manastır and Hilmi Paşa.[2] It is interesting that in all these manifestos Niyazi spoke, not as a representative of the CUP as one might expect, but simply as the leader of 'my 200 men'. This could mean that the Committee had not as yet taken over the direction of the insurrection, and that Niyazi had taken the initiative on his own. The Committee was essentially an urban organization and it was in the towns that it aided the rebellion.

The manifesto of 3 July to the authorities of Ohri stated that the reason for the insurrection was to combat 'the injustices and inequities which our fatherland has been suffering for many years . . . and to force the government to restore the constitution of 1293 [1876]'.[3] Next day, Niyazi issued another manifesto to the authorities warning them that 'the task of feeding and supporting those working for the sacred cause . . . of restoring the constitution was incumbent' on the people'.[4] He appealed to the local people to furnish his men with their basic needs just as they would in wartime. In a separate manifesto to the people of Ohri he asked them to stop paying taxes to the government and to pay them to his men instead. In return he promised to guarantee the security of life, honour, and property.[5] Finally, on 6 July Niyazi appealed to the Bulgarian community around Resne. He asked for their co-operation and active help in the struggle for the Con-

Constantinople, 9 July 1908, enclosure in Barclay to Grey, no. 378 con., Therapia, 9 July 1908, F.O. 371/544/24315; Cevat, op. cit. 159; Knight, op. cit. 153 ff.

[1] Uzunçarşılı, *Bell.* xx/77 (1956), 108; and Heathcote to Barclay, Monastir, 5 July 1908, enclosure in Barclay to Grey, no. 378, ibid.

[2] Niyazi, op. cit. 83–8; Bernard Lewis, *The Emergence of Modern Turkey*, 3rd ed. (1965), 202; Kuran, *Osmanlı*, 465.

[3] Niyazi to the Authorities of Ohri, 3 July 1908, a French translation of the original enclosed in Barclay to Grey, no. 400 con., Therapia, 20 July 1908, F.O. 371/544/25649.

[4] Ibid., 4 July 1908.

[5] Niyazi to the People of Ohri, 4 July 1908 (op. cit., p. 5, n. 5).

stitution, which, he pointed out, would benefit all regardless of race or religion.[1] On the eve of the insurrection Niyazi wrote to a relative to whom he had entrusted his family: 'Rather than live basely, I have preferred to die. I am therefore going out now, with two hundred patriots armed with Mausers, to die for our country.'[2] Niyazi was not being melodramatic. Death was a more probable conclusion for this adventure than salvation of the fatherland.

Niyazi's example was followed by other junior officers—Sadık Bey, Captain Habib, Ziya, Fahri, and İbrahim Şakir to mention a few—the most notable of all being Major Enver, a young officer attached to Hilmi Paşa's staff.[3] Eyüb Sabri, another junior officer, who acquired a reputation as a hero of the movement, is said to have joined Niyazi early in July. In fact he did not take to the hills around Ohri until 20 July, three days before the Constitution was restored.[4] The real importance of these minor military insurrections was that they soon involved the CUP. Without this initiative the Committee might have remained dormant for some time to come; but the Sultan's counter-measures forced it to act. The Committee's first act of participation was its manifesto of 6 July 'to the *vali* of the illegal government' in Manastır.[5] Thereafter the initiative passed into the hands of CUP organizations in the towns of Macedonia where the outcome of the constitutional movement was decided.

When the news of Niyazi's insurrection reached Istanbul, the Palace became aware of the extent of the constitutional movement. To begin with, the Sultan and his advisers had looked upon the situation in Rumelia as the work of a discontented group. They had been content to crush the conspiracy by means of the secret police. But now that the conspiracy had become a rebellion, the Sultan called in the army to crush it. The first reaction of the

---

[1] Niyazi to the Bulgarians of Resne, 5 July 1908; Niyazi, op. cit. 104–8; translation from the Bulgarian original enclosed in ibid., no. 408 con., Therapia, 22 July 1908, F.O. 371/544/25912.

[2] Niyazi, op. cit. 73; letter dated 20 June 1334 o.s. (3 July 1908); B. Lewis, *Emergence*, 204.

[3] Niyazi, op. cit. 236; Kuran, *Osmanlı*, 466; Knight, op. cit. 183; Heathcote to Barclay, enclosure in Barclay, no. 400 (op. cit., p. 6, n. 3); see also Ramsaur, 134; and Enver's letter in the *Neue Freie Presse*, 8 July 1908, quoted in *The Times* of 16 July.

[4] Uzunçarşılı, *Bell.* xx/77 (1956), 161–4.

[5] Text of the manifesto in Tunaya, *Partiler*, 137–9; French translation in Barclay, no. 408; Cevat, op. cit. 159.

Palace was to begin an inquiry and to learn exactly what was happening around Manastır.[1] Meanwhile General Şemsi Paşa was ordered to proceed to the scene of the rebellion, and to crush the movement with all means available.[2] On 7 July Şemsi Paşa was passing through Manastır on his way to deal with the rebellion. He had just telegraphed his plan of operation to the Palace, when, as he was getting into his carriage outside the post office, he was assassinated.[3] This event has rightly been regarded as the first positive step towards the constitution. It struck a blow at the Sultan's despotism by killing one of his most trusted generals. At the same time it saved Niyazi Bey from pursuit and destruction, and gave the constitutional movement a chance to broaden its base. It is quite probable that had Şemsi Paşa been permitted to proceed against Niyazi, he would have crushed the rebellion.

The assassination of Şemsi Paşa was a desperate and dangerous step for the Committee to take. It was one thing to assassinate a Palace spy, but quite another thing to kill a general of the Ottoman army. In resorting to such action, the Committee risked conflict with Şemsi Paşa's, men. After the assassination, the British Consul in Manastır wrote:

For a time there was great excitement in the town, especially as to the probable action of the late General's own men, a body of some thirty Albanians armed with mausers and apparently dressed as soldiers, but, as I am assured, not belonging to the army. There was, of course, good reason to fear that the band of bashibozouks might wish to avenge their master. . . .[4]

The CUP was greatly alarmed at the measures which might be taken to crush their movement. To the rank and file in the army the rebellion at Resne was presented by the Palace as a Serbian insurrection, while the CUP was presented as being pro-Christian and anti-Islam.[5] To the Powers, the CUP was described as a nationalist movement which was both anti-Christian and anti-European. The

[1] Kuran, *Osmanlı*, 466; Uzunçarşılı, *Bell.* xx/77 (1956), 108.
[2] Kuran, *Osmanlı*, 466; Cevat, op. cit. 159.
[3] Kuran, *Osmanlı*, 469; Cevat, op. cit. 154; Uzunçarşılı, *Bell.* xx/77 (1956), 109–10; B. Lewis, *Emergence*, 204; Süleyman Külçe, *Firzovik Toplantısı ve Meşrutiyet* (1944), 37–45; and Ali Hamdi, 'Fedai Âtıf Bey ve Şemsi Paşanın Katli', *Resimli Tarih Mecmuası*, lxv (May 1955), 3828–31.
[4] Heathcote to Barclay, Monastir, 8 July 1908, enclosure in Barclay to Grey, no. 388 con., Therapia, 15 July 1908, F.O. 371/544/25086.
[5] Knight, op. cit. 196.

başı-bozuks (civilian irregular troops) with Şemsi Paşa's force were
to be used against the Christian population in Macedonia either to
bring about a civil war or a massacre of the Christians, in both
cases making foreign intervention inevitable.[1]

Right from the start the CUP worked to destroy its anti-
Christian, anti-foreign image. On 12 July, a captain in the army,
a member of the Committee, visited the British Consul in Manastır:

He declared that no hostile action whatever is intended against the
Christians. His object in calling on me was to enquire what would be
the view of the matter taken by the British Government, especially if
some Constitutional Government could be settled here locally. He
laid great stress on the desire of his party to return to the traditional
policy of friendship with Great Britain, and in this connection he said
that no enquiries of this nature were to be addressed to the Consulates
of the other Powers here.[2]

On the same day the Committee at Manastır sent manifestos in
French to all the Consulates of the Great Powers. The manifestos
pointed out that agents of the Palace were active in sowing seeds of
distrust amongst the diverse elements of the Empire and the CUP
had counteracted these. The fundamental aim of the Committee
was to have the Constitution of 1876 restored. The Committee
was in no way hostile to the non-Muslims, whose rights it would
guarantee constitutionally. If it did use force it was only against
the enemies of liberty and in self-defence. It was averse to blood-
shed but feared that the Government at Istanbul might precipitate a massacre of the non-Muslims and place the responsibility
for it on the Committee. The CUP bands, far from attacking
villages had protected them from the incursions of other bands,
and they had always propagated fraternity amongst all the elements. The Government had shown its complete lack of scruples
by dispatching *başı-bozuks* with Şemsi Paşa. The employment of
başı-bozuks, who understood no law and only sought to pillage,
proved the mistake of the Great Powers in giving friendly counsels to the Porte.[3]

[1] See the Committee's denial of these charges in their manifesto to the European Consuls in Manastır, enclosure in Barclay, no. 408 (op. cit., p. 7 n. 1).
[2] Heathcote to Barclay, Monastır, 13 July 1908, enclosure in Barclay, no.
400 (op. cit., p. 6, n. 3).
[3] Manifesto, Barclay, no. 408 (op. cit., p. 6, n. 3).

The replacement for Şemsi Paşa, *müşir* Osman Paşa, arrived in Manastır on 12 July 1908. But he proved to be ineffective against the Committee because his troops were no longer loyal and refused to fire on their comrades. At the same time, the supporters of the Government in the administration were becoming demoralized.[1] The Committee, meanwhile, was consolidating its position. The Bulgarian population in Rumelia was by and large on the side of the Committee. The Muslims were slowly won over too. By mid July, the Committee's position in Rumelia seemed impregnable. About ten days before the Constitution was restored, Hilmi Paşa wrote to the Palace that almost all of the officers of the Third Army were connected with the CUP. He advised the Sultan to release the two officers he was holding on suspicion of conspiring against the Palace, or events in Macedonia would take a turn for the worse. The two officers were duly released.[2] The Committee kept the forces loyal to the Sultan in check by a policy of terrorism. On 6 July, Hakkı Bey, a member of Mahir Paşa's inquiry commission, was assassinated in Salonika. On 10 July, the army chaplain from Manastır was shot in Salonika *en route* for Istanbul. Two days later, Sadık Paşa, the Sultan's A.D.C., was shot aboard the ship *Sidon* while going to the capital. Osman Hidâyet Paşa, Commandant of the Manastır garrison, was shot while reading a proclamation from the Sultan.[3] The situation seemed to be out of the Sultan's control. He tried to restore his authority by sending loyal troops from Anatolia against the rebels. Between 15 and 24 July, 18,000 Anatolian troops were sent, but they proved to be no more effective than the Macedonians.[4]

On 20 July, the Muslim population of Manastır rose in support of the constitution and seized the military stores.[5] The *vali* of Manastır, Hıfzı Paşa, had already written to the Palace and said

[1] Annual Report, 1908, enclosure in Lowther, no. 105 (op. cit., p. 1 n. 1); Cevat, op. cit. 159.

[2] Hilmi Paşa's letter in Uzunçarşılı, *Bell.* xx/77 (1956), 135; other officials also wrote to the Palace about the serious situation in Macedonia. See Cevat, op. cit. 159.

[3] Menteşe, *Cumhuriyet*, 17 Oct. 1946; Danişmend, *Kronoloji*, iv. 361; Barclay to Grey, no. 425 con., Constantinople, 28 July 1908, F.O. 371/544/26958.

[4] Cevat, op. cit. 159; Annual Report, 1908 (op. cit., p. 1, n. 1); Uzunçarşılı, *Bell.* xx/77 (1956), 111; C. R. Buxton, op. cit. 52; and Pears, *Forty Years*, 203, write that the Committee had sent Nâzım Bey to İzmir, where he infiltrated the ranks of the army in the guise of a tabacco seller (or *hoca*) and subverted the troops.

[5] Annual Report (op. cit., p. 1, n. 1); Knight, op. cit. 218–19.

that further resistance to the constitutionalists was futile and that the Sultan should restore the constitution. He had been rebuked for his advice and he had therefore tendered his resignation.[1] Risings took place at Gribava, Elasma, Kizano, Köyler, and Şerifiye, and the Albanians assembled at Firzovik in the province of Kosova and took an oath to restore the constitution. They sent an ultimatum to the Sultan demanding the restoration of the Constitution of 1876, threatening to march on Istanbul to depose him if he did not do so.[2]

The Firzovik Incident, generally regarded as an important landmark in the struggle for the constitution, had very strange origins. It began as a demonstration against an excursion, planned and organized by the Austro–German Railway School, to the village of Sarayiçi, renowned for its natural beauty. The workmen who had been sent ahead to prepare the picnic site were driven out, and the demonstrations continued against the local Ottoman officials.[3] The Austro–German excursion was cancelled but the news of the demonstrations at Firzovik reached the *vali* of Kosova, Mahmud Şevket Paşa. He sent the commander of the Kosova *gendarmerie*, a certain Gâlip Bey, to investigate. Gâlip Bey, who happened to be a member of the CUP, informed the general headquarters of the Committee of the prevailing situation, and asked them to exploit it in favour of the constitution. The Albanians were completely unorganized, but amongst them was a certain Hacı Şaban Efendi, a supporter of the CUP. He took charge of the disorganized rabble and harnessed it into a demonstration in favour of the constitution. The result was the demand for the constitution and the ultimatum to the Sultan.[4]

The situation in Macedonia was now completely out of the Palace's control. Hilmi Paşa again sent a cipher telegram to the Sultan on 22 July explaining the gravity of the situation. He reported that the mission of *müşir* Şükrü Paşa and *birinci*

[1] Cevat, op. cit. 160; Barclay to Grey, no. 176 con., Constantinople, 23 July 1908, F.O. 371/544/25618; Knight, op. cit. 192–5.

[2] Külçe, *Firzovik*, 60–1; Tunaya, *Partiler*, 139–41; see also Tunaya, *Hürriyetin İlânı* (1959), 7; Uzunçarşılı, *Bell.* xx/77 (1956), 124–5; Cevat, op. cit. 160.

[3] Vice-Consul Satow to Consul-General Lamb (Salonika), Uskub, 11 July 1908, enclosure in Barclay to Grey, no. 393 con., Therapia, 17 July 1908, F.O. 371/544/25304; see also Külçe, *Firzovik, passim*, and Uzunçarşılı, *Bell.* xx/77 (1956), 124–5.

[4] Uzunçarşılı, *Bell.* xx/77 (1956), 125–6; Cevat, op. cit. 160.

ferik Rahmi Paşa to Rumelia had revealed nothing new. He therefore suggested that the Sultan send one or two chosen ministers and vezirs who could examine the situation on the spot and suggest the remedy.[1] However, by 22 July it was too late for such measures; the Committee had decided to proclaim the constitution. Having established it in Macedonia they hoped to extend it to the rest of the Empire, by force if necessary. As a prelude to a peaceful proclamation, Eyüb Sabri and his men kidnapped Marshal Osman Paşa from Manastır,[2] and next day (23 July) the constitution was proclaimed.[3] On the same day, only a few hours later, the constitution was proclaimed in some of the other towns, such as Preşova, Köprülü, Üsküp, and Serez. A description of a typical proclamation has been left by the British Vice-Consul at Drama:[4]

By the usual train from Salonica there arrived at Drama at or about 1.30 p.m. a hundred soldiers and about twenty officers commanded by a young staff officer named Rushen Bey. . . . Rushen Bey delivered a speech in which he laid great stress on the absolute necessity of establishing a constitutional Government if the Turkish Empire was to be saved from utter ruin, on the abolition of the distinction between race and creed under the Ottoman Government and gave the words '*la patrie, liberté, égalité, fraternité*' as their motto. He then turned to the soldiers and said: 'You are now going into the town to proclaim a constitutional Government; anyone who resists, no matter what his rank and position, is to be shot dead. . . .'

Meanwhile, in the *Konak*, in the mosque, and in the Greek church, the great majority of the population, both Greek and Mussulman, had been swearing fidelity to the Constitution. . . . Finally at 4 p.m. it was proclaimed that the Constitution was accepted, and telegrams were sent to the Sultan, signed greatly against his will by Zia Pasha, the *Mutessarif*.

Salonika, though the ideological centre of the constitutional movement and the headquarters of the Committee of Union and Progress, was the last important town in Macedonia to proclaim the constitution. The Committee had planned to proclaim the

---

[1] Uzunçarşılı, *Bell.* xx/77 (1956), 135–6.

[2] Ibid. 161–4; Cevat, op. cit. 160.

[3] Uzunçarşılı, *Bell.* xx/77 (1956), 161–4; Cevat, op. cit. 160; Tunaya, *Partiler*, 141–2.

[4] Bonham to Barclay, Drama, 23 July 1908, enclosure in Barclay to Grey, no. 423 con., Therapia, 28 July 1908, F.O. 371/544/26956. See also Uzunçarşılı, *Bell.* xx/77 (1956), 168–70.

constitution in Salonika on 27 July if circumstances permitted. But the march of events was so rapid that the date was forwarded to 25 July. On the morning of 24 July, Hilmi Paşa received a telegram from the Grand Vezir, informing him of the Sultan's decision to accede to the wish of his people and restore the constitution. A little after 9 a.m. Hilmi Paşa read the Sultan's *irade* (proclamation) proclaiming the constitution to the salute of a hundred and one guns.[1]

Events in the capital followed a different pattern. After Şemsi Paşa's assassination and the refusal of Anatolian troops to crush the rebellion, the Palace became demoralized and gave up the policy of repression for one of conciliation. In the classical manner this change was manifested by the dismissal of the Grand Vezir— and in this case the 'Minister of War' as well. On 22 July Ferid Paşa and Rıza Paşa were dismissed and replaced by Said and Ömer Rüştü Paşas. Significantly, Ömer Rüştü was appointed Minister of War and not *serasker*, making it appear as though Abdülhamid was establishing a new form of government voluntarily.[2] The Sultan could now make concessions without loss of face; it would appear as if Ferid Paşa had been the stumblingblock. After the constitution was re-established Abdülhamid took the credit for it, telling Midhat Paşa's son that 'the constitution had been established for the good of the country and the nation [in 1876]. . . . But traitors withdrew it and deceived him.'[3] Further discussions took place on the night of 23 July, and telegrams from Macedonia were read reporting the proclamation of the constitution. Faced with what amounted to a *fait accompli*, the Sultan decided to accede to the demand of the rebels and Hilmi Paşa was informed accordingly. On the same day an imperial *irade* was issued in Istanbul restoring to the Ottoman Empire the Constitution of 1876.[4] A new era began.

---

[1] Said Paşa's telegram to Hilmi Paşa, enclosure in Barclay to Grey, no. 430 con., Therapia, 29 July 1908, F.O. 371/545/26961. See also Steeg to Louis, op. cit., *DDF*, xi, no. 419, 719–22.

[2] *Hatt-ı Hümayun* appointing Said Paşa in *Sabah*, 23 July 1908. See also Uzunçarşılı, *Bell.* xx/77 (1956), 136–8; Cevat, op. cit. 160.

[3] Midhat, *Hatıralarım*, 197.

[4] *Hatt-ı Hümayun* restoring the constitution in *Sabah*, 25 July 1908 and its translation enclosed in Barclay to Grey, no. 179 tel. con., Constantinople, 24 July 1908, F.O. 371/544/25753; Uzunçarşılı, *Bell.* xx/77 (1956), 138–43. See also Yusuf Hikmet Bayur, *Türk İnkilâbı Tarihi*, i (1940), 240 ff.

II

THE CONSTITUTIONAL RÉGIME
AND THE COUNTER-REVOLUTION
OF 1909

THE proclamation of the Constitution on 23/4 July 1908[1] was a success beyond all expectations of the Committee of Union and Progress.[2] But as a result of the Sultan's sudden capitulation, the country and its administration were thrown into confusion.[3] The government was completely demoralized and administration virtually came to a standstill. Members of the Cabinet no longer knew what powers they had, and therefore lost all sense of initiative.[4] Meanwhile the people, not knowing what freedom meant, thought that all the old institutions of law and order had come to an end. Having suffered injustices for so long, they decided to take matters into their own hands. The people of Trabzon demanded the dismissal of their *vali* or threatened to drive him out. Fearing the consequences if he refused, Memduh Paşa, the Minister of the Interior, accepted their demand and dismissed the *vali*. In Bursa and Konya, Abdülhamid's agents were arrested and expelled and the *vali*s were given a list of corrupt officials whose dismissals were demanded. The men who took the initiative against the administration were usually political offenders who had been banished to remote provinces by Abdülhamid.[5] Some of them organized Unionist

---

[1] The text of the *irade* (imperial decree) proclaiming the constitution and inviting the Chamber of Deputies to assemble is given in A. S. Gözübüyük and Suna Kili, *Türk Anayasa Metinleri* (1957), 59–60. *Sabah*, 25 July 1908.

[2] Hüseyin Cahit Yalçın, *Talât Paşa* (1943), 16; also Alfred de Bilinski, 'The Turkish Revolution', *NC*, lxiv (1908), 353. 'The re-establishment by Abd-ul-Hamid of the Constitution . . . came as a surprise to everybody, not excepting the chiefs of the Young Turk party, who did not expect such a sudden fruition of their patriotic labours.'

[3] Ali Fuat Türkgeldi, *Görüp İşittiklerim* (1951), 1–4; Yalçın, *Talât Paşa*, 16–17.

[4] Türkgeldi, op. cit. 2–3; Yalçın, *Talât Paşa*, 18.

[5] Türkgeldi, op. cit. 4; Gilbertson to H. C. A. Eyres, Broussa, 28 July 1908,

clubs and represented the provinces of their exile in Parliament. In the capital itself, there was no authority capable of controlling the people who had decided to punish members of the old regime.[1] In this situation there was grave danger of the country drifting into anarchy unless some form of authority was quickly established.

The CUP was the only body with sufficient authority and prestige to control the situation. Within a few days of the revolution, the Committee tried to bring about the destruction of the Palace clique and the vast espionage network.[2] On the advice of Said Paşa, the Grand Vezir, the Sultan proclaimed a general amnesty for all political prisoners and exiles.[3] Within a short time, the Committee had succeeded in clearing the administration of corrupt officials and in replacing them with more liberal men.[4]

At this stage it seemed quite possible for the Committee to assume power directly. The traditional authority of the Sultan had collapsed, while the Committee had the prestige of having carried out a successful insurrection and the mystique of a secret society. But the Committee did not do so. Instead it left power in the hands of the existing Cabinet, and set itself up as a vigilance committee safeguarding the constitution, exercising its power and influence only when it felt the necessity. The Committee's critics have charged it with intervention in government, of exercising power without responsibility.[5] Though there is much truth in this charge, it does not explain why the Committee acted in this way.

The explanation lies in the social background of the Young Turks and in their basic conservatism. They were by and large conservative in outlook with little or no interest in promoting social change. The importance of the 1908 *coup d'état* is not that

and Vice-Consul Doughty-Wylie to Barclay, Konia, 27 July 1908, in F.O. 195/2280. For the breakdown of discipline in the student community, see Kenan Akyüz, *Tevfik Fikret* (1947), 89–90.

[1] Yalçın, *Talât Paşa*, 17.

[2] Midhat Şükrü Bleda, 'Bir Canlı Tarih Konuşuyor', *Resimli Tarih Mecmuası* (June 1953), 2392; Uzunçarşılı, *Bell*. xx/77 (1956), 172–4, gives the text of the decree ending espionage. Barclay to Grey, no. 199 tel. conf., Constantinople, 29 July 1908, F.O. 371/544/26307. File 544 is full of detailed reports of the first days of the constitution.

[3] Uzunçarşılı, *Bell*. xx/77 (1956), 172–4.

[4] Annual Report, 1908, 5–7 (see p. 1, n. 1).

[5] Kâmil Paşa's interview in *Neue Freie Presse*, 18 Feb. 1909, quoted in *FR*, lxxxiv (1909), 397–8. Also Yalçın, *Talât Paşa*, 20; Bleda, *Res. Tar. Mec*.

it was revolutionary in profession; it was not. Its aim was to restore a constitution which had been granted thirty-two years earlier and thereby save the State. The revolutionary nature of the movement emerged later partly as a result of the failure of its pragmatic policies, and partly as an outcome of incidental reform and the social change this brought about.[1] The CUP was a direct extension of the reform movement of the nineteenth century, especially the Young Ottomans,[2] and like them it was concerned only with the problem of how to save the Empire.[3] Fundamentally the Young Turks provided the same answer as the Young Ottomans of the 1860s and 1870s; to introduce constitutional government, thereby curbing the power of the Sultan, and at the same time satisfying the aspirations of the minorities by giving them equal rights within the law.[4] Socially the Young Ottomans had been in a position to assume power once they had forced the Sultan to concede the constitution. They did, after all, come from 'a ruling élite, prepared by education to command and to govern'.[5] The Young Turks shared their social values but not their social position. During the period of Abdülhamid's despotic rule, the base of the reform movement had become much broader. This was brought about by Abdülhamid's reforms.[6] Whereas the Young Ottomans were members and products of the ruling institution, the Young Turks belonged to the newly emerging professional classes; lecturers in the recently founded government,

[1] Bleda (op. cit., p. 15, n. 2); Yalçın, '1908 İnkılâbı İnkılâpçı Değildi', YT, ii/19. 179–80; B. Lewis, Emergence, 208 ff.; and A. H. Mithat, Hatıralarım, 229–33.

[2] The best study of the Young Ottomans is Şerif Mardin's The Genesis of Young Ottoman Thought (1962). There is also Ramsaur, Young Turks, and Tunaya, Partiler, 89–157.

[3] Tunaya, Partiler, 167–74, briefly discusses the different solutions that were offered in answer to how can this state be saved? See also B. Lewis, Emergence, 208–9.

[4] The Young Turks rather naïvely thought that all the complaints of the different elements came from maladministration, oppression, and a lack of freedom. If all these causes of discontent were removed through the Constitution and parliamentary government, the Turkish nation would be saved. Yalçın, Talât Paşa, 14. Yalçın concludes: 'They had never seen in their lives what a parliament looked like, or how it met and discussed. But they secretly believed in the Constitution and the Parliament as one believes in a mighty talisman'.

[5] B. Lewis, Emergence, 201; Mardin, Genesis; deals with the social background of the prominent 'Young Ottomans'. See also Mardin's article in MEJ, xiv (1962), 169–82.

[6] For Abdülhamid's reforms, see B. Lewis, Emergence, 174–90.

colleges, lawyers trained in western law, journalists, minor clerks in the bureaucracy, and junior officers trained in the western-style war colleges. Most of them were half-educated[1] and products of the state schools. The well-educated ones had no experience of administration and little idea about running a government. There was not a single experienced statesman amongst them.[2]

The Young Ottomans, belonging to the ruling élite thought they could save the Empire if they were given the opportunity to govern.[3] The Young Turks, a generation later, did not see in themselves the capacity to rule.[4] Therefore they never considered taking up high governmental posts. Furthermore, the Young Turks knew how conservative was the social environment in which they were operating. Hüseyin Cahit Yalçın, who had been a Unionist deputy for Istanbul as well as a prominent journalist, expressed the Committee's concern for this problem:

This country [he wrote] could not have accepted a young man without rank, decorations, a beard, glory and reputation, rising to the Grand Vezirate. Since the public opinion of the country was such, and since they the Young Turks themselves were made up of the same stuff, it would be unfair to blame them for not assuming power. . . . In July 1908, the CUP could not make a captain or a major Minister of War, nor Talât Bey, a head postal clerk, Grand Vezir. Conditions and circumstances made this impossible. . . . If this in fact had happened, anarchy would certainly have broken out in the country. . . . The members of the CUP realised this and did not take up positions of power.[5]

It is generally assumed that since the Ottoman Empire did not have a class structure like that of Europe, the driving forces in the politics of the individual were his religious and ethnic affiliations. While this analysis is valid for earlier periods of Ottoman history, it no longer holds true for the late nineteenth and early twentieth centuries on account of the social changes that had taken place. Generally speaking, therefore, the importance of the social issues has been underplayed or even ignored in the study of the Young Turk period and social conflict has often been shrouded in religious and ethnic symbols.

Not all observers, however, have fallen into this trap. In *The*

---

[1] Kemal H. Karpat, *Turkey's Politics* (1959), 14 n. 31; Yalçın, *Talât Paşa*, 13–14.   [2] Yalçin, *Talât Paşa*, 14.   [3] B. Lewis, *Emergence*, 201.
[4] Yalçın, *Talât Paşa*, 14.   [5] Ibid. 34–5.

Times of 24 August 1908, the Istanbul correspondent—while recognizing that European classes were not altogether applicable to Ottoman society—described the Young Turk movement as essentially middle class. 'The high officials, generally speaking,' he wrote, 'were hostile to the movement. . . . The lower classes . . . were, as a rule, indifferent. It was among the junior officers of the army and navy, the middle and lower grades of the civil service, the professional classes, and the *ülema*, that the movement for reform carried all before it.' But the opponents of the Committee argued that the Unionists were unfit to rule because they were too young and because they lacked the Ottoman traditions of the Sultanate and the Caliphate. In this very argument the aspect of social class was, of course, implicit. Parallel with the whole question of age and traditional status was the fact that only a few Unionists had the necessary experience or social background to go into the higher ranks of the bureaucracy. Here they were in marked contrast with the Young Ottomans who had already held high positions, and whose principal complaint was that they were not permitted to reach the top. Mehmed Cavit, a high-ranking Unionist who later became Minister of Finance, explained to the First Secretary of the British Embassy that the Young Turks 'were all young men who lacked experience in administrative work, however much they might have studied; also the respect, which in all countries is conceded to age, is far greater here than elsewhere'.[1] This lack of experience proved to be no more than a phobia, for when the Unionists began to assume positions of power they conducted themselves in a remarkably mature manner.

There were other obstacles preventing the Committee from assuming power. One was the lack of a centralized and co-ordinated nation-wide organization. Any real organization that it had was centred in the Macedonian provinces with headquarters at Salonika.[2] When the insurrection succeeded, the limited number of branches in the rest of the Empire were quite unprepared to take control of the administration.[3] During the period of despotism there had been many secret societies. But because of the repression and because of their very nature, they were scattered,

---

[1] Mr. Hohler's conversation with Cavit in Lowther to Grey, no. 384 con., Pera, 26 May 1909, F.O. 371/772/20299. See also A. N. Mandelstam, *Le Sort de l'Empire ottoman* (1917), 24.
[2] See above, Chapter I, *passim*.   [3] Yalçın, *Talât Paşa*, 16.

isolated, and unknown to each other.[1] Once the constitution was proclaimed they all came out into the open, with different policies and without any recognized leadership.[2] Under these conditions the Committee was unable to assume power openly, and power was left formally in the hands of the government of Said Paşa. In reality, this power became the bone of contention between three forces, the Palace, the Sublime Porte, and the Committee.[3]

The first encounter between the executive and the Committee took place early in August. It took place over the right to appoint the Ministers of War and Marine. By implication, Article 27 of, the 1876 Constitution vested this prerogative in the person of the Grand Vezir, his appointments having to be sanctioned by an imperial *irade*.[4] The Sultan appointed only the Grand Vezir and the *Şeyhülislâm*[4]. Article 10 of the *Hatt-ı-Hümayun* of 1 August gave the Sultan the right to make all four appointments.[5] The issue was not merely constitutional; its implications went much deeper. It meant that the person who appointed the two ministers of the armed forces, controlled the armed forces themselves. The Committee, having its main support from the junior officers of the army and navy, realized that its position would be undermined if the Sultan succeeded in establishing a foothold in their preserve. They therefore opposed Clause 10 of the *Hatt* most fiercely and attacked Said Paşa for having drafted it. Said Paşa and his Minister of the Interior, Memduh Paşa, were already regarded with suspicion for having released common criminals along with political prisoners, and also for allowing some of the corrupt officials of the old regime to escape.[6] The Committee had

[1] Ibid. 12.

[2] Ibid. 12. Sarrou, op. cit. 34–5, relates how, immediately after the revolution, the CUP sent a delegation to see the Sultan. Abdülhamid agreed to see the president of the delegation, only to be told that the Committee had no president.

[3] H. C. Yalçın, 'Kudretsiz Bir Hükûmet, Müvesvis Bir Padişah', *YT*, ii/16.75.

[4] Gözübüyük and Kili, op. cit. 27.

[5] The text of the *Hatt-ı-Hümayun* in *Tanin*, 2 Aug. 1908 and *Sabah*, 2 Aug. 1908. The other fourteen clauses of the charter guaranteed the inviolability of domicile, freedom from arbitrary arrest, the grant of permission to travel abroad, and to form commercial associations with foreign subjects. It announced the equality of all Ottomans, without distinction of race or religion, and proclaimed full liberty. It announced that projects for the reorganization of ministries, particularly the ministry of war, and provinces would be prepared and submitted to Parliament.

[6] Türkgeldi, op. cit. 3. According to Türkgeldi, Memduh Paşa only intended to release political prisoners. But at the instigation of Baba Tahir, owner of the *Malûmat*, ordinary criminals threatened violence if they were not released. Mem-

seen these acts as attempts to discredit and endanger the revolution. Clause 10 confirmed their suspicions.[1] The Committee was not alone in opposing Said Paşa and Clause 10. Cemalüddin Efendi, the *Şeyhülislâm*, also found it both unconstitutional and contrary to the oath Abdülhamid had sworn, promising to uphold the constitution.[2] In the Cabinet, Said Paşa justified the clause on the ground that since the Sultan was Commander-in-Chief of the armed forces, it was within his sacred rights to appoint the two ministers.[3] His critics in the Cabinet argued that these offices were not military but civil, and in the past civil servants like Celâl Paşa had held them.[4] Unable to accept Said Paşa's explanation, the *Şeyhülislâm* sent in his resignation, but the Sultan refused to accept it. Said Paşa, faced with such determined opposition, decided to resign himself.[5]

Even before 1 August, the Committee had asked the Sultan, through Hüseyin Hilmi Paşa, to be permitted to send a deputation to the capital in order to discuss the situation.[6] Permission was reluctantly granted and a deputation composed of Talât, Cavit, and Rahmi Beys arrived from Edirne on 1 August.[7] They had a long interview with Said Paşa, but the latter was so rude and outspoken that he even shocked his Minister of the Interior, Hacı Âkif Bey.[8] They then saw Kâmil Paşa and asked that Recep Paşa, *vali* of Tripoli (North Africa), be made War Minister in his ministry.[9] Finally, the deputation visited the Sultan and asked for the formation of another ministry under Kâmil Paşa, with Recep Paşa as Minister of War, and the revision of the *Hatt-ı-Hümayun* of 1 August. Although Kâmil Paşa had accepted Recep Paşa, the

duh Paşa, wishing to avoid further trouble, gave the order to release all criminals, Türkgeldi, op. cit. 2–3. 'Kanunu Esasi Ve Yeni Hatt-ı Hümayun', *Tanin*, 3 and 4 Aug. 1908. Yalçın, *Talât Paşa*, 17, gives the CUP side of the story. Also Lowther to Grey, no. 208 tel. con., Constantinople, 2 Aug. 1908, F.O. 371/544/26789.   [1] Türkgeldi, op. cit. 3.

[2] *Şeyhülislâm* Cemalüddin Efendi, *Hatırat-ı Siyasîye* (1336/19 0), 10–12.

[3] Ibid. To Fitzmaurice, whom he saw on 10 Aug., he said he had to humour the susceptibilities of the Sultan by not insisting on devolving the right to command the land and sea forces, theoretically vested in His Majesty, on ministers appointed by the Grand Vezir. See Lowther to Grey, no. 459 con., Therapia, 10 Aug. 1908, F.O. 371/445/28455. For Said Paşa's defence, see the *Levant Herald*, 25 Aug. 1908.

[4] Cemalüddin, op. cit.   [5] Ibid.; Cevat, op. cit. 8.

[6] Uzunçarşılı, *Bell.* xx/77 (1956), 148–9.

[7] Ibid; Lowther to Grey, no. 448 con., Therapia, 4 Aug. 1908, F.O. 371/545/27644.

[8] Türkgeldi, op. cit. 5.   [9] Uzunçarşılı (op. cit., p. 20 n. 6).

Sultan refused to do so.[1] He regarded Recep Paşa as being too ambitious and independent and therefore preferred to retain Riza Paşa as Minister of War. But under the pressure of the Committee and through the persuasion of Cemalüddin, the Sultan finally gave in.[2]

Said Paşa resigned on 5 August and Kâmil Paşa was appointed Grand Vezir on 6 August and asked to form a Cabinet.[3] Next day there appeared in the Sabah a declaration by the Committee promising full support to the new Cabinet, and asking the people to co-operate in maintaining law and order so as not to provoke foreign criticism.[4] Thus ended the first attempt to find a way out of the anomalous situation. Co-operation between the Committee and the Porte frustrated the Palace's attempt to monopolize power once more. Henceforth power passed into the hands of the Porte, while the Committee continued to play the role of guardian of the constitution, though still not taking an active part in the administration of the Empire.

The business of government and reform began with Kâmil Paşa's ministry. Most of his ministers, except two, were new men, described by the British Ambassador as 'men of experience, ability and energy, enjoying the popularity of all classes'.[5] There was still, however, no one from the Committee.

On 16 August, Kâmil Paşa's programme appeared in the press.[6] It stated that he resolved to govern according to the constitution. But since it was not possible to wait for the Chamber of Deputies to assemble before executing this programme, he intended to modify certain laws of the old regime which were not in conformity with the constitution.

[1] Cemalüddin, op. cit. 12.

[2] Ibid.; for Abdülhamid's assessment of Recep Paşa, see Cevat, op. cit. 8–9 and 10–11.

[3] For Said Paşa's resignation and Kâmil Paşa's appointment, see Tanin and Sabah of 6 and 7 Aug. 1908; Cemalüddin, op. cit. 12–13; Cevat, op. cit. 8; French translation of Hatt in Lowther to Grey, no. 473 con., Therapia, 12 Aug. 1908, F.O. 371/455/28469.

[4] Lowther, loc. cit.; Sabah, 6 and 7 Aug. 1908.

[5] Lowther to Grey, no. 473 con., Therapia, 12 Aug. 1908; F.O. 371/545/28469. The two men Kâmil retained from Said Paşa's Cabinet were Cemalüddin Efendi (Şeyhülislâm) and Tevfik Paşa (Minister of Foreign Affairs). For a list of the Cabinet, see Türkgeldi, op. cit. 5 and Cevat, op. cit. 190–1.

[6] Text of programme in Sabah, 16 Aug. 1908, 'Meclisî Vükelânın Programı'; translation enclosed in Lowther to Grey, no. 494 con., Therapia, 18 Aug. 1908, F.O. 371/546/29298.

On account of the gravity of the financial situation, existing financial laws would be reformed and a rational budget prepared for the coming year. All ministries would be reformed and surplus functionaries would be pensioned off. The army and navy would also be reorganized.

Since reform would require a larger expenditure, the existing system of taxation would have to be reorganized and resources allocated more rationally. Commercial treaties would be revised.

In the spirit of progress, a programme for the development of commerce, industry, public works, and agriculture was under preparation. Scientific progress and education would be encouraged and a law guaranteeing the rights of property would be passed. In the spirit of equality guaranteed by the constitution, military service would be extended to all Ottomans, including non-Muslims.

The Government, already enjoying good relations with all nations, would base its policy on the maintenance of these good relations, as well as the maintenance of the integrity and honour of the Ottoman Empire. The Government would work to bring to an end, with the consent of the interested Powers, the privileges and rights, outside the scope of international law, enjoyed by foreigners in the Ottoman Empire by virtue of the capitulations. To do this the Government would make great efforts to bring all branches of administration to a point where they would inspire confidence amongst all, and therefore would make the privileges enjoyed by foreigners unnecessary.

Kâmil Paşa's programme was nothing less that the proclamation of intent to reform the Ottoman Empire into a modern centralized state.[1] This intention had been stated on earlier occasions, notably in 1839, 1856, and 1876. But little had been done to translate intent into action. By 1908 the situation had changed both in the Empire and the rest of the world. Within the Empire, the threat of secession by the non-Turkish elements was growing day by day, bringing with it the menace of foreign intervention. In Macedonia, where this threat was strongest, there emerged a new social group which saw reform, not as a means of preserving its power as an élite, but as a means of saving the state and bringing it in line with the modern world. With its broader social base, this group was

---

[1] See also the CUP's official programme for 1908, in Tunaya, *Partiler*, 208–10.

less compromising in its relations with the traditional elements and their values, and accepted more readily the necessity of cultural and social change as an essential part of modernization. Externally, Japan's success in becoming and being accepted as a modern power by the rest of the world was possibly the most influential factor in raising Turkish hopes in modernization.[1]

The Young Turks set out to streamline the entire system of administration. The traditional *millet* system, 'whereby the individual carries his law from place to place', being incompatible with the centralized state, was sentenced to death.[2] All Ottomans, regardless of ethnic origins or religion, were granted the same rights and duties. Extra-territorial rights enjoyed by foreigners, being incompatible with the idea of one law for all, were attacked. But the success of this programme hinged on the ability of the new regime to put its finances in order. No one realized this more than the Young Turks.

Kâmil Paşa's programme established a climate of optimism, and it remained only for Parliament to justify it. Meanwhile the Government worked at half-speed, only carrying out measures necessary to keep the administration going. The Palace had followed the policy of appeasing its opponents and rewarding its followers by giving sinecures. As a result, almost all departments of administration were overcrowded with incompetent and corrupt officials.[3] In the interest of both efficiency and economy, Kâmil Paşa made large reductions in the administrative personnel in almost all departments.[4] This measure caused considerable dissatisfaction, and even within the Cabinet not all members were

---

[1] The Young Turks already saw themselves as the 'Japan' of the Near East, and in Nov. 1908 asked the English for an alliance, using the Anglo-Japanese Alliance as a precedent. See Ahmed Rıza and Nâzım Bey's interview with Grey in Grey to Lowther, private, London, 13 Nov. 1908, F.O. 800/185 A (*Grey Papers*). The Young Turks also considered obtaining Japanese experts instead of European ones to help them with the task of modernization. But nothing came of it. See *Yeni Gazete*, cited in Lowther to Grey, no. 546 con., Therapia, 6 Sept. 1908, F.O. 371/559/31790. Sir Charles Hardinge commented that 'the idea would be deeply resented by several of the Great Powers'.

[2] R. E. Ward and D. A. Rustow, *Political Modernisation in Japan and Turkey* (1964), 3–4.

[3] Nâzım Bey's interview in *Pester Lloyd*, 12 May 1910, enclosure in Howard to Grey, no. 40 con., Budapest, 14 May 1910, F.O. 371/1010/19028. Also Annual Report, 1908, 58–9, (op. cit., p. 1 n. 1).

[4] A list of dismissed officials was published in the *Levant Herald*, 10 Aug. 1908; also see Annual Report, 1908, 58–9.

in favour.[1] The Young Turks, however, preferred to spend a few thousand pounds to pension off incompetent and corrupt officials since retaining them reduced efficiency and could cost much more in the long run.[2] This policy took many years to execute. By May 1910, 'about 80 per cent of the Government appointments had been reformed'.[2]

The new regime faced its first major crisis in October 1908. On the 5th, Bulgaria declared her complete independence. Next day, Austria-Hungary announced the annexation of Bosnia and Herzegovina to her Empire. On the same day, Crete announced her decision to unite with Greece.[3] There was little that the Porte could do but protest to the signatories of the Congress of Berlin (1878), since the first two actions were a violation of that treaty, and the position of Crete was also guaranteed by the Powers.[4] The Powers soon made it known that they would not intervene on Turkey's behalf.[5]

These hostile acts aroused great indignation throughout the Ottoman Empire. There were violent articles and much sabre-rattling in the press, but the only positive action taken was the boycott of Austrian goods. As the crisis coincided with the month of *Ramazan*, the Cabinet was not meeting and therefore the matter was not officially discussed.[6] Kâmil, however, convened a meeting at his home and informed his ministers of his attempts to form alliances with Serbia, Rumania, and Greece. Serbia had been in favour, Rumania against, and Greece ambiguous.[7] Kâmil then asked his War Minister if the army could be mobilized for war. Ali Rıza Paşa gave a negative answer, and it was

---

[1] Ekrem Bey, Minister of *Evkâf* and later of Education, also a prominent writer, poet, and critic, resigned from the ministry because he disagreed with this policy of massive purges. See Fahir İz, 'Ekrem Bey', *EI*[2].

[2] Nâzım Bey's interview; F.O. 371/1010/19028 (op. cit., p. 23 n. 3).

[3] Y. H. Bayur, *Tarihi*, i (1940), 245 ff., deals with these problems from the Turkish side. Foreign Office correspondence dealt extensively with these problems too in F.O. 371/550 ff. and F.O. 371/747 ff.

[4] Lowther to Grey, no. 294 con., Constantinople, 5 Oct. 1908, F.O. 371/550/34514.

[5] Grey to Lowther, no. 284 con., Foreign Office, 5 Oct. 1908, F.O. 371/551/34595. The British Government was the only one favourably disposed towards the Porte, and the Porte was guided by her advice. Grey informed Rifat Paşa, the Ottoman Ambassador in London, that Britain would not recognize Bulgarian or Austrian actions until she knew the opinions of the other signatories, especially Turkey. He advised the Porte against war and promised to support Turkish proposals for compensation.

[6] Türkgeldi, op. cit. 10–11.   [7] Ibid. 11.

therefore decided to seek a political solution.[1] The Porte sent telegraphic protests to the Powers and asked them to safeguard the interests of Turkey by summoning a conference.[2] On 7 October, Kâmil telegraphed the Macedonian provinces enjoining them to see that there was no violence against Bulgarians residing in the Empire, or any incidents on the border.[2] In the capital he called a press conference and asked all papers to be moderate and keep down tension.[2] By and large the Porte took a moderate line and the situation continued to smoulder for the next six months, ending with financial compensation for the Ottoman Empire. The effect of these foreign complications on the internal situation, however, was of much greater importance.

The crisis in the Balkans provided some of the disaffected elements with an opportunity to attack the new regime. The first manifestation of reaction took place on 7 October, and, not surprisingly, it took a purely religious form. A large *Ramazan* crowd led by Hoca Ali Efendi, better known as 'Blind Ali' (*Kör* Ali), marched to the Palace. He asked to see the Sultan, and when Abdülhamid appeared at the window, Ali Efendi asked for the constitution to be abolished, for the *Şeriat* to be restored, and for the Sultan to lead his flock once again.[3] He also asked for the closing down of drinking houses, the prohibition of photography, and an end to Muslim women walking around in the town.[4] Reactionaries were busy in other parts of the capital as well. In Ayasofya Square they put up placards abusing the *Şeyhülislâm* and calling upon true believers to murder him as the exponent of theories subversive to the dominant faith of which he was supposed to be the guardian.[5] They created scenes in mosques and theatres, and even attacked Muslim women in the streets on the pretext that, as a result of the new liberal regime, they were not

---

[1] Ibid. 12, Rıza Paşa's actual answer was: 'We don't even have shoes for our soldiers to wear.' The British Ambassador gave another reason for not declaring war: 'The necessity of keeping large bodies of troops here to crush any possible reactionary movement.' Lowther to Grey, no. 296 con., Constantinople, 6 Oct. 1908, F.O. 371/551/34666.

[2] Lowther to Grey, no. 301 con., Constantinople, 7 Oct. 1908, F.O. 371/551/34753.

[3] Cevat, op. cit. 15–16; Tunaya, *İslâmcılık Cereyanı* (1962), Kör Ali Vakası, 129–30; Yalçın, '31 Martin Provası Ve Kendisi', *YT*, i. 136–7; also 'Kör Ali', *Tanin*, 9 Oct. 1908.

[4] Cevat, op. cit. 16.

[5] Lowther to Grey, no. 670 con., Therapia, 14 Oct. 1908, F.O. 371/560 36131. See also Yalçın and Tunaya, op. cit.

properly veiled.[1] Meanwhile Murad Bey, a notorious character from the pre-constitutional era and editor of the *Mizan*, formed an anti-constitution group in league with a Nazif Sururi and Cemil Molla, the son of a former *Şeyhülislâm*.[2] This conspiracy was discovered by the Porte and Murad Bey was arrested and exiled while his accomplices were imprisoned.[3]

The final and potentially the most explosive act of the October reaction was the mutiny at the Taşkışla barracks.[4] This mutiny was triggered off by an order from the Commander, transferring the 7th and 8th regiments of the 2nd Division of the Imperial Guards Corps to Jedda.[5] Some eighty-six soldiers who were about to be posted to Jedda refused to go and demanded immediate discharge from the army. They piled up their arms outside the barracks and refused to obey the orders of their general, Şükrü Paşa, to go back in.[6]

The CUP had already issued, in the *Şurayı Ümmet* of 22 October, a proclamation stating that it was allied to the army and was therefore able to crush any reaction that might take[7] place. On 31 October, the day of the mutiny, the CUP issued another statement.[8] The Committee blamed the mutiny on the fact that the rebellious troops had been pampered by the Palace and therefore discipline had broken down. It demanded severe punishment for the eighty-six soldiers who had violated military discipline by disobeying orders.[8] Mahmud Muhtar Paşa, Commander of the first Army, called in loyal troops from the Macedonian battalions, and the mutiny was crushed at the cost of three killed and as many wounded.[9] Muhtar Paşa wanted to make an example

---

[1] Lowther, to Grey, no. 670 (op. cit., p. 25 n. 5); Türkgeldi, op. cit. 11, relates how Kör Ali's men smashed the windows of the *Şeyhülislâm*'s carriage.

[2] Türkgeldi, op. cit. 12. For a more detailed account of the conspiracy and the past activities of these men, see Lowther, to Grey no. 670. See also Celâl Bayar, *Ben de Yazdım*, i (1965), 176–8.

[3] Türkgeldi, op. cit. 12.

[4] Cevat, op. cit. 19–20; Yalçın, 'Provası', op. cit.; Knight, op. cit. 264 ff., gives a contemporary account from the Young Turkish point of view. Foreign Office correspondence, both from Constantinople and from the Military Attaché deal with this incident in some detail. See F.O. 371/544 and F.O. 195/2290.

[5] Cevat, op. cit. 19; Major Surtees to Lowther, 54 M.A., Constantinople, 2 Nov. 1908, F.O. 195/2290.

[6] Cevat, op. cit. 19; Surtees to Lowther, 54.

[7] *Şurayı Ümmet*, 22 Oct. 1908.

[8] A statement from the CUP concerning the Taşkışla incident, 31 Oct. 1908, in *İkdam*, 1 Nov. 1908.   [9] Cevat, op. cit. 19.

of these men by hanging their corpses for public inspection. But this caused alarm at the Palace and the Porte, and Kâmil Paşa virtually gave him the choice of revoking his decision or resigning. Muhtar Paşa revoked his decision.[1]

The reaction was suppressed without undue difficulty largely because it had been spontaneous, and lacked both leadership and organization. Since the success of any reaction would have favoured only the Palace, the Porte became the ally of the Committee to prevent any such contingency. The Porte dealt promptly with men like Murad Bey, who might have given sophistication and leadership to the reactionary movement.[2] Kâmil Paşa was extremely confident of his position and underestimated the potential power of the Committee. He 'never thought it capable of seizing the absolute power, . . . and [he] used it as a weapon of defense against the Sultan'.[3]

The only reason for co-operation between the Committee and Kâmil was political expediency. The Committee, unable to take control openly, needed someone independent of the Palace and at the same time liberal in outlook, to rule instead. Kâmil was willing to tolerate the Committee while it continued to neutralize the Palace. But this delicate balance could not be maintained indefinitely because both parties could win the dominant position only at the expense of the other.

The Committee was counting on doing this by winning the elections and gaining control of the Chamber of Deputies. Immediately after the July Revolution the Committee sent out emissaries to the provinces to explain the nature of their movement and to set up organizations for securing the election of their candidates.[4] The Committee also tried to reach agreements with the non-Turkish communities on their candidates who would stand for election, and in many cases it was successful in doing so.[5] Candidates were usually elected with the approval and support

[1] Cevat, op. cit. 19–20.

[2] When Murad Bey was exiled, it was decided, however, to pay him his salary while he was away. Türkgeldi, op. cit. 12.

[3] İsmail Kemal, *The Memoirs of İsmail Kemal Bey* (1920), 323.

[4] Annual Report, 1908 (op. cit., p. 1 n. 1).

[5] For the Committee's compromise with the Greeks, see Fazlı Bey's interview with the Greek Patriarch, in Lowther to Grey, no. 535 con., Therapia, 1 Sept. 1908, F.O. 371/546/30971. The Armenians had also decided to co-operate with the CUP. See Fitzmaurice's interview with Patriarch Izmirlian; in Fitzmaurice to Lowther, no. 54 D, 30 Nov. 1908, F.O. 195/2281. For agreements in

of the Committee, and it was difficult to win a seat without this support.[1] Most of its nominees were usually selected from among professional men in the towns and landed proprietors[2]. But in spite of, or perhaps because of, the Committee's active role in the elections of 1908, all elements in the Empire were fairly well represented and satisfied with their representation.[3] Out of 288 deputies, there were 147 Turks, 60 Arabs, 27 Albanians, 26 Greeks, 14 Armenians, 10 Slavs, and 4 Jews.[4]

Apart from the CUP, the only other party to contest the elections was the Liberal Union (*Osmanlı Ahrar Fırkası*).[5] It was officially founded on 14 September 1908,[6] and therefore had very little time to organize itself for the elections. In the elections which were held in late November and December, the Liberals failed to win a single seat in the capital, even with such illustrious candidates as Prince Sabaheddin and Kâmil Paşa.[7] Their only successful candidate, Mahir Said Bey, came from Ankara.[8] In March 1909, Manyasizâde Refik, the Committee's candidate for Istanbul, died and his seat in the Chamber fell vacant. In the by-election both parties fought for the seat, and the Liberal's candidate, Ali Kemal, a prominent journalist, was defeated by

Macedonia see Consul Lamb to Lowther, in Lowther to Grey, no. 647 con., Therapia, 9 Oct. 1908, F.O. 371/546/36109.

[1] Mandelstam, op. cit. 17.

[2] Knight, op. cit. 281. Hüseyin Cahit [Yalçın] was chosen by the CUP to stand for election as one of its candidates for Istanbul. Until then he was not a member of the Committee. See H. C. Yalçın, 'İttihadı Terakki Cemiyetine Nasıl Girdim?', *YT*, i, 23–4.

[3] By and large the non-Turkish elements were content with the way the elections had been conducted. See Lowther to Grey, no. 793 con., Pera, 23 Nov. 1908, F.O. 371/546/41691. The Greeks, however, were the exception. They complained against the irregularities committed by the Committee at their expense. Lowther to Grey, no. 801 con., Pera, 24 Nov. 1908, F.O. 371/546/41699. H. C. Yalçın wrote that if the CUP had not intervened in the elections in Istanbul, it is doubtful if there would have been a single Turkish deputy from there. He wrote that the Greeks were very well organized and had a long experience in electioneering; see 'Türkiyeyi Yaşatmak ve Batırmak İstiyenler', *YT*, i, 214.

[4] This information is based on a study of the 'Young Turk' Parliaments 1908–18, still in preparation, by Dankwart A. Rustow and Feroz Ahmad. See also Tunaya, *Partiler*, 165 n. 4; Mandelstam, op. cit. 16; and H. K. Bayur, *Sadrazam Kâmil Paşa—Siyasi Hayatı* (1954), 296.

[5] Tunaya, *Partiler*, 239 ff.   [6] Ibid. 239.

[7] Tunaya, 'Elections in Turkish History', *MEA* (Apr, 1954), 117, and *Cumhuriyet*, 18 Feb. 1954. Also see Tunaya, *Partiler*, 241; R. E. Koçu, 'Türkiyede Seçimin Tarihi, 1876–1950', *Tarih Dünyası*, i (1950), 181.

[8] Tunaya, *Partiler*, 241.

Rifat Paşa.[1] The Committee's supremacy in the Chamber seemed assured. It strengthened its position in Parliament by weakening the Sultan's control over the Senate. Article 60 of the constitution gave the Sultan the prerogative of appointing Senators.[2] But in December 1908 the Committee put sufficient pressure on the Sultan to force him to exclude from the Senate men with reputations tarnished under the old regime.[3]

According to Article 43, Parliament should have assembled on 1 November.[4] But on account of the difficulties of organizing the elections, there was a delay of over a month and a half. Finally, when Parliament opened on 17 December, some deputies still had not arrived.[5] 'His Majesty the Sultan, contrary to all recent custom, and also contrary to the somewhat general expectation, came to Stamboul by land, ...He entered the Chamber, and His Majesty's First Secretary read the Speech from the Throne.'[6]

In his speech, the Sultan explained why he had prorogued Parliament in 1878. He claimed that his advisers had pointed out to him the difficulties of constitutional government. They had recommended that the execution of the constitution ought to be postponed until the people were ready for it. The Chamber had then been prorogued and its re-assembly deferred to a time when people were better educated. To improve education, he said, he had established schools all over the Empire and the level of education had been raised. When the people again expressed their desire for the constitution, 'being satisfied that the fulfilment of this wish would promote the present and future happiness of my Empire and Country, I proclaimed the constitution anew without hesitation, in spite of those who hold views and opinions opposed to this'. He concluded by expressing an absolute and unalterable decision to govern according to the constitution.[7] Abdülhamid was obviously trying to improve his standing with Parliament by

[1] Ibid. 241 n. 8.   [2] Gözübüyük and Kili, op. cit. 31.
[3] Lowther to Grey, no. 873 con., Constantinople, 19 Dec. 1908, F.O. 371/546/45087. Full list of senators enclosed.
[4] Gözübüyük and Kili, op. cit. 29.
[5] Babanzâde İsmail Hakkı, 'Tarihî bir Gün', Tanin, 18 Dec. 1908. H. C. Yalçın, 'Meşrutiyetin İlk Mebuslar Alayı', YT, i. 390. Lowther to Grey, no. 686 con., Pera, 17 Dec. 1908, F.O. 371/546/44631.
[6] Lowther to Grey, no 686. Cevat, op. cit. 28–9. Kâmil Paşa, writes Cevat, threatened to resign if the Sultan did not personally go to the opening of Parliament, op. cit. 28. The text of the Speech in Takvim-i Vekayi, and Tanin, 18 Dec. 1908.   [7] Takvim-i Vekayi, 18 Dec. 1908.

placing the blame for his past misdeeds on his advisers. If this was his aim he achieved considerable success. On 31 December, he entertained the deputies to dinner at the Palace. According to one account, he won over a large number of them, including his most uncompromising critic and opponent, Ahmed Rıza.[1]

Both Chambers replied to the Sultan's speech.[2] Both praised the Sultan for his wisdom and generosity in restoring the constitution, and condemned his advisers for having misguided him. The Senate alone called attention to the importance of the Cretan question, which was totally ignored by both the Sultan and the Chamber.[3] With regard to the conflict with Bulgaria and Austria, the Chamber promised assistance and support to the Cabinet in seeking a solution consistent with the honour and the rights of the nation. Internally it promised to strive to put in order the finances of the Empire, and also to give attention to establishing security and peace so that means of prosperity and happiness would be insured to everyone in the Empire. The Chamber stressed the need for a uniform justice as well as free patriotic education in the public schools. In conclusion Cavit Bey read:

Nothing but love of fatherland and nation comes from our hearts. Our whole aspiration is to do good work for the state and nation. Our guide is the torch of equality and union; our aim—justice and right. We have undertaken to uphold the rights of thirty million people. In discharging the duty delegated to us, we have no other anxiety than the reproach of conscience and the fear of God.[4]

With the opening of Parliament and with the establishment of a constitutional regime, the Sultan ceased to count as a power to be reckoned with. The Committee, at least, no longer regarded him as a possible threat and were content to let him continue as a constitutional ruler.[5] Power was, for the time being, divided

---

[1] H. C. Yalçın, 'Sultan Hamidin İlk ve Son Ziyafeti', YT, i. 46–7; also Lowther to Grey, no. 29 con., Pera, 14 Jan. 1909, F.O. 371/760/2283.

[2] The Senate's address was read on 26 Dec., and appeared in Takvim-i Vekayi, 27 Dec. 1908. The Chamber's address was read two days later and appeared in Takvim-i Vekayi, 29 Dec. 1908.

[3] Takvim-i Vekayi, 27 Dec. 1908. Lowther thought that this omission seemed to indicate that Turkey proposed to ignore the Cretan declaration, and to rely on the Protecting Powers for a settlement of the question in a manner favourable to herself. Lowther to Grey, no. 686 (op. cit., p. 29 n. 6).

[4] Takvim-i Vekayi, 29 Dec. 1908.

[5] Ahmed Rıza and Nâzım Bey's interview. Grey to Lowther, pr., London, 13 Nov. 1908, F.O. 800/185 A. See also Hüseyin Cahit's conversation with Francis McCullagh, in McCullagh, The Fall of Abd-ul-Hamid (1910), 16.

between the Porte and the Committee, and had the Porte exercised a little patience, the Committee might have eliminated itself on account of factionalism within its ranks. Kâmil, however, resented interference in government from the CUP, especially as it was a body with no legal standing in the country.[1] He had strongly resented Ahmed Rıza and Nâzım Bey's mission to European capitals where they spoke as if they represented the Ottoman Government.[2] When the Committee entrusted Kâmil Paşa with the entertainment of the Balkan Committee, without even consulting him, Kâmil was offended and insulted.[3] Essentially it was the question of a new force challenging the position of the traditional one; the traditional element could not but resent this intrusion into its domain.

Kâmil Paşa had never attached much importance to the CUP. Even after its success in the Istanbul elections, Kâmil did not think it would be able to command a majority in Parliament.[4] He had seen the Committee only 'as a weapon of defense against the Sultan'. The Sultan had been the only real danger to the power of the Porte in the past, and Kâmil saw him as the only danger in the future. He had never thought the Committee capable of seizing absolute power;[5] he obviously calculated that it would present no problem after it had been used to eliminate the Palace. Meanwhile Kâmil appeased the Committee by making ministerial changes. On 30 November he brought in Manyasizâde Refik, the first Unionist to enter the Cabinet, as Minister of Justice. Hüseyin Hilmi Paşa, who had made a reputation for himself as a liberal and who had sympathized with the Young Turks while he was Inspector-General of Macedonia, became Minister of the Interior.[6]

---

[1] *İkdam*, the principal organ of the Liberal Union, accused the CUP of being an illegal body interfering with the government, and challenged it to become a political party instead of a secret society. See 'Cemiyetler, Fırkalar', *İkdam*, 13 Feb. 1909. The Committee had already decided to form a parliamentary party, though it continued to maintain the secret organization as well. See Article 3 of 1908 Congress, Tunaya, *Partiler*, 206.

[2] Lowther to Grey, no. 855 con., Pera, 13 Dec. 1908, F.O. 371/546/43987. See above p. 23 n. 1. For other examples of Unionist interference see Y. H. Bayur, *Tarih*, ii/iv. 203–8 and H. K. Bayur, op. cit. 249–50.

[3] Ibid. (all references) and İnal, *Osmanlı Dervinde Son Sadrıazamlar* (1940–1953). 1404.

[4] Kâmil's conversation with Lowther, in Lowther to Grey, no. 415 con., Constantinople, 12 Dec. 1908, F.O. 371/557/43443.

[5] Kemal, op. cit., 323.

[6] Lowther to Grey, no. 408 con., Constantinople, 30 Nov. 1908, F.O. 371/

The Committee was not entirely happy with Kâmil Paşa either. During the months of November and December, while elections were being held, Kâmil threw in his lot with the Liberal Union.[1] Therefore throughout these months, the Committee's press attacked the Grand Vezir, accusing him of failing to carry out his promise of internal reform, of 'slackness and inefficiency both in domestic and foreign policy, and of an attempt to transfer the despotism of the Palace to the Porte'. He was rightly held responsible for failing to come to an agreement with Bulgaria and Austria,[2] as Kâmil was using these negotiations to strengthen his hand in Parliament and to constitute a Cabinet of his own choice.[3]

In spite of all the criticism, there is no evidence that the Committee wanted to bring about Kâmil's downfall. Talât had informed the British Ambassador that the Committee 'had great confidence in Kiamil Pasha, who had wide experience and great moderation of views, though unfortunately he was somewhat old, though still possessing much energy. . . . They had every intention of doing their best to maintain him in power.'[4] The Committee had good reasons for retaining Kâmil. He was an old and experienced statesman with liberal views and independent ideas. He was respected by almost everyone and actively supported by the British Embassy. This last factor was important because at this stage, and indeed up to the Balkan Wars, the Young Turks leaned on England more than on any other power. Therefore, if the Committee were critical of Kâmil, it was because he was disregarding their policies and trying to end their influence. Rather than overthrow him, they preferred to retain him providing he did not try to become all-powerful.

On 13 January 1909, Hüseyin Cahit, deputy for Istanbul, and said to be a most fervent critic of Kâmil, interpellated the latter on his policy since he assumed office. Kâmil Paşa's statement was read

561/41872; also same to same, no. 818 con., Constantinople, 2 Dec. 1908, F.O. 371/561/42605. Also *The Times*, 1 Dec. 1908; İnal, op. cit. 1665. It is worth noting that Manyasizâde Refik had been appointed Minister of Police without portfolio in Aug. 1908, but he rejected this appointment.

[1] Kemal, op. cit. 321 ff.
[2] 'Lân Atîk bir Sadrâzâm', *Şurayı Ümmet*, 15 Dec. 1908, and Lowther to Grey, no. 894 con., Pera, 29 Dec. 1908, F.O. 371/760/330.
[3] Kemal, op. cit. 324.
[4] Lowther to Grey, no. 541 con., Therapia, 2 Sept. 1908, F.O. 371/559/31787.

before the Chamber.[1] Even Hüseyin Cahit was satisfied with the explanations and the Cabinet received the vote of confidence.[2] Dr. Ârif İsmet Bey, deputy for Biga, summed up the general feeling in the Chamber when he said that 'the Grand Vezir is Young Turkey's only experienced vezir'.[3] The interpellation and the subsequent vote of confidence was seen by the opposition as a great triumph for themselves and therefore a defeat for the Committee. It distorted the relations between Kâmil and the Committee, and made them appear like an open struggle for power.

The almost unanimous vote of confidence seemed to justify Kâmil's estimate of his own position in the Chamber. But it also led him to underestimate the Committee's strength. If the Liberal Union saw this event as a defeat for the CUP, the CUP did not see it as a victory for the Liberal Union. There was a faction in the Committee which wanted to see Kâmil Paşa overthrown. But the Unionists as a party had decided not to make the interpellation a party issue. 'A deputation composed of Enver Bey and Talât Bey, the Vice-President of the Chamber, called on the Grand Vezir to inform him that the Committee as a body disassociated itself from the hostile attitude towards him taken up by some of its members.'[4] Kâmil saw this as a sign of weakness. Thus with the Chamber behind him and the negotiations with Bulgaria and Austria still continuing, Kâmil decided that it was a favourable moment to strengthen his position by appointing his own men to the posts of Ministers of War and Marine.[5]

Kâmil Paşa made these changes on 10 February. Nâzım Paşa, Commander of the Second Army stationed at Edirne, replaced Ali Rıza Paşa as Minister of War. Vice-Admiral Hüseyin Hüsnü Paşa replaced Ârif Paşa as Minister of Marine.[6] These changes were communicated to the Palace, and the Sultan was asked to issue an *irade* sanctioning them immediately. If the Sultan wanted

---

[1] 12th Session, 2nd sitting, 13 Jan. 1909, in *Takvim-i Vekayi*, 16 Jan. 1909. Hüseyin Cahit, 'Sadrâzâm Paşanın İzahatı', *Tanin*, 14 Jan. 1909. Ali Kemal, 'Kâmil Paşanın Beyanatı', *İkdam*, 14 Jan. 1909.
[2] Türkgeldi, op. cit. 17–18; Hüseyin Cahit, ibid.
[3] Türkgeldi, 18.
[4] Lowther to Grey, no. 29 con., Pera, 14 Jan. 1909, F.O. 371/760/2283.
[5] Kemal, op. cit. 324.
[6] H. K. Bayur, op. cit. 293 ff.; Türkgeldi, op. cit. 18–19; Cevat, op. cit. 35, McCullagh, *Fall*, 33 ff. Detailed account in Lowther to Grey, no. 93 con. Pera, 11 Feb. 1909, F.O. 371/760/6295.

to interview his new Minister of War, he was available at the Palace.[1] On receiving this urgent request, Abdülhamid issued the *irade* at once, though he remarked to his First Secretary: 'I know Kâmil Paşa, this man wants to become a dictator.'[2] The result of these changes was a crisis of the first magnitude. On 12 February, Hilmi Paşa tendered his resignation, protesting that he could not be a member of a Council of Ministers in which the President made such changes without consulting his colleagues.[3] His resignation was followed by those of Hasan Fehmi, Manyasizâde Refik, and Ziya Paşa.[4] On the same day a Salonika paper carried the story that Abdülhamid had been deposed and Yusuf İzzettin had become Sultan.[5] In the capital, there was only a rumour of such a plot, implicating the ex-Minister of War. The Committee was quick to deny this and issued a proclamation saying so.[6] If the purpose of these rumours was to create a diversion and draw attention off the ministerial changes, it failed miserably. The Committee was most alarmed at Kâmil's action and was determined to take him to task in the Chamber. The *Tanin* described Kâmil Paşa's action as a *coup d'état*, an encroachment on the rights of Parliament, and a violation of constitutional principles.[7]

The Chamber assembled on 13 February to interpellate Kâmil Paşa on the dismissal of the two ministers. Amid the great excitement in the Chamber that eventful Saturday, it was rumoured that Kâmil would not appear to answer the interpellation.[8]

---

[1] Cevat, op. cit. 36; Kemal, op. cit. 324, suggests it was chance that Nâzım Paşa was to pass through Istanbul at the time.

[2] Cevat, op. cit. 36; McCullagh, *Fall*, 32.   [3] Kemal, op. cit. 324.

[4] Türkgeldi, op. cit. 20. Ziya Paşa had intended to resign from the Ministry of Finance because he found his task too difficult, ibid.

[5] Cevat, op. cit. 36.

[6] Ibid.; text of the Committee's proclamation in *İkdam*, 13 Feb. 1909; also see *The Times*, 15 Feb. 1909. The rumour of a plot seems to have been quite widespread in the capital, and Lowther took it seriously. See Lowther to Grey, no. 93 (op. cit., p. 33 n. 6). Kâmil Paşa later denied his belief in the existence of any conspiracy, but claimed that as head of the Government, he was bound to take notice of rumours. Interview in *Neue Freie Presse* of 18 Feb. 1909, cited in *FR*, lxxxiv (1909), 397–8.

[7] *Tanin*, 12 Feb. 1909 and 'Meşrutî İdareye Mühim bir Darbe', *Şurayı Ümmet*, 12 Feb. 1909.

[8] 21st Session, 13 Feb. 1909 in *Takvim-i Vekayi*, 18 Feb. 1909 and 19 Feb. 1909; *İkdam*, 14 Feb. 1909; H. C. Yalçın, 'Deniz Kuvvetlerinin Zoruyla Çekilen Sadrâzâm', *YT*, ii/14. 46–7. The proceedings of that day are also described in Türkgeldi, op. cit. 18–21; and Lowther to Grey, no. 102 con., Pera, 15 Feb. 1909, F.O. 371/760/7050.

Nevertheless, the Grand Vezir was summoned to appear before the House and give his explanation. But Kâmil replied that as the change of the Minister of War was connected with the important foreign complications, he could not give any explanation immediately, and therefore asked for the interpellation to be postponed until Wednesday the 17th.[1] The Committee saw the postponement as a political manœuvre designed to win enough time to prepare public opinion and to strengthen his position.[2] The Chamber rejected this explanation, probably influenced by the two petitions sent by the fleet anchored off Beşiktaş, demanding an explanation from the Grand Vezir and assurances that the constitution was in no danger.[3] Another invitation was sent and declined. The Chamber then decided to have a vote of no confidence against the Grand Vezir. While all this was going on, a third note arrived from Kâmil Paşa. Kâmil claimed his right under Article 38 of the constitution, to postpone any explanation until the 17th. He claimed he had to do this on account of considerations of foreign policy, and threatened to place his resignation before the Sultan if the Chamber continued to pursue the matter. He warned the Chamber that if he were forced to resign, he would publish his explanation in the press and the Chamber would have to bear the responsibility for any prejudice that might be caused to the state.[4] The threat came too late and the Chamber passed the vote of no confidence by 198 to 8 votes.[5] Kâmil Paşa, meanwhile went to consult Şeyhülislâm Cemalüddin, and both decided to offer their resignations. But even this was too late, because when Cemalüddin offered his resignation to the Sultan, the latter had already accepted his dismissal.[6] After the vote, Ahmed Rıza and Talât went to the Palace and informed the Sultan of the Chamber's

---

[1] For a pro-Kâmil account of the crisis, see H. K. Bayur, op. cit. 293 ff. and 301; Yalçın, YT, ii/14. 46–7; Kemal, op. cit. 325 relates that when the message from the Chamber reached him Kâmil was in conference with the Austrian Ambassador and therefore could not go to the Chamber at once.

[2] Yalçın, YT, ii/14.

[3] Ibid. The officers of the First Army, commanded by Nâzım Paşa, the new Minister of War, also sent a telegram saying while they respected Nâzım Paşa as their Commander, they refused to accept his appointment as Minister of War. Türkgeldi, op. cit. 19.

[4] Yalçın, YT, ii/14. 47; Lowther, no. 102 (op. cit. p. 34 n. 8); Türkgeldi, op. cit. 20.   [5] Yalçın, YT, ii./14. 47; İkdam, 14 Feb. 1909.

[6] Türkgeldi, op. cit. 20–1. According to Talât Bey this was a package deal; Arab deputies agreed to vote against Kâmil if the Committee agreed to dismiss the Şeyhülislâm. No reference to this in Cemalüddin.

decision. Next day, 14 February, Hüseyin Hilmi Paşa was appointed Grand Vezir.[1]

The events in Parliament were dramatized in the columns of *Tanin* of 14 February 1909. Hüseyin Cahit described how on the previous day

. . . the Chamber of Deputies went through a memorable day. . . . Restored after thirty years of oppression Parliament faced a formidable challenge. . . . On the one side stood absolutism and on the other liberty. Which was it to choose? Had the problem been so clearcut the choice would have been simple: resist absolutism and support liberty. But there were also experienced enemies to be faced . . ., and therefore there was great anxiety as to how Parliament would emerge from this ordeal. Had it succumbed yesterday, a fatal blow would have been struck at this unfortunate nation. Fortunately the prompt and decisive action of the deputies saved both the nation and the constitution.

Apparently the Unionists saw Kâmil's bid for power as the first real threat to their position and there was a sigh of relief when they emerged unscathed from their ordeal.

Kâmil Paşa's fall was a great setback for the Liberal Union and all other anti-CUP elements. Only a month earlier, the Chamber had shown its approval of Kâmil and his policies by giving him an almost unanimous vote of confidence. Yet, on the second occasion only eight deputies had the courage to vote against the Committee; about sixty, according to Kâmil, were intimidated by the Committee and left the Chamber without voting.[2] The Committee had shown its supremacy in Parliament, and to defeat it constitutionally now seemed out of the question.[3] The only way left was to overthrow it by violence.

During the next two months there was a bitter press campaign against the Committee, and the Unionist organs paid back in the same coin. Kâmil's fall was seen by the British Embassy and British interests in Turkey as a blow to their prestige, and therefore the British press also joined in the campaign against the

---

[1] Cevat, op. cit. 36–8. *Sabah*, 15 Feb. 1909; İnal, op. cit. 1665.

[2] Kâmil Paşa's defence in *İkdam*, 3 Apr. 1909, 'Sadr-ı Sabık Kâmil Paşa Hazretlerinin İzahnamesi', and *Tanin* and *Serbesti*, 4 Apr. 1909. French translation enclosed in Lowther to Grey, no. 249 con., Pera, 6 Apr. 1909, F.O. 371/761/13689.

[3] İsmail Kemal told Sir G. Lowther that the Liberals could only be sure of fifty votes in the Chamber. Lowther to Hardinge, no. 16 pr., Constantinople, 2 Mar. 1909; F.O. 800/184 (*Hardinge Papers*).

Committee. The *Levant Herald*, an English language paper in Istanbul, generally associated with the British Embassy, defended Kâmil stoutly and attacked the Committee, thereby provoking some of its members to demand the expulsion of its editor.[1] The opposition was quick to exploit the British attitude towards the Committee, and was greatly encouraged by it. Anti-CUP articles in the English press 'were welcomed by large sections of the population and were reproduced with comments by anti-Committee organs'.[2]

In view of their weak position in the Chamber, the opposition set out to strengthen it by winning over the British Embassy. Members of the opposition visited the Ambassador and kept him informed as to the political climate prevailing in the country, or more especially in the capital. Sir G. Lowther wrote in one dispatch:

> Many who had concealed their real views began to pluck up courage and give expression to disgust at the unconstitutional and violent action of those who had brought about Kiamil Pasha's fall. Many again, strangely enough, look to England to help them rid themselves of this new despotism of men who, they say, have not even the traditions of the Sultanate and Kaliphate, while some Deputies have confidentially approached me to express their alarm at the disastrous turn things are taking, and to appeal to England to ward off the dangers which must inevitably supervene from the dictation of a secret Committee. . . .
>
> The organs of the latter are indulging in fierce attacks on the pro-Kiamil papers, and some of their articles have a veiled anti-English tinge. The bulk of the public feeling is as pro-English as before, and would be inclined to set down any internal and external trouble or mishap as the consequence of the Committee's misguided and unconstitutional behaviour. The Sultan, too, at a recent audience confidentially expressed to me his deep anxiety at the present situation. . . .[3]

The Young Turks were aware of the value of English support, and conversely the undesirability of her hostility. They knew that the British Embassy attached great importance to Kâmil's ministry, and that his fall could certainly be seen as a blow against

[1] Annual Report, 1909, 3, in Lowther to Grey, no. 55 con., Pera, 31 Jan. 1910, F.O. 371/1002/4235.
[2] Lowther to Grey, no. 151 con. Pera, 3 Mar. 1909, F.O. 371/761/8914; Annual Report, 1909 and McCullagh, *Fall*, 31 and 56.
[3] Lowther, no. 151, ibid; Cevat, op. cit. 39–41.

British influence. They tried to counteract this impression as well as the opposition's propaganda by informing Sir Gerard that they had opposed Kâmil only for his unconstitutional acts, and they promised to withhold their support from any ministry which might succeed him unless they pursued Kâmil's policy of friendship to England.[1] On 14 February, Hilmi Paşa declared that his policy towards England would be the same as Kâmil's and that Turkey would continue to act on the advice of His Majesty's Government.[2] These manifestations of friendship towards England, though motivated by political expediency, were far from insincere. They represented the very basis of whatever foreign policy the Young Turks had since July 1908. The Committee's desire to conclude an alliance with England has already been mentioned elsewhere.[3] But Sir Gerard refused to respond in a favourable manner. He adopted a cold and patronizing attitude towards the Committee.[4]

The CUP, somewhat apprehensive of the prevailing situation, tried to adopt a conciliatory attitude towards the opposition. The Manastır branch sent a telegram to the Sultan, reassuring him of their loyalty and devotion, and denying the existence of any plot.[5] Paradoxically, it was not the Unionist press which attacked the Sultan, but the *Serbesti*, an anti-Committee paper owned by the Sultan's brother Reşad Efendi.[6] To the Liberals, the Committee offered a truce, urging them in the name of patriotism to cease attacking the Committee, and to co-operate in finding a remedy for the prevailing situation.[7] After all the Liberal Union was no less under attack from Islamic elements than was the

---

[1] Hüseyin Cahid, 'Kabinenin Sukutu ve İngiltere', *Tanin*, 15 Feb. 1909; Annual Report, 1909, 2; Sir Gerard refused to receive the Committee's deputation, telling them that if they had a communication to make they should make it through official channels. See 'X', 'Les courants politiques dans la Turquie', *RMM*, xxi (1912), 193.

[2] Lowther to Grey, no. 53 tel. con., Constantinople, 15 Feb. 1909, F.O. 371/760/6275.

[3] Sir E. Grey, op. cit., F.O. 800/185A (see p. 23 n. 1).

[4] To Sir Charles Hardinge he wrote: 'I have been a little cold with the Committee which I think has done them good for they are aware that our support is essential—on the slightest sign of their doing good work I shall be more cordial. . . .' Lowther, no. 16 (op. cit., p. 36 n. 3).

[5] W. S. Edmonds to Lowther, no. 145 sal., Monastir, 16 Feb. 1909, F.O. 195/2328.   [6] Cevat, op. cit. 40.

[7] Hüseyin Cahit, 'İttihad ve Terakki Cemiyeti ve Ahrar Fırkası', *Tanin*, 28 Mar. 1909, and 'Birleşme', *Tanin*, 12 Apr. 1909; Kemal, op. cit. 330–1; Lowther to Grey, no. 151 con., Pera, 3 Mar. 1909, F.O. 371/761/8914.

CUP;[1] the social policy of some Liberals went further than that of the Committee. But the Liberals declared that they would co-operate only if the Committee ceased to be a secret organization, and refrained from all interference in the affairs of the Government and the army.[2] İsmail Kemal, who had been sounded by both Talât and Hilmi Paşa, replied: 'as it was the Committee and the new Government representing it that had brought things to this pass, it was for them and not for us [the Liberal Union] to seek for a remedy'.[3] Thus the campaign against the Committee continued unabated.

On 6 March, the *Serbesti* published a document implicating the Committee in blackmail to extract money from corrupt officials of the old regime.[4] A few days later, the same paper wrote that Niyazi, one of the heroes of the July Revolution, had seceded from the Committee, on account of dissatisfaction with it. But this was promptly denied by Niyazi.[5] The situation was aggravated by the murder of Hasan Fehmi, editor of the *Serbesti*. The opposition held the Committee responsible. The failure to find the murderer placed the odium on the CUP.[6] On 7 April, the funeral was used by the opposition as a demonstration against the Committee, and it also revealed the shape events were taking.[7]

Meanwhile, the Committee and the Government were trying to strengthen their position through legislative measures. On 3 March, a law was passed to the effect that notice of public meetings must be given to the authorities at least 24 hours prior to the meeting.[8]

---

[1] The Muhammedan Union, see above, always spoke of the CUP and the Liberal Union as one, both supporting the ideal of Ottomanism, Tunaya, *Partiler*, 270, 274–5. The Liberals were aware of the danger of reaction and in the October Mutiny at Taşkışla, the *İkdam*, the most prominent of the Liberal Union papers, had welcomed the suppression of the reaction; see above, p. 26 n. 8.

[2] Lowther, no. 151 (op. cit., p. 37 n. 2).   [3] Kemal, op. cit. 331.

[4] Lowther to Grey, no. 181 con., Pera, 12 Mar. 1909, F.O. 371/769/10792.

[5] Niyazi's repudiation in *Yeni Asır*, Salonika, 17 Mar. 1909; in Consul-General Lamb to Lowther, no. 89 sal., Salonica, 18 Mar. 1909, F.O. 195/2328.

[6] Tunaya, *İslâmcılık*, 128; Cevat, op. cit. 46; Lowther to Grey, no. 259 con., Pera, 9 Apr. 1909, F.O. 371/774/14539, McCullagh, *Fall*, 73–4. On 23–4 McCullagh suggests the possibility of the Palace's involvement in the murder. Also Cevat, op. cit. 40.

[7] Ali Kemal, 'İlk Kurban', *İkdam*, 8 Apr. 1909; Cavit, *Tanin*, 2, 3 Sept. 1943; Halide Edib, *Memoirs of Halide Edib* (1926), 276; *The Times*, 8 Apr. 1909.

[8] *İkdam*, 4 Mar. 1909; Lowther to Grey, no. 176 con., Pera, 10 Mar. 1909, F.O. 371/761/9958; and Abdülhamid, *İkinci Abdülhamid'in Hatıra Defteri* (1960), 136–7.

Hilmi Paşa had intended to have a law passed curbing the freedom of the press, but the opposition to this was so great that the debate, on 25 March, proved to be inconclusive.[1] Finally, as a precautionary measure, the Committee decided to remove the rest of the *Yıldız* Guards and replace them with Anatolians. But the Arab and Albanian troops, loyal to the Sultan, resisted, and had to be subdued by the Macedonians.[2]

While the Committee was consolidating its position, the reactionary forces were getting organized too. On 5 April 1909, the occasion of the Prophet's birthday, the Society of Muhammed (*İttihadı Muhammedî*) was officially established; it had been operating earlier through its organ the *Volkan*, and its political programme was published on 3 March in the columns of its paper.[3] Its doctrines and programme of action were clerical and strongly opposed to the idea of union based on the Ottoman ideal.[4] It stood for the rule of the *Şeriat*, and if there were to be any union, it must be based on the ideal of Islam.[5] The Society was therefore against the westernizing reformism of both the CUP and the Liberal Union. Its propaganda was aimed at the religious and conservative elements in the Empire, and through its organ, the *Volkan*, the Society was able to exercise considerable influence on the traditional deputies in the Chamber and the rank and file in the army.[6]

It was in this atmosphere that the counter-revolution of 13 April took place. On the night of 12/13 April the troops of the First Army Corps mutinied, overpowered their officers, and led by *softas* marched to the Ayasofya Square, near Parliament, demanding the restoration of the *Şeriat*.[7] The Government had been long aware of the dangerous situation prevailing in the

[1] Cevat, op. cit. 39; Lowther to Grey, no. 223 con., Pera, 30 Mar. 1909, F.O. 371/761/12788.

[2] Cevat, op. cit. 44–5; *The Times*, 7 Apr. 1909; Lowther to Grey, no. 231 con., Pera, 2 Apr. 1909, F.O. 371/769/13671.

[3] Kuran, *Osmanlı*, 500; Tunaya, *Partiler*, 261 ff.

[4] Proclamation and programme of the Society in Tunaya, *Partiler*, 270 and 271 ff.

[5] Tunaya, *Partiler*, 271, clause 3.

[6] Ibid. 263 and Ahmet Rıza Beyin Hatıraları, *Cumhuriyet*, 1 Feb. 1950.

[7] Cevat, op. cit. 48; the counter-revolution is an event of great importance in Turkish history, and is a subject of journalistic interpretations every year on the date of its anniversary. The Foreign Office Correspondence dealt with the event in considerable detail in F.O. 371/770 ff., as well as Consular correspondence in F.O. 195. For a fuller bibliography, see B. Lewis, *Emergence*, 212.

capital. But the actual turn of events took it completely by surprise.[1] Hilmi Paşa called a meeting of his ministers and sent out
his Chief of Police to talk to the *softas*, who were leading the
rebellious soldiers, to find out exactly what they wanted. The more
articulate of the *softas* demanded the dismissal of the Minister of
War and the President of the Chamber, Ahmet Rıza, as well as
the restoration of the *Şeriat*, and the restriction of Muslim women
to their homes.[2] The *Şeyhülislâm*, who was sent by the Sultan to
talk to the soldiers, found their demands almost identical, save
that they wanted a pardon from the Sultan for their actions.

In the Chamber there was utter chaos. The Committee deputies
had fled for fear of their lives, and *softas* and soldiers were everywhere.[3] Hilmi Paşa, finding his position untenable, went to the
Palace with his Minister of War and Minister of Education, and
tendered the resignation of his Cabinet.[4] The resignation was
promptly accepted. The Sultan had also accepted all the demands
of the soldiers, and he dispatched Ali Cevat, his First Secretary,
to Ayasofya Square to read the Sultan's proclamation both in the
Chamber and before the soldiers, so that order could be restored.[5]
The next morning, on 14 April, the royal order appointing
Tevfik Paşa Grand Vezir was drawn up. In the text the Sultan
included the appointment of the two ministers of the armed forces
as his prerogative.[6] Tevfik Paşa refused to accept office under
these conditions and the Sultan stepped down.[7] But, in fact, the
Sultan had already appointed *müşir* Edhem Paşa, Minister of
War.[8]

The CUP seemed to have been completely routed. Hilmi Paşa
had resigned; members of the Committee had either fled from the
capital or were in hiding, and their newspaper offices in Istanbul sacked. The Liberal Union had filled the vacuum. It seems

---

[1] Colonel Surtees to Lowther, in Lowther to Grey, no. 307 con., Constantinople, 28 Apr. 1909, F.O. 371/771/16541.
[2] Hilmi Paşa's report in Cevat, op. cit. 89–90, no. 4.
[3] Kemal, op. cit. 332.
[4] Cevat, op. cit. 48, 90–2, document 6, gives the minutes of the resignation.
It relates the events of the days and explains that 'it is necessary to resign for
the good of the country'; Yunus Nâdi, extracts from 'İhtilâl ve İnkılâb-ı
Osmanî', in *Cumhuriyet*, 4 Apr. 1959.
[5] Cevat, op. cit. 49.
[6] Ibid. 57; Nâdi, *Cumhuriyet*, 4 Apr. 1959; *Serbesti*, 15 Apr. 1909.
[7] Cevat, ibid. 57, Türkgeldi, op. cit. 28.
[8] Cevat, op. cit. 53–4.

worth while to examine the sudden collapse of an organization, which a few days earlier had appeared all-powerful.

The strength of the Committee was always exaggerated, and it never amounted to very much in Istanbul. The Committee had enjoyed considerable support when it was struggling against the despotism of the Palace. But once the despotism was destroyed, only the expectations of a very few were satisfied, and the dissatisfied elements went into opposition. Like many of the independence movements of our own day, the Committee was split into factions once it had achieved its basic aim; those members dedicated to the ideal of reform and the creation of a modern state were always in a minority.[1] The Committee had also created a number of dissatisfied elements. There was the large number of opportunists who had supported the CUP in the hope that they would gain high positions when the Palace was toppled. Their ambitions were frustrated by the Committee's decision not to assume office (in the Government). Large numbers were thrown out of work when Abdülhamid's espionage network was abolished and when the ministries were reorganized. All these together formed a strong anti-CUP group. The secular policies of the Young Turks alarmed and alienated the religious elements. In particular, the rank and file in the army, complained of not being allowed time for ablutions and prayers, and resented being given orders and sworn at by young officers whom they regarded as mere boys.[2] Thus almost all traditional elements in Ottoman society were opposed to the Committee, none more than the Palace and the Porte. They resented the intrusion of men with no authority into preserves of power which were traditionally theirs. This may account for the ready acceptance of the rebels' demands by the Sultan and the Porte. After all, the counter-revolution was the traditional alliance between the soldiers and the *softas*, so reminiscent of the days of Janissary rule.[3]

But because the name of the Society of Muhammed is intimately linked with the counter-revolution, the movement has been regarded as having been purely religious, and its political

---

[1] Yalçın, *YT*, ii. 180.   [2] Cevat, op. cit. 47; McCullagh, *Fall*, 67 ff.

[3] McCullagh, *Fall*, 59. The *ulema* denounced the Muhammedan League and its organ, the *Volkan*, 'which does not contain good and sincere Mussulmans, but alas! but intriguers who seem bent on exploiting religion', ibid. 61. Hikmet Bayur, *Tarih*, i, 297 n. 1, found it strange that an Islamic paper should have a French name.

significance has been almost completely lost. It is doubtful if the rebellion could have been so restrained and well controlled had its inspiration been only religious fanaticism. The rebels searched out only members of the Committee and with the same care sacked only the offices of the Unionist press. The Liberal Unionists, as much open to attack from religious fanaticism, were not harmed, let alone the Christian deputies and foreigners. A religious outbreak, which would normally have struck terror in the hearts of Christians, was praised in the Greek press. The *Neologos* wrote:

The Army has gained the great prize for patriotism, and April 13, 1909 ought to be henceforth marked with no less splendour than July 24, 1908. The Army was inspired yesterday by its love for the country and by no other sentiment.[1]

Religion was the vehicle for the political struggle which had been continuing since July 1908. Islam had played a vital role in Ottoman society and continued to do so, and used as a weapon against the Committee, it provided the opposition with the largest audience. The religious aspect of the counter-revolution ended with the meaningless demand for the *Şeriat*; hereafter the politicians took over. The Committee regime floundered and the Liberals took its place. İsmail Kemal was elected the President of the Chamber, Mizancı Murad, whom Kâmil Paşa had exiled in October 1908, offered to support Tevfik and help establish him in power.[2] Even the new ministry was regarded as a stopgap until the situation became calm, and Kâmil Paşa could be appointed Grand Vezir once again.[3] Then the triumph of the Liberals would be complete.

The Committee was totally defeated; it only remained for the Liberals to convince the Third Army in Macedonia that the rebellion had been spontaneous and in no way unconstitutional. But this was far from easy. The Committee was still all-powerful in Macedonia and the Third Army was loyal to the constitution. The Palace was bombarded with telegrams from the Macedonian provinces, accusing Abdülhamid of destroying the constitutional government and the constitution, and threatening retaliation.[4]

[1] McCullagh, *Fall*, 59; Danişmend, *31 Mart Vak'ası* (1961), 210–11.
[2] See above, p. 27 n. 2.
[3] Lowther to Hardinge, no. 25 pr., Constantinople, 14 Apr. 1909, F.O. 800/184 (*Hardinge Papers*).
[4] Cevat, op. cit. 62; Danişmend, *31 Mart*, 210–11.

Macedonia refused to recognize Tevfik Paşa's Cabinet and the Committee demanded the arrest of certain members of the Liberal Union, namely İsmail Kemal, Mizancı Murad, Kâmil's son, Said Paşa, the Sultan's Second Chamberlain, Emin Bey, and some prominent newspapermen.[1] On 17 April, the Committee passed on from words to action. The 'Action Army' (*Hareket Ordusu*) left Salonika, ostensibly to restore discipline among the rebellious troops, and to restore order in the capital. The Sultan welcomed this, and thought it was a good idea so long as force was not used.[2] But in the Cabinet the news caused panic. Some members thought it would be wise to send a deputation to meet the 'Action Army' before it reached the capital and to reassure the troops that the constitution had not been harmed.[3]

Deputations were sent to negotiate with the Salonika Army but they met no favourable response; one of the deputations was not even allowed to return to the capital.[4] The British Ambassador, at the request of İsmail Kemal, instructed his consuls in Macedonia 'to assure the population that the constitution was not compromised', thereby hoping to prevent intervention from Macedonia.[5] But the Committee's influence was too pervasive, and such propaganda was either suppressed or countered with propaganda of their own.[6] As a final bid to prevent the occupation of the capital by the 'Action Army', the Porte asked Sir Gerard to permit Fitzmaurice to join the delegation which was going to negotiate with the Salonika force. The Porte calculated that English support would strengthen their bargaining position and undermine the opposition.[7] Fitzmaurice went with the delegation, but when he reached Stambul he found that other counsels prevailed and that it was decided that the deputation should go without him.[8]

This deputation proved to be a failure too, and the troops from Salonika continued to surround the capital. Finally, on the night

---

[1] Türkgeldi, op. cit. 29–30.   [2] Cevat, op. cit. 65–6.
[3] Türkgeldi, op. cit. 30.
[4] Kemal, op. cit. 343; Lowther to Grey, no. 287 con., Constantinople, 20 Apr. 1909, F.O. 371/771/15582.
[5] Kemal, op. cit. 343; Lowther, no. 287, ibid.
[6] Lowther, ibid.
[7] Lowther to Grey, no. 129, tel. pr., Constantinople, 17 Apr. 1909, F.O. 371/770/14474. Fitzmaurice was the Chief Dragoman at the British Embassy.
[8] Lowther to Grey, no. 287 con., Constantinople, 20 Apr. 1909, F.O. 371/771/15582.

of 23/24 April, the 'Action Army' began operations, and after some skirmishing the capital was occupied.[1] On 22 April, the two Chambers sat together at Yeşilköy as a National Assembly. They ratified the proclamation of the investing army, guaranteed the constitution and security in the country, and declared that the actions of the army were in conformity with the aspirations of the nation.[2] Five days later, the National Assembly proclaimed its decision to depose Abdülhamid and replace him with his brother Mehmed Reşad.[3] The National Assembly's decision was ratified by a *fetva* extracted from an unwilling *Şeyhülislâm*,[4] and this marked the end of the counter-revolution, though mopping-up operations continued.

The suppression of the counter-revolution proved to be a mixed blessing for the CUP. The Liberal Union was destroyed as a party though not in spirit; but the Committee did not emerge unchallenged. The events of 13 April had shown the Committee's inability to control the situation and to maintain law and order. The chaos that followed forced the army to intervene as the instrument of law and order, and not as the instrument of the CUP.[5] Until April 1909, the soldier had played the subordinate role to the politician, and only junior officers had been members of the Committee. The revolt brought in the senior officers. Mahmud Şevket Paşa took care to point out that he and his army were not acting as agents of the Committee, and that his only aim was to see law and order maintained and discipline in the army restored.[6] Significantly his Chief of Staff was no other than Mustafa

---

[1] Colonel Surtees, no. 307 (op. cit., p. 41 n. 1), also a more detailed account in Lowther to Grey, no. 303 con., Pera, 28 Apr. 1909, F.O. 371/771/16537.

[2] The proclamation of the 'Action Army'; *İkdam*, 21 Apr. 1909. Proclamation of the National Assembly, *Takvim-i Vekayi*, 24 Apr. 1909.

[3] The charter announcing the decision to depose Abdülhamid in *Takvim-i Vekayi*, 28 Apr. 1909; Cevat, op. cit. 153–4. Abdurrahman Şeref, Minister of Education in Hilmi Paşa's Cabinet relates how this decision was taken in a secret sitting of the National Assembly. *Abdurrahman Şeref Beyin Eseri*, 19–25; cited in Cevat, op. cit. 145–6; Menteşe, *Cumhuriyet*, 22 Oct. 1946; Ahmed Rıza, *Cumhuriyet*, 3 Feb. 1950.

[4] B. Lewis, *Emergence*, 213; Türkgeldi, op. cit. 36. Text of the *fetva* in Cevat, op. cit. 148.

[5] Şevket Paşa's proclamation, *Takvim-i Vekayi*, 26 Apr. 1909. Also Colonel Surtees's interview with Şevket Paşa, in Surtees to Lowther, no. 307 (op. cit., p. 41 n. 1), and no. 38 M.A., Constantinople, 12 May 1909, F.O. 195/2323 and no. 39 M.A., Constantinople, 14 May 1909, F.O. 195/2323. Also Consul Lamb to Lowther, no. 135, Salonica, 21 Apr. 1909, F.O. 195/2328.

[6] Proclamation and Surtees (op. cit., p. 41 n. 1).

Kemal, a junior officer unconnected with the CUP, and said to be a firm believer in the principle that the army should stay out of politics.[1] But the failure of the politicians to maintain law and order brought in the soldier, and the establishment of martial law made a military dictatorship seem inevitable.[2] Though this did not take place, the effects of the soldiers' growing role in the politics of the Empire became apparent in the period that followed.

[1] For Mustafa Kemal's role in the 'Action Army', see H. K. Bayur, *Tarih*, i. 299; and Abidin Daver, 'Hareket Ordusu Istanbula Nasıl Girmişti', *Cumhuriyet*, 24 Apr. 1951.
[2] Mandelstam, op. cit. 25.

III

(i) THE MILITARY AND THE CUP

IT was pointed out at the end of Chapter II that the failure of the politicians to maintain law and order in April 1909 had brought the professional soldier into the arena of politics.[1] But the army, not knowing how to run the Empire, left the civilians to govern. It retained, however, the power to veto any measures it did not approve of. Though the CUP was the only political association existing at the time, the army's power of restraint was so effective, that the government was still far from being a 'one party dictatorship', as it has sometimes been described.[2] Nor did the fact that all opposition parties were banned bring to an end all opposition to the Committee's policies. There may have been no Liberal Union Party (*Ahrar Fırkası*) in May 1909, but there were many Liberal Unionists.

The political situation of May 1909 was neatly summed up by Lieutenant-General Pertev Paşa, Chief of Staff to Mahmud Şevket Paşa. On being asked what the intentions of the military authorities were with regard to the existing political situation, Pertev Paşa replied:

I will tell you, my dear friend, there is no secret; it is intended that Mahmoud Shevket Pasha, who, as you know, is now practically Military Dictator, shall become Inspector-General of the first three *Ordus*. There is no intention of interfering with the Committee of Union and Progress, to which we all belong—myself included—but we only acknowledge loyalty to its principles in so far that we have sworn to protect the Constitution . . . and no more officers will join the Committee.[3]

---

[1] See above, p. 45.

[2] Recai G. Okandan, *Amme Hukukumuzun Ana Hatları* (1959), 345, writes: 'The Unionists took advantage of the April revolt (*31 Mart Vak'ası*) and disbanded rival political parties, proclaiming a one party dictatorship', and Bayur, i. 301, wrote: 'In short, having saved the nation from a grave danger, the CUP emerged even stronger than before.' See also Danişmend, *Kronoloji*, iv, 381.

[3] Pertev Paşa's conversation with Conyers Surtees (Military Attaché) in C. Surtees to Lowther, no. 39, Pera, 14 May 1909, F.O. 371/776/19410.

The army was certainly the most important single factor in the politics of the Ottoman Empire. But it was not politically monolithic. In political terms it was divided into three quite distinct groups. The largest and least important was the rank and file. This group, like the civilian populace, could be influenced at any moment by the propaganda of the popular demagogue. Therefore it had to be kept isolated from political influence. The second group, that of the junior officers, had been educated in the Hamidian military colleges, where politics had unofficially and illegally dominated the curriculum.[1] They were, therefore, at least in 1909, supporters of constitutional government and the CUP, and what it stood for, namely, union and progress. The third group was that of the senior officers, men like Şevket, Mahmud Muhtar, and Pertev Paşas, to mention only a few. They were professional soldiers who symbolized discipline. They were determined to create an army free from the influence of politics so that the events of 13 April could never happen again. In accordance with this principle, Şevket Paşa had led the 'Action Army' in order to restore order in the capital and discipline in the army.[2]

All power was virtually in the hands of Mahmud Şevket Paşa.[3] Though he did not exercise this power directly, at first it was always exercised under his personal supervision.[4] The Committee of Union and Progress was at this stage almost powerless. Its entire organization in the capital had been completely smashed during the counter-revolution. Rather than compete for power, the CUP was occupied with trying to regain some of its old influence.[5] It could do no other than to play second fiddle to Şevket Paşa, and it was in his shadow that it later made its comeback.

Though Şevket Paşa came from Salonika to uphold the constitution, he soon made it abundantly clear that he himself intended to be free of all constitutional checks. The first manifestation of this came on 18 May when Şevket Paşa became the

[1] Ahmet Bedevî Kuran, *Harbiye Mektebinde Hürriyet Mücadelesi* (n.d.), *passim.*   [2] Cevat, op. cit. 65–6.

[3] Halid Ziya Uşaklıgil, *Saray ve Ötesi*, i (1940), 42 and 45.

[4] Mahmud Kemal İnal, *Osmanlı Devrinde Son Sadrıazamlar*, 14 pts. (1940–1953), 1884, where he cites Mahmud Muhtar Paşa's work, *Maziye bir Nazar*, n. 1, and the 'Political Memoirs of an Old Minister' (unnamed), which appeared in *Tan* on 21 Dec. 1937.

[5] Uşaklıgil, *Saray ve Ötesi*, i (1940), 44. For the destruction of the CUP organization in the capital, see above, p. 41 ff.

Inspector-General of the first three army corps.[1] There was no precedent for this post and it seems to have been specially created for the prevailing political situation. Being purely military in function, it placed Şevket Paşa outside the authority of the Minister of War and the Cabinet, especially while martial law was in operation, and martial law was prolonged until March 1911.[2] In the following year, when the Committee tried to rationalize the finances of the Empire by means of a budget, Şevket Paşa refused to allow the Ministry of Finance to inspect military expenditure.[3]

Mahmud Şevket Paşa's desire to be independent of the Cabinet probably sprang from the soldier's innate suspicion of the civilian, especially with regard to military affairs. The Porte also resented the army's independence and its interference in government, since this violated the principles of modern centralized government which the Committee had set out to introduce in July 1908. But in spite of such major differences, the army and the Committee had something in common which enabled them to work together. They both shared the patriotic ideal of territorial integrity, or as Halide Edib so aptly described the CUP, they were both 'Empire men'.[4]

It was in this political atmosphere that Hüseyin Hilmi Paşa was appointed Grand Vezir for the second time.[5] Tevfik Paşa, however acceptable he may have been, had to go simply because he had come to power during the April revolution. Hilmi Paşa was restored to his old position because he had been overthrown by the counter-revolutionaries.[6] His re-appointment was not popular with all sections of the Committee. They made this

---

[1] Lowther to Grey, no. 360 con., 18 May 1909, F.O. 371/776/19411; see above, p. 47 n. 3.

[2] Imperial *İrade* of 11 Aug. 1909, prolonging martial law until Mar. 1911, in Lowther to Grey, no. 654 con., Therapia, 11 Aug. 1909, F.O. 371/779/30767.

[3] See below, p. 71 ff.   [4] Edib, *Memoirs*, 266.

[5] *Hatt-ı Hümayun*, dated 15 Rebiülahır 1327 (5 May 1909), appointing Hilmi Paşa Grand Vezir in İnal, op. cit. xi. 1671. Five days earlier, Tevfik Paşa had been confirmed in his office of Grand Vezir by a *Hatt-ı Hümayun* dated 1 May 1909. See *Stamboul*, 2 May 1909.

[6] Uşaklıgil, *Saray ve Ötesi*, i (1940), 80–1, suggests that Hilmi Paşa was brought back as a symbol of the Committee's influence and strength. Talât Bey cited by Türkgeldi, op. cit. 40, said that the resignation of Tevfik Paşa's Cabinet was regarded as being essential on account of the great excitement in the provinces. It is not likely that the Committee had much to say in Hilmi Paşa's appointment. The Cabinet did not include a single Unionist, while it had Ferid Paşa as Minister of the Interior, and he was definitely hostile towards the Committee.

quite clear on 24 May when Hilmi Paşa came before the Chamber
to present his programme and to ask the House for a vote of
confidence.[1] He came under heavy attacks, but finally the Chamber
gave him the vote 191 to 5. The Committee probably thought it
expedient to do so because a Cabinet crisis at such a critical
stage would have proved fatal to parliamentary government.
There seems to be some truth in what a Cabinet minister is
reported to have told the British Ambassador: 'that had the
Committee not arranged to give a vote, Mahmoud Shevket
Pasha might have felt obliged to send the House about its business.'[2] It was much too early to challenge the army. Before it
could take on such a task, the Committee had to re-establish
itself on the capital.

In July 1908, the Committee of Union and Progress had been
faced with the problem of what to do with the power they had so
suddenly acquired. The Unionists were essentially conservative
and had no intentions of destroying the existing governmental
machinery. Therefore they left the elder statesmen in power, and
set themselves up as guardians of the constitution. But in April
1909 the ease with which the non-Unionist Cabinet of Hilmi Paşa
succumbed to the rebels made the Committee realize the need to
strengthen their position by direct participation in government.
They did not intend to take over the Cabinet overtly. They thought
they could solve the problem by introducing Unionist deputies into
the different ministries as under-secretaries.[3] In this way the Committee would be able to influence the minister without offending
traditional prejudice, and also acquire the necessary experience to
be able to take over the ministries at a later date. The Committee
had already secured its position in the Palace by having Hâlid
Ziya appointed as the Sultan's First Secretary and Tevfik Bey as
his Second Chamberlain.[4] The under-secretaries were expected to
serve a similar though more important function in the Cabinet.

Some members of the Committee discussed this idea for the
first time during the counter-revolution.[5] But nothing was done

---

[1] 'Heyet-i Vükelanın Programı', in Tanin, 25 May 1909, 2.
[2] Lowther to Grey, no. 378 con., Pera, 25 May 1909, F.O. 371/761/20293.
[3] H. C. Yalçın, Talât Paşa, 37.
[4] Uşaklıgil, Saray ve Ötesi, i (1940), 20–4; also Mehmed Kaplan, 'Hâlid
Ziya', in İA, v/1, Istanbul, 1948, 146.
[5] Mehmed Cavit, 'Meşrutiyet Devrine ait Cavit Beyin Hatıraları', Tanin,
8 Sept. 1943.

until the revolution had been crushed. On 6 May (23 *Nisan* 1325),
Cavit and Talât went to see Mahmud Şevket Paşa in order to
win him over to their side. But the latter dismissed them with a
few patronizing words[1]. They then went to see the Grand Vezir,
but Hilmi Paşa was no less discouraging. He told them that in
no country were under-secretaries to be found in the Cabinet.[2]
Discouraged but undaunted, the Committee decided to take the
matter before the Chamber.

If deputies were to be allowed to hold the office of under-
secretary, Article 67 of the constitution would have to be modified.
This article laid down that a deputy could not hold, at the same
time, any other government appointment. Though a minister
could be elected a deputy, other officials elected as deputies were
obliged to resign their office if they accepted their mandate as
deputy.[3] A motion of amendment had first to be passed by the
Chamber of Deputies by a two-thirds majority of its members,
then approved by the Senate by a similar majority, and finally
sanctioned by Imperial *İrade*, before it came into force.[4] In theory,
a vote in the Chamber should have been easy to obtain. There
was no opposition in June 1909, and the House was packed with
Unionists. But the Committee itself was divided over the issue of
under-secretaries. In the Party and the *Cemiyet* there were those
who did not approve of the idea of choosing under-secretaries
from among their members.[5]

The problem was brought before the Chamber on 1 June
1909.[6] Hilmi Paşa read the modified version of the article and then
submitted the text to the Committee for the revision of the

<hr />

[1] Ibid., Cavit wrote of the interview with Şevket Paşa: 'He became patronizing; he considered us rather young and thought that we were trying to attain
position. "You will become under-secretaries, do not be in a hurry; when you
gain experience you will even become ministers", he said.' See also Yalçın,
Talât Paşa, 37.

[2] Cavit, op. cit., *Tanin*, 8 Sept. 1943, wrote: 'Hilmi Paşa claimed that in no
country were under-secretaries to be found in the cabinet.' Yalçın thought that
the old generation did not wish to dig its own grave by preparing younger men
to take over. See Yalçın, *Talât Paşa*, 37; Türkgeldi, op. cit. 43; and Hüseyin
Cahit, 'Müsteşarlar meselesi', *Tanin*, 19 May 1909.

[3] Gözübüyük and Kili, op. cit. 32. The official text of the constitution in
French is in G. Aristarchi, *Législation ottomane*, v (1878), 17.

[4] Gözübüyük and Kili, op. cit. Article 116, 38; Aristarchi, op. cit. 24-5.

[5] Yalçın, *Talât Paşa*, 37.

[6] 84th Session, 1 June 1909 in *Takvim-i Vekayi*, 3 June 1909, 8 and 'Chronique parlementaire', *Stamboul*, 2 June 1909, 2; 'A la Chambre ottomane',
Levant Herald, 2 June 1909, 2.

constitution. There was a debate in the Chamber on 12 June which was so long and heated, that finally a closure had to be voted. The issue was then put to the vote by a show of hands. (This seems to have been Ahmed Rıza's device to steam-roll the issue in favour of the Committee.) But when he announced that it had been accepted by a majority, there was an uproar in the House.[1] Several deputies demanded a vote by ballot on the whole question. It was decided, at last, to vote by ballot on the question whether the post of under-secretary was compatible with the mandate of a deputy. The result of the vote was 113 for and 74 against, and since this did not constitute a two-thirds majority the question was left undecided.[2] On Thursday, 17 June, discussion was again re-opened. But the opposition was still too strong and Talât withdrew the motion on behalf of the Committee.[3]

In view of this failure to have Article 67 modified, the Unionists revised their entire policy. They decided to place some of their more prominent and talented members directly into the Cabinet. The policy of moderation and coexistence vis-à-vis the Hilmi Paşa Cabinet was brought to an end. And an attempt was made to introduce unity and discipline into the Society, since experience had shown that measures in the Chamber were defeated because the Committee deputies failed to support them.

Manyasızâde Refik was the first Unionist to become a minister.[4] But on account of his untimely death he had not been able to play a role of any significance.[5] It was not he but Cavit Bey, deputy for Salonika and a prominent member of the CUP, who was the first real Unionist in the Cabinet. He joined the Cabinet in June 1909 as Minister of Finance, and in the years that followed played a role of great importance.[6]

---

[1] 91st Session, 12 June 1909 in Takvim-i Vekayi, 22 June 1909; Report of the Proceedings of the Turkish Parliament during the month of June 1909, enclosure in Lowther to Grey, no. 624 con., Therapia, 4 Aug. 1909, F.O. 371/761/29787, 9–10.

[2] Ibid.; both Stamboul and the Levant Herald of 18 June 1909 give the result as 108 to 75.

[3] 95th Session, 17 June 1909 in Takvim-i Vekayi, 27, 28 June 1909, 12 ff. and 3 ff., respectively. See also 'Chronique parlementaire', Stamboul, 18 June 1909, 2. This time the debate was on another issue and not on the under-secretaries at all. The opponents of the scheme argued that the measure had been defeated in the Chamber, or at least had not obtained the two-thirds majority needed to change the Constitution. Therefore it was now unconstitutional to reopen the issue.

[4] Tunaya, Partiler, 177. [5] See above, Chapter II.

[6] Lowther to Grey, no. 497 con., Therapia, 28 June 1909, F.O. 371/777/25107.

In July 1909, the Committee seem to have considered the possibility of bringing down the Hilmi Paşa Cabinet, and in its place setting up a new Cabinet much more Unionist in complexion. Unable to have a Grand Vezir from amongst their number, they secretly approached Kâmil Paşa and offered him his old office on condition that he include some Unionists in his Cabinet, especially Talât Bey as Minister of the Interior.[1] Kâmil did not reject this proposal but pointed out the shortcomings of the Committee's candidates,[2] and at this point the matter seems to have been dropped.

Meanwhile attacks on the Cabinet continued. The *Tanin* of 20 July accused the Cabinet of containing members attached to the old regime, and demanded that the government be handed over to active, honourable, and trustworthy men, men of the new regime[3]. Three days later, on the anniversary of the revolution, the Central Committee in Salonika issued a proclamation.[4] As Ottomans, all the different elements in the country were called upon to sink their differences in the interests of the nation as a whole. They were urged to replace the Cabinet, which was full of men imbued with the traditions of the old regime, by a younger Cabinet whose youth and enterprise alone could save the country.[4] As a consequence of these attacks, Ferid Paşa, whose name was intimately connected with the old regime, resigned as Minister of the Interior, and his place was taken by Talât.[5]

Hüseyin Cahit wrote: 'Cavit Bey may be counted as the first Minister of Finance since the Revolution of July 10.' Rütbesiz Nâzır', *Tanin*, 27 June 1909. For a brief account of Cavit's activities during this period see D. A. Rustow, article on Djawid Bey in *EI*[2].

[1] Lowther to Grey, pr., Constantinople, 20 July 1909, F.O. 800/78. Sir Gerard's informant was Kâmil Paşa himself. On its intention to replace Hilmi Paşa with a candidate of its own, the Committee wrote to the Eastern Question Association in Putney: 'Hilmi has upset our projected Bulgarian alliance and will not hold long as Grand Vizir if he does not give way. Talaat would not consent to be nominated Grand Vizir and he is right to keep out of it for a time. Kiamil Pasha is friendly to us now, but his chances are not improved for re-appointment as Grand Vizir in consequence of his name having been pushed forward by your Embassy which ought to desist if it really wishes to help him' (N) [Nâzım?]. Committee of Union and Progress to Mr. Atkin (Secretary of the Eastern Question Association), Salonica, 2 Sept. 1909, in F.O. 371/780/33878.

[2] Lowther to Grey, ibid. Kâmil's objection to Talât becoming a minister was that he had been an employee in the telegraph office on £3 a month.

[3] *Tanin*, 20 July 1909. 1.

[4] 'İttihat ve Terakki Cemiyetinin Osmanlılara Beyannamesi', text in *Tanin*, 24 July 1909.

[5] Lowther to Grey, no. 263 con., Constantinople, 7 Aug. 1909, F.O. 371/761/29709.

With Cavit and Talât in the Cabinet the Committee's position
was more secure. The Committee now set out to remedy the
factionalism and lack of unity amongst its members in the Chamber. As early as December 1908, even before Parliament had met,
Sir Gerard Lowther had predicted that deputies elected on the
Committee's ticket would not always vote with it in the Chamber.[1] This prediction was vindicated when the Committee was
forced to disown its dissident members who insisted on voting
against Kâmil Paşa on 13 January 1909 and on many other
occasions.[2]

The Committee, realizing its weak position in the Chamber,
tried a political manœuvre. At an official dinner of the CUP at
the Pera Palas Hotel on 12 March, Hilmi Paşa announced that
the Committee had renounced its old role since the opening of
Parliament in order to form a political party.[3] The purpose of this
announcement was to appease the dissidents in the Chamber who
wanted independence of action, and the opposition who challenged
the Committee to come out into the open. Having made this concession to its deputies, the Committee hoped they would vote in
accordance with its wishes. On 12 June, the same day as Article 67
was to be discussed in the Chamber, the press published the official
Charter of the Parliamentary Party of Union and Progress.[4] The
concession did not have the desired result and Article 67 was not
modified. Unity seemed to be as far away as ever. Just before the
Second Congress of the CUP, Hüseyin Cahit wrote an article on
the position of the Society and the Party. He called for unity and
discipline and pointed out that those deputies who had been
elected under the auspices of the Committee, had a duty to obey
its orders. But to those deputies and members of the Committee
who did not like its programme, he offered the alternative of
making their own programme and forming a separate party.[5] In
February 1910 some Unionist deputies, as if acting on Cahit Bey's

[1] Lowther to Grey, no. 855 con., Pera, 13 Dec. 1908, F.O. 371/546/43987.
[2] See above, Chapter II.
[3] *Levant Herald*, 15 Mar. 1909. This was the first official announcement of
a parliamentary party within the CUP. A few hours before the outbreak of
13 Apr. it was repeated with a view to calming down the opposition and avoid-
ing the fast approaching calamity. See Tunaya, *Partiler*, 183; and McCullagh,
Abd-ul-Hamid, 74.
[4] Meclisi Mebusanı Osmanîde Müteşekkil İttihad ve Terakki Fırkasının
Nizamnamei Dahilisi, text in Tunaya, *Partiler*, 210–11.
[5] 'Cemiyet ve Fırka', *Tanin*, 7 Sept. 1909.

advice, formed the *Ahâli Fırkası* (People's Party) and ended the myth of a monolithic Committee once and for all.[1]

The conflict between the civilians and the military was much more complex, and is therefore more difficult to put one's finger on. In theory both elements were allied against reaction and committed to the constitution. In practice they differed on the question of power. The military, having restored a constitutional regime, recognized the civilians' legal right to power. The civilians, in their turn, conceded to the military the right to interfere in politics by consenting to the establishment of martial law, which in practice placed the military above the civilian administration. The result was an ambiguous situation with two legal authorities enjoying undefined powers.

Hüseyin Cahit's article of 26 October was an attempt to find a solution to this situation favourable to the Committee.[2] He appreciated the army's role in defending the constitution, but pointed out that further interference was unnecessary now that a constitutional regime was firmly established. He warned that continued interference would be harmful both to the state and to military discipline.[2] Because of the changed situation, the Committee had decided that in future soldiers would not be members of the Committee, its clubs, or in any way be connected with it. But at the same time they would not leave the Committee.[3] This double talk can only be taken to mean that while the Committee expected the senior officers to opt out of politics, it expected junior officers to continue supporting it.

Mahmud Şevket Paşa was of the opposite view. He expected all (junior) officers to terminate their affiliations with political parties and societies, since political involvement undermined the unity and discipline of the army.[4] The Imperial proclamation of 29 May, appealing to officers in the armed forces to stay out of politics, made this quite plain.[5] In a speech at the Second Army headquarters at Edirne in November, Şevket Paşa personally urged his officers to abstain from politics. As an example of exploiting the army for political ends, he pointed to Colonel

---

[1] Tunaya, *Partiler*, 294–5.

[2] Hüseyin Cahit, 'Askerler ve Cemiyet', *Tanin*, 26 Oct. 1909.

[3] Ibid., see also Tunaya, *Partiler*, 183–4.

[4] Consul Lamb to Lowther, tel., no. 135 sal., Salonica, 21 Apr. 1909, F.O. 195/2328.

[5] *Hatt-ı Hümayun* dated 16 May 1325 in *Tanin*, 30 May 1909, 2.

Sadık's election as the Committee's delegate in negotiations between the Committee and the Porte.[1]

The differences between the military and the Committee were not always expressed in such open terms. More often they were shrouded in the Anglo-German rivalry then taking place in the Ottoman Empire. The Committee looked to Britain and the military to Germany, and any criticism of Germany in the Committee press could be taken to imply criticism of the military.

This also partially explains the Committee's feelers to Kâmil Paşa in July 1909.[2] Kâmil was a notorious Anglophile, and was known to have the support and goodwill of the British Embassy at Istanbul. He also had the prestige and experience necessary to become independent of Şevket Paşa, something which Hüseyin Hilmi did not seem to be anxious to do. July 1909 seemed a good time for the Committee to attempt to bring about a *rapprochement* with Britain. An Ottoman Parliamentary Delegation was visiting Paris and London,[3] while General von der Goltz was in Istanbul to reorganize the army.[4]

In December, a project to amalgamate the Hamidieh, an Ottoman navigation company on the River Euphrates, and the Lynch Company, a British concern, became another occasion to air the conflict between the Committee and Şevket Paşa.[5] The Committee press ascribed the opposition to the fusion scheme to German instigation. Şevket Paşa and von der Goltz were accused of planning to overthrow the CUP in order to set up a military regime devoted to German interests.[6] There were further attacks

[1] Mr. Marling to Grey, no. 896 con., Constantinople, 10 Nov. 1909, F.O. 371/761/41733.

[2] See above, p. 53.

[3] Lowther to Grey, no. 510 con., Therapia, 1 July 1909, F.O. 371/778/25436; and *The Times*, 16 July 1909.

[4] Lowther to Grey, no. 552 con., Therapia, 14 July 1909, F.O. 371/775/27099.

[5] There is a very detailed documentary account of the 'Lynch Affair' in F.O. 371/759.

[6] *Le Jeune Turc*, 12 décembre 1909, enclosure in Marling to Grey, no. 967 v. con., Constantinople, 14 Dec. 1909, F.O. 371/781/46061. The main opponent of the fusion scheme was Babanzâde İsmail Hakkı, deputy for Baghdad. He was a very prominent Unionist and opposed to fusion on the grounds that Britain was already powerful in Iraq, and control of the river system would make her even more powerful. As a good Unionist, he wanted the Porte to strengthen its hold in Iraq, rather than make it weaker. The whole problem was, of course, linked with the Baghdad Railway and German interests therein.

on Germany in the *Tanin*, particularly in the issue of 17 December.[1] These attacks were so displeasing to the military that it was thought that Cahit Bey would be summoned before the court martial.[2] Though it did not take place, the court martial suspended the *Tanin* on 22 December.[3] The military made it quite clear who had the real power.

In the Chamber, the 'Lynch Affair' aroused much spirited debate.[4] Finally, Hilmi Paşa, who favoured the fusion scheme, asked for a vote of confidence. The vote he received was almost unanimous.[5] Yet, in spite of his mandate from the Chamber, Hilmi Paşa tendered his resignation on 28 December.[6] The resignation was accepted and the office offered to Hakkı Paşa, Ambassador in Rome. After some hesitation and negotiations, Hakkı Paşa accepted, and the *Hatt* announcing his appointment was issued on 12 January 1910.[7]

(ii) THE PERIOD OF CONSTITUTIONAL REFORM

The first session of the Ottoman Parliament ended on 27 August 1909.[8] It was a long and eventful session, and for the sake of convenience may be divided into three quite distinct periods. The first period lasted from the opening of Parliament on 17 December 1908 to the fall of Kâmil Paşa on 13 February 1909.[9] During this period Parliament was more concerned about the crisis brought on by Austria-Hungary's annexation of Bosnia and Herzegovina, and Bulgaria's declaration of independence, than with legislation. Moreover, the Chamber was still too inexperienced

---

[1] Hüseyin Cahid, 'Almanlar ve Osmanlılar', *Tanin*, 17 Dec. 1909. See also Mr. Marling to Grey, no. 994 con., Constantinople, 26 Dec. 1909, F.O. 371/992/178.

[2] Marling to Grey, no. 994.   [3] *Yeni Tanin*, 23 Dec. 1909.

[4] 'Chronique parlementaire', *Stamboul*, 30 nov. 1909, 2. The interpellation of Hilmi Paşa on this subject was asked for by three deputies from Mesopotamia. See also 'Chronique parlementaire', *Stamboul*, 13 Dec. 1909; 'L'affaire Lynch à la Chambre', also the *Levant Herald*, 30 Dec. 1909.

[5] *Stamboul*, 14 Dec. 1909; *Levant Herald*, 14 Dec. 1909.

[6] *Yeni Tanin*, 29 Dec. 1909; and also *Sabah* and *İkdam* of the same date.

[7] A.A.A. (Adıvar), 'İbrahim Hakkı Paşa', *İA*, V/ii (1951), 892. *Hatt-ı Hümayun* in *Yeni Tanin*, 13 Jan. 1910.

[8] *Tanin*, 28 Aug. 1909.   [9] See above, Chapter II.

and inarticulate and lacked the unity necessary for legislating. The second period began with Kâmil's fall and ended with the deposition of Abdülhamid II and the accession of Mehmed V in May 1909. The failure of the revolt of 13 April temporarily discredited the conservative, anti-reformist element in the Empire, and gave an impetus to the radical, reformist group in the Chamber. It was, therefore, during the third period, lasting from the beginning of May to 27 August, that most of the legislative work was done.

In his closing address to the Chamber Ahmed Rıza, its President, summed up the legislative work of the first session.[1] The Government had submitted seventy-three Bills to the Chamber. The Chamber had passed fifty-three of these after discussion, and the remainder had gone to various committees. Deputies had submitted 668 motions to the House, of which 158 were accepted and passed on to the competent ministries by special committees appointed for the purpose.[1] Ahmed Rıza was simply pointing out that the Chamber had legislated on almost every kind of problem, from the vital to the trivial. The Chamber had passed such an important law as the 'Law of the Provisional Budget of 1909',[2] as well as laws of minor importance, such as the 'Law Prohibiting the Use of Spirits or Wine in Beverages'.[3] Essentially the purpose of the legislation enacted in this period was threefold. Firstly, to write into the constitution the political changes which had taken place since July 1908. Secondly, to modernize and give unity to the Ottoman Empire and its administrative machine. Finally, and closely bound up with the second aim, to enact such legislation as to make the capitulations unnecessary, and thus bring about their abolition.

The question as to whom was the supreme authority in the Empire had already been decided in favour of the Chamber of Deputies. The amendments legalized the *fait accompli*. Of the 119 articles of the 1876 Constitution, twenty-one were modified, one annulled, and three new ones were added.[4] Not all the modifications recorded a change in the power structure; some, Article 28 for example, were phrased differently.[5] But the amendments

---

[1] Ahmed Rıza's speech in *Tanin* 28 Aug. 1909.
[2] *Takvim-i Vekayi*, 16 Mar. 1909.   [3] *Takvim-i Vekayi*, 30 Aug. 1909.
[4] H. N. Kubalı, 'Kanun-i Esasi', in *İA*, vi. 170.
[5] The 1909 amendments of the 1876 Constitution are published in *Takvim-i Vekayi*, 4 Sept. 1909. The text of these amendments in the modern Turkish

of Articles 3, 7, 27, 77, and 113 virtually mark the end of the Sultan's power and prerogatives. The modified versions of Articles 29, 30, 35, 38, 44, 53, and 54 show how completely the Porte had fallen into the shadow of Parliament.

Article 3 which had vested unconditional sovereignty in the House of Osman was revised. Sovereignty was made conditional on the Sultan's oath before the General Assembly to respect the *Şeriat* and the constitution, and to remain faithful to the country and to the nation.[1] The Sultan's prerogative to nominate and revoke ministers was omitted from Article 7. Though he was permitted to nominate persons to high office, he had to do so in conformity with special laws. He retained most of his old prerogatives, though the right to make a treaty of almost any kind, which had been his in the past, was now made subject to the approval of Parliament.[2]

The appointment of ministers was taken out of the hands of the Sultan. He still retained his prerogative to appoint the Grand Vezir and the *Şeyhülislâm*. But the duty of choosing the rest of the Cabinet was vested in the Grand Vezir, who was expected to submit his list to the Sultan for his sanction.[3] In the same way, the President and the two Vice-Presidents of the Chamber of Deputies were no longer appointed by the Sultan. They were elected by the deputies and the result of the election was submitted to the Sultan for his sanction.[4] Finally, Article 113, that notorious article which had given the Sultan the right to banish anyone who was regarded as a danger to the security of the state, and which had been used to exile Midhat Paşa, the architect of the 1876 Constitution, was so completely modified that the Sultan was not even mentioned in it.[5]

The result of the modification of these five articles was that the Sultan 'reigned but no longer ruled'. His function in the government of the Ottoman Empire was restricted to confirming decisions already taken by the Cabinet or Parliament.

script is given in Gözübüyük and Kili, op. cit. 70–3, and the complete text of the 1876 Constitution on 25–38. For convenience all future references to the Constitution will be made to Gözübüyük and Kili and Aristarchi, op. cit.

[1] Gözübüyük and Kili, op. cit., old article on 25, modified version 70 (Article 3); Aristarchi, op. cit. 7.

[2] Gözübüyük and Kili, op. cit. (Article 7), 25 and 70; Aristarchi, op. cit. 7–8.

[3] Gözübüyük and Kili, op. cit. (Article 27), 27 and 70; Aristarchi, op. cit. 10.

[4] Gözübüyük and Kili, op. cit. (Article 77), 33 and 72; Aristarchi, op. cit. 18.

[5] Gözübüyük and Kili, op. cit. (Article 113), 37 and 73; Aristarchi, op. cit. 24.

The Unionists were as determined to curb the powers of the Porte as those of the Palace. That is why they had taken such a firm stand against Kâmil Paşa, bringing about his fall in 1909. The amendments were a manifestation of the weakened position of the Porte. Article 29 limited the discretionary power which had been the Grand Vezir's in the past.[1] Ministers were made responsible to the Chamber of Deputies, jointly for the over-all policy of the Government, and individually for the policy of their departments.[2]

In case of any disagreement between the Cabinet and the Chamber, the Cabinet had either to submit to the ruling of the Chamber or resign. If the Cabinet resigned and a new ministry was formed which adopted its predecessor's posture, and if the Chamber rejected it with a vote of no confidence, the Sultan was bound to dissolve the Chamber and order new elections in accordance with the constitution. But if the new Chamber maintained the decision of its predecessor, then the ministry was obliged to abide by the ruling. In short, the last word was always with the Chamber.[3] The Cabinet became totally dependent on the goodwill of the Chamber. The Chamber could summon, by a majority vote, a minister and interpellate him on any matter. If after the interpellation a vote of no confidence was passed, the minister would fall. If the minister happened to be the Grand Vezir, his Cabinet would fall with him.[4]

In the past, all proposals for new legislation had gone through the Cabinet, which had drawn up the Bill. But Article 53 was revised in 1909. Initiative for legislation could now come directly from both Chambers, and legislation could be carried out without the Cabinet's intervention, though it had to be sanctioned by the Sultan before it became law.[5] Article 54 strengthened Parliament's hold over the legislative process even further.[6]

If one of the aims of amending the constitution was to weaken the executive and strengthen the legislature, it was fulfilled beyond all expectations. Ever since July 1908 the Unionists had placed

[1] Gözübüyük and Kili, op. cit. (Article 29), 27 and 71; Aristarchi, op. cit. 10.
[2] Gözübüyük and Kili, op. cit. (Article 30), 28 and 71; Aristarchi, op. cit. 10.
[3] Gözübüyük and Kili, op. cit. (Article 35), 28 and 71; Aristarchi, op. cit. 11.
[4] Gözübüyük and Kili, op. cit. (Article 38), 29 and 71; Aristarchi, op. cit. 12.
[5] Gözübüyük and Kili, op. cit. (Article 53), 30–1 and 72; Aristarchi, op. cit. 14–15.
[6] Gözübüyük and Kili, op. cit. (Article 54), 31 and 72; Aristarchi, op. cit. 15.

the hopes of their reform movement in a strong Parliament, which they expected to act as a counterbalance to the more conservative forces in the Palace and the Porte. How powerful they had succeeded in making Parliament only became clear in 1912, when the Committee found the Chamber of its own creation unmanageable. But in 1909, for better or for worse, the centre of gravity had definitely shifted in favour of the legislature.

Apart from the constitutional amendments, the Chamber passed other legislation whose aim seems to have been to curb some of the freedom released by the Revolution of 1908, and to prevent recurrence of a counter-revolution of the type that had just been suppressed. With these legislative measures the Unionists also tried to centralize the Government and to bring unity to the Empire by 'ottomanizing' all the diverse elements therein. Thus within the span of a few months the Chamber passed the 'Law on Vagabondage and Suspected Persons',[1] the 'Law on Public Meetings',[2] the 'Laws on the Press and Printing Establishments',[3] the 'Law on Strikes',[4] the 'Law concerning the Conscription of non-Muslims',[5] the 'Law of Associations',[6] and the 'Law for the Prevention of Brigandage and Sedition'.[7]

The purpose of these laws was to place in the government's hands the power to curb any movement expressing dissatisfaction against its policies. The 'Law on Vagabondage and Suspected Persons' curbed any kind of individual action, while the 'Law on Public Meetings' made any public protest impossible. Before any meeting, the organizer was expected to present a written declaration stating his name and profession, and indicating the place, date, and time of the meeting. The 'Laws on the Press and Printing Establishments', while not actually censoring the newspapers, acted as a great restraint on the freedom of the press. The anti-strike law checkmated any action that might have been taken by the growing labour movement. And the 'Law of Associations',

---

[1] *Takvim-i Vekayi*, 14 May 1909, Text (French) in Lowther to Grey, no. 588 con., Therapia, 26 July 1909, F.O. 371/779/28919.

[2] *Takvim-i Vekayi*, 17 June 1909. Translation of law in Lowther to Grey, no. 466 con., Therapia, 22 June 1909 F.O. 371/777/23981.

[3] Printed as two separate laws in *Takvim-i Vekayi*, 31 July 1909. Texts of both laws in Lowther to Grey, no. 655 con., Therapia, 11 Aug. 1909, F.O. 371/779/30768.

[4] *Takvim-i Vekayi*, 15 Aug. 1909. [5] Ibid. 11 Aug. 1909.

[6] Ibid. 23 Aug. 1909. French text in *Stamboul*, 24 Aug. 1909.

[7] Y. H. Bayur, *Tarih*, i. 306.

the 'Law for the Prevention of Brigandage and Sedition', and
the 'Law on the Conscription of non-Muslims' were a belated
attempt to end the difference existing among the various ethnic
groups in the Empire and to bring about unity. The first law
forbade the formation of political clubs or associations which had
an ethnic basis or a national name.[1] The second law authorized
the formation of special military units to be used for disarming and
repressing Greek and Bulgarian bands in Rumelia and Armenian
bands in eastern Turkey.

Those measures which had aimed at centralization met with a
certain amount of success. But the growth of nationalism among
the subject peoples of the Empire made it too late in the day
to realize 'the "ottomanist" dream of the free, equal, and peaceful association of peoples in a common loyalty to the dynastic
sovereign of a multi-national, multi-denominational empire'.[2] Even
while the association law was being discussed in the Chamber,
Dalçef Efendi, a Bulgarian deputy, had pointed out 'that union of
different elements would not be brought about by the passing of
laws, but by community of interests'.[3] This was exactly what was
lacking in the Ottoman Empire.

The Unionists were concerned with one other problem; the
creation of a modern state. For this it was essential to abolish the
capitulations, 'long resented as a symbol of inferiority and sub-
servience',[4] and absolutely incompatible with the status of a
modern state whose sovereignty they violated. Knowing that they
were not powerful enough to abrogate the capitulary rights of
foreigners unilaterally, the Unionists tried to overcome this
weakness by legislation. By introducing sound legislation, they
hoped to make the administration of the Empire efficient so that
foreigners would no longer need to claim their special privileges.
At the same time, the new laws would violate the capitulations in
such a discreet way that the Great Powers would either be forced
to ignore the violation or they would not be able to intervene
effectively. In a short time, it was hoped, a precedent would be

---

[1] Article 120, one of the articles newly added laid down this principle in the
constitution itself. See Gözübüyük and Kili, op. cit. 73.

[2] B. Lewis, *Emergence*, 214.

[3] 'Report of the Proceedings in the Ottoman Parliament during July and
August 1909', 6, enclosure in Lowther to Grey, no. 799 con., Therapia, 29
Sept. 1909, F.O. 371/761/36622.

[4] B. Lewis, *Emergence*, 249.

set, and the capitulations would either wither away or would be renounced by the Powers voluntarily.[1]

But the Unionists, far from being anti-foreign, had sought foreign assistance in reforming and modernizing the administration of the Empire. A few months after the revolution, the Porte obtained the services of Crawford, a British customs official, to reorganize the Ottoman Customs. His work was appreciated so much that the Porte asked for his term to be extended for a further two years.[2] In the same way the Porte wanted its post and telegraphic services modernized so that foreign post offices could be abolished. The Ministry of Post and Telegraph was opened on 23 July 1909, and in his speech, Nâil Bey, significantly, spoke of the foreign post offices as an infringement of Turkish sovereignty, and asked for efficiency so that they could be removed.[3] A few weeks later, Sterpin was engaged as director-general of the new ministry,[4] and a new article was added to the constitution guaranteeing the inviolability of mail in the Ottoman post.[5] In August, Count Ostrorog was appointed *conseiller de justice*. His duties were mainly those of drafting laws for presentation to the Chamber, and bringing the Ottoman code of law in line with that of Europe.[6]

The Porte's attempt to violate the capitulations did not go unnoticed. The British Ambassador pointed out to his government that each law often infringed upon the treaty rights of foreigners.

---

[1] Even in the nineteenth century 'one of the main purposes of these changes was to meet foreign criticisms of Ottoman justice, and thus prepare the way for the abrogation or limitation of foreign judicial privileges recognized by the capitulations'. B. Lewis, *Emergence*, 179. During this period there was considerable optimism that the capitulations would soon be abolished. Thus, while discussing the privileges that various elements enjoyed in the field of education, Talât Bey said in the Chamber that he 'failed to understand how, at a time when the capitulations were about to be abolished, school privileges could be retained'. Debate, 8 June 1909, 'Report of the Proceedings of the Turkish Parliament during the month of June, 1909', in Lowther to Grey, no. 624 con., Therapia, 4 Aug. 1909, F.O. 371/761/29787; and *Tanin*, 9 June 1909.

[2] Grey to Lloyd George (Chancellor of the Exchequer), London, 29 July 1909, F.O. 371/763/34737.

[3] Lowther to Grey, no. 594 con., Therapia, 26 July 1909, F.O. 371/779/28925.

[4] Sterpin, a Belgian, was engaged because Belgium had no post office in the Ottoman Empire, and he was therefore acceptable to everyone. Lowther to Grey, no. 656 con., Therapia, 10 Aug. 1909, F.O. 371/779/30769.

[5] Article 119, Gözübüyük and Kili, op. cit. 73.

[6] Lowther to Grey, no. 632 con., Therapia, 6 Aug. 1909, F.O. 371/779/30745.

To overcome this he suggested that each law as passed be examined and action taken as required.[1] It was the result of such diplomatic surveillance that the Porte withdrew Article 13 of the 'Law on Vagabondage and Suspected Persons'. This article sanctioned flogging as a punishment for vagabondage, and the foreign missions refused to allow their subjects to be flogged by the Ottoman authorities.[1] The foreign embassies maintained their surveillance over all new legislation passed by the Chamber, and frustrated the Porte's attempt to abrogate the capitulations. The capitulations continued to haunt the Turks until 24 July 1924 when they were abolished by the Treaty of Lausanne.[2] While they remained in force, the Ottoman Empire retained its status of a 'semi-colony'.[3]

[1] Lowther to Grey, no. 665 con., Therapia, 14 Aug. 1909, F.O. 371/779/31623.

[2] B. Lewis, *Emergence*, 249.

[3] Hüseyin Avni, *Bir Yarm Müstemleke Oluş Tarihi* (1932), Istanbul, *passim*.

IV

THE GROWTH OF OPPOSITION

THE role of the Committee of Union and Progress in the politics of the period under review has been exaggerated to an extent that discourages any attempt to look beyond the obvious. Almost all political happenings have been reduced to the machinations of the Committee. In conformity with this convenient pattern, Hilmi Paşa's resignation on 28 December 1909— a fortnight after receiving an overwhelming vote of confidence— has also been put down to Unionist pressure and intrigue.[1] It is true that the Unionists had not been happy with Hilmi during both his terms of office. He had succumbed to the counter-revolutionaries on 13 April without offering any resistance. After the counter-revolution had been crushed he was restored to power by Şevket Paşa, and throughout the rest of the year he remained virtually neutral in the masked struggle between the Committee and the military. All this may have provided sufficient motive for some Unionists to seek his resignation. But it is doubtful if they were in a position to bring it about.

Besides there is no reason why we should not believe Hilmi Paşa's own testimony regarding his resignation. To the press he declared that he had resigned purely on personal grounds, that the Committee had put no pressure on him as was being suggested, and that there was no disagreement between him and the Committee. Hilmi's declaration was confirmed by Halil Bey, President of the Parliamentary Party of the CUP.[2] But the truth probably lies

---

[1] Y. H. Bayur, *Tarih*, i. 318; Danişmend, *Kronoloji*, iv. 381; Okandan, op. cit. 345; İnal, op. cit. 1572 ff.; Tunaya, *Partiler*, 178 n. 16, cites an article by Babanzâde İsmail Hakkı as evidence of Unionist collusion; *Sabah*, *İkdam*, and *Stamboul* of 29 Dec. 1909; and Lowther to Grey, no. 8 con., Constantinople, 1 Jan. 1910, F.O. 371/1000/928; Uşaklıgil, *Saray ve Ötesi*, ii (1940), 24.

[2] *Yeni Tanin*, nos. 14 and 15, 7 and 8 Jan. 1910 respectively; *Stamboul*, 8 Jan. 1910; *The Times*, 29 and 30 Dec. 1909; in the issue of the 30th *The Times*'s correspondent cited Hilmi Paşa's interview with Reuter's correspondent. İnal, op. cit. 1672–3. It is worth noting that in Aug. 1912, because Ahmed Muhtar Paşa's Cabinet was persecuting Unionists, Hilmi Paşa resigned his portfolio as Minister of Justice; see Abdurrahman Bey cited in İnal, op. cit. 1674.

somewhere in the middle. While not discounting completely the Committee's role, especially its harassment of the government in the Chamber, it is necessary to look for more convincing reasons for Hilmi Paşa's resignation.

One factor was Hilmi Paşa's own reluctance for office during such troubled and uncertain times. He had had most of his experience in provincial administration, and had made his reputation as Inspector-General of Macedonia.[1] After the revolution he was Minister of the Interior in Kâmil Paşa's Cabinet, and when Kâmil fell in February 1909, he succeeded him as Grand Vezir.[2] Hilmi's first term in office was a period of great political unrest culminating in the mutiny of April 1909. It was during this period that he expressed his regret at not having gained more experience under such well-tried Grand Vezirs as Said and Kâmil Paşas, before himself assuming that post.[3]

Hilmi's second term as Grand Vezir passed under the shadow of Mahmud Şevket Paşa and martial law, and he was deprived of virtually all independence of action.[4] The debate in the Chamber on the 'Lynch Affair' was the straw that broke the camel's back.[5] Hilmi (and Cavit), finding the behaviour of the Chamber unreasonable and unpredictable, decided to settle the matter once and for all. In this situation and mood Hilmi went to submit his resignation to the Sultan. To Halid Ziya, the Sultan's First Secretary, he exclaimed: 'It is not possible to have an understanding with the Party. No Grand Vezir can remain in office without relying on the majority. . . .'[6] But Hilmi was not simply throwing in his hand and admitting defeat. Through Halid Ziya he placed before the Sultan a number of alternatives. He suggested that the Sultan could reject his resignation. If the resignation was accepted, however, the Sultan could reappoint Hilmi and ask him to form a new Cabinet. If the new Cabinet did not obtain the confidence of Parliament the Sultan could then dissolve the Chamber and order fresh elections. On the other hand, the Sultan could accept Hilmi Paşa's resignation, summon the Presidents of the Senate and Chamber of Deputies and appoint the new Grand Vezir on

---

[1] İnal, op. cit. 1654–64; Uşaklıgil, *Saray ve Ötesi*, ii (1940), 23–4.

[2] İnal, op. cit. 1655; see above, Chapter II.

[3] Türkgeldi, op. cit. 23.

[4] Abdurrahman Efendi, quoted in İnal, op. cit. 1673; 'A Minister's Political Memoirs', *Tan*, 21 Jan. 1937, quoted in İnal, op. cit. 1844.

[5] See above, p. 56–7.   [6] Uşaklıgil, *Saray ve Ötesi*, ii (1940), 24.

their advice.[1] Mehmed Reşad thought it was more expedient to simply accept Hilmi's resignation and then let events take their course.

There was another factor which seems to have had something to do with Hilmi Paşa's resignation: the 'Lynch Concession'. Hilmi Paşa's overwhelming vote of confidence over the 'Lynch Affair' created a new problem. Technically it left Hilmi free to grant the concession to the English firm. But 'national' interest prevented him from doing so. Talking about the political implications of granting a concession for a railway from Baghdad to the Persian Gulf, Hilmi had said: 'This question puts us between the hammer and the anvil. For political reasons I cannot grant this concession to the British. . . .'[2] The same political reasons applied to the granting of the 'Lynch Concession'. The fear of British expansion in Iraq was strong among Arab deputies and within Iraq itself. Politically it was too potent a factor for the Porte to ignore. Even while the question was being discussed in the Chamber, there had been protest meetings in Baghdad against the concession being granted to an English concern.[3] The situation in Baghdad and Basra became so serious that the Porte considered proclaiming martial law.[4] It would be dangerous to grant the concession to the Lynch Company, but also 'very difficult for us to reject the British . . . whose help we depend on in various questions'.[5] Under such conditions Hilmi's resignation offered the best way out of this impasse; it would free his successors from established policy and decisions.[6] Thus Hakkı Paşa was able to reverse Hilmi's 'decision' concerning the 'Lynch Concession', and he even cancelled some other concessions ear-marked for British enterprise in and around Iraq.[7]

[1] Ibid. 29–30

[2] E. T. S. Dugdale (ed. and trans.), *German Diplomatic Documents, 1871–1914*, iii (London, 1930), 367; Ambassador von Marschall to the German Foreign Office, Constantinople, 25 Oct. 1909 (hereafter cited as *GDD*).

[3] Y. H. Bayur, *Tarih*, i. 318; *Stamboul*, 22 Dec. 1909; *The Times*, 11 Dec. 1909. *The Times* correspondent wrote: '. . . Ismail Hakki Babanzadeh and Deputies from the Arab districts, who cherished a sincere, if unfounded, belief that the scheme of amalgamation covered an ingenious design on the part of Great Britain to effect the economic conquest of Irak. . . .'; and von Marschall, Constantinople, 26 Oct. 1909 and 6 Nov. 1909, *GDD*, iii. 368 and 385 respectively. [4] *Levant Herald*, 29 Dec. 1909.

[5] Hilmi Paşa's conversation with von Marschall, *GDD*, iii. 367.

[6] *Levant Herald*, 29 Dec. 1909.

[7] Lowther to Grey, no. 25 con., Constantinople, 15 Jan. 1910, F.O.

There was considerable speculation about Hilmi Paşa's successor. Hakkı, Kâmil, Said, and Ferid Paşas are said to have been considered, but Hakkı was chosen because he was the least controversial and most acceptable candidate. The fact that he had been legal adviser to the Porte and ambassador to Italy gave him roots in traditional institutions and made him acceptable to the conservative element. His liberal education in political science and law and his early career as a lecturer brought him 'closer to youth, to innovation and Europeanization than the earlier vezirs'.[1] Not being a partisan of any faction, he was able to bargain with all sides. He demanded absolute freedom in forming his Cabinet and once this condition was met he accepted office. One of his first acts as Grand Vezir was to appoint Şevket Paşa Minister of War, thereby hoping to end the anomaly of having the administrator of martial law and the Inspector-General of the first three army corps outside Cabinet control.[2] But Şevket Paşa's inclusion in the Cabinet created problems of its own.

Yusuf Hikmet Bayur has noted that the year 1910 was the first and last year when the Ottoman Empire was free of irksome external problems (excepting Crete) and the pressure of foreign governments.[3] But this favourable external situation did not make for internal political stability; if anything it aggravated it. Milanovich, the Serbian Minister for Foreign Affairs, who visited Istanbul early in 1910, observed that 'the position of Hakki Pasha was . . . not paramount; there was the Committee, and there was, above all, the army, not to speak of the various elements which were not friendly to the new order of things'.[4] This, briefly, was the political situation prevailing in the capital. The

371/1000/1348; Grey to Lowther, no. 37, tel. con., Foreign Office, 17 Feb. 1910, F.O. 371/1004/5693; Memorandum: Sir H. B. Smith's interview with Hakkı Paşa, enclosure in Smith to Nicolson, Constantinople, 30 Dec. 1910, F.O. 371/1240/636.

[1] Yalçın, Talât Paşa, 36; İnal, op. cit. 1763 and 1783–4; Uşaklıgil, Saray ve Ötesi, ii (1940), 44 ff.; 'Sadrazam Kim Olacak?', İkdam, and Tanin of 29 Dec. 1909; Lowther to Grey (op. cit., p. 65 n. 1).

[2] A. A. A. (Adıvar), 'İbrahim Hakkı Paşa', İA, v/ıı (1951), 892. İnal, 1871 and 1884; 'Political Memoirs', Tan, 21 Jan. 1937; Mahmud Muhtar Paşa, Maziye bir Nazar, cited in İnal, 1884; Yeni Gazete, 3 Jan. 1910, quoted in Stamboul of 3 Jan. 1910, Lowther to Grey (op. cit., p. 65 n. 1), and also no. 27 con., Constantinople, 16 Jan. 1910, F.O. 371/1000/3550.

[3] Y. H. Bayur, Tarih, i. 316.

[4] Nicolson to Grey, no. 158 con., St. Petersburg, 26 Mar. 1910, F.O. 371/1008/11717.

discord between the military and the politicians continued un-abated. But a development of greater political significance was the reappearance of conservative groups, both within the CUP and without; groups which had lain dormant since May 1909. The formation of the People's Party (*Ahâli Fırkası*) on 21 February 1910 was the first manifestation of this.[1] At the time it aroused little comment because everyone was preoccupied with martial law. But it was not long before people realized the long-term consequences of the growth of a conservative opposition.

The continued existence of martial law made a mockery of constitutional government. Hakkı Paşa tried to modify this situation by bringing Şevket Paşa into the Cabinet, and in his programme read before the Chamber on 25 January he promised to end martial law 'now that the situation was normal once more'.[2] Not only did he fail to carry out this promise, but his idea of using Şevket Paşa to strengthen the position of his Cabinet also boomeranged. Şevket's presence in the Cabinet weakened the reformist group, especially with regard to financial reform.

The Committee had set itself the task of reforming the administration of the Empire, and naturally financial reform came very high in the order of priorities. Mehmed Cavit, Minister of Finance

[1] *İkdam*, 22 Feb. 1910; Tunaya, *Partiler*, 294–303; A. B. Kuran, *Osmanlı*, 522–3. During this period 1909–11 other conservative groups were also formed. There was the *Mütedil Hürriyetperveran Fırkası* also known as *Mütedil Liberaller* or Moderate Liberals, Tunaya, *Partiler*, 254–61, and the *Osmanlı Demokrat Fırkası* (*Fırkai İbad*) or the Ottoman Democratic Party, ibid. There was also the New Party or *Hizb-i Cedid*. All these liberal-conservative groups acted together against the Committee and therefore hardly functioned as separate groups. Finally, in Nov. 1911 all opposition groups united to form the *Hürriyet ve İtilâf Fırkası* or the Freedom and Accord Party, see below. There were also some left-wing groups. In Sept. 1910 the *Osmanlı Sosyalist Fırkası* (Ottoman Socialist Party) was formed. See Tunaya, *Partiler*, 303–14; G. Haupt, 'Le début du mouvement socialiste en Turquie', *Mouvement social*, no. 45 (1963), 121–37; Joshua Starr, 'The Socialist Federation of Salonik', *Jewish Social Studies*, vii (1945), 323–36; on the activities of one of the founders and president of the Socialist Party, Hüseyin Hilmi, see M. S. Çapanoglu, *Türkiye'de Sosyalizm Hareketleri ve Sosyalist Hilmi*, Istanbul, 1964. The socialist movement had very little success; its leaders were persecuted and exiled and the party soon disappeared. Karpat, *Turkey's Politics*, 1959, 353–4 n. 16, writes: 'This persecution was explained as stemming from the fact that since the country had no industry, socialism was an artificially planted movement in Turkey.' Another rather smugly held idea emerges in parliamentary debates that Ottoman (Muslim) society was essentially egalitarian and classless and therefore socialism had no relevance in the Ottoman Empire.

[2] Hakkı Paşa's programme in *Yeni Tanin*, 26 Jan. 1910; French translation in *Stamboul* of same date.

in Hakkı Paşa's Cabinet, had set out to educate the 'public' on on the importance of financial reform even during the first days of the constitution.[1] When he became Hilmi Paşa's Finance Minister in June 1909, he set up a special committee to prepare the budget for the following year. The estimated budget was presented in December and soon after Hilmi Paşa resigned.[2] Hakkı Paşa, however, promised to apply scrupulously his predecessor's budget, and at the same time promised to increase revenue by reforming the system of taxation, and by reaching an agreement with the Powers which would permit the Porte to raise certain tariffs on imports. He said his Cabinet would try to cut down expenditure, but never at the expense of the dignity and prestige of the Empire, nor at the expense of good administration. He added that he realized that the Ottoman Empire was a Great Power with a vast coastline and extensive borders. Therefore he would always give the utmost attention to the needs of the army and the navy.[3]

The partial reform of the system of taxation in 1909 had produced encouraging results.[4] At the end of 1910, in spite of all the difficulties, the achievements of Cavit's financial administration were generously praised by Sir Adam Block, President of

[1] Mehmed Cavid, 'Bütçe Nedir?', in *Sabah*, 10 Aug. 1908.
[2] Estimated budget is given in Marling to Grey, no. 999 con., Constantinople, 28 Dec. 1909, F.O. 371/993/183. Actual budget given in W. W. Cumberland, The Public Treasury, E. M. Mears, *Modern Turkey* (New York, 1924), 390.
[3] Hakki Paşa's programme, *Yeni Tanin*, 26 Jan. 1910.
[4] Improvement in revenues in 1909; extract from the *Tanin*, 10 Mar. 1910, in Lowther to Grey, no. 186 con., 29 Mar. 1910, F.O. 371/1007/11227, in Turkish liras:

	1910	1909	Increase	Decrease
Real property tax	26,625,980	15,780,892	10,872,088	
Tax on profits (*Temettü*)	2,052,256	1,717,755	334,501	
Tithes	85,718,059	76,568,397	9,149,662	
Sheep tax	1,093,004	525,435	567,569	
Military service exemption tax	837,626	7,190,565		6,352,939
Other sources	38,050,110	18,484,901	19,565,209	
Total	154,404,035	120,267,945	40,489,029	6,352,939
Customs	24,249,854	21,734,404	2,515,450	
Posts and telegraphs	6,291,014	6,312,270		21,256
Total	184,944,903	148,314,619	43,004,479	6,374,195

the Public Debt.[1] But despite this substantial increase in revenues, it was still not possible to meet the deficit in the budget or to carry out any real and lasting reforms because the military dominated the political scene. Their heavy demands on the budget and their interference in the administration would not permit this. General von der Goltz, addressing the German Asiatic Society on his return from Turkey, observed that internal reform in the Ottoman Empire was not possible while the Porte faced the possibility of external aggression. In the prevailing situation the only real desire of the Young Turks was to increase their military strength.[2] While this idea was endorsed by the Committee, it was dogma to the military. Men like Cavit, however, criticized on rational grounds the policy of sacrificing other much-needed reforms to the exigencies of a renovated army and navy. They asked why the military expenditure could not be curtailed and more money devoted to productive ends.

The debate on the military budget commenced on 16 June. Mahmud Şevket Paşa spoke in support of his estimate. Security, he declared, was the first need of the Empire; without security, public works and the reorganization of finances would prove futile. He pointed out that as defence was not a party issue, deputies ought to forget party affiliations when voting. He requested that the military budget be voted unanimously, so that everyone might see that the Ottoman nation had resolved to maintain its power. He concluded by asking the Chamber to vote an extraordinary credit amounting to five million liras, as well as the ordinary budget of nine and a half million.[3] Cavit Bey spoke against the inflated military budget, and appealed to the Chamber to reject it in its present form. He pointed out that the already large deficit would swell dangerously if the budget were allowed through. But Şevket Paşa dismissed Cavit's arguments about a lack of money by concluding: 'we shall begrudge the army nothing'.[3] Cavit's arguments made no impression on the Chamber

---

[1] Achievements of the new regime: Sir Adam Block's view, *The Times*, 15 Dec. 1910; see also *Tanin*, 24 Dec. 1910.
[2] Goltz's speech reported in *The Times*, 9 Dec. 1910.
[3] 115th Session of the Chamber of Deputies, 16 June 1910, *Takvim-i Vekayi*, viii. 2303 ff.; *Tanin*, *Yeni İkdam*, and *Stamboul* of 17 June 1910; Annual Report, 1910, in Lowther to Grey, no. 103 con., Constantinople, 14 Feb. 1911, F.O. 371/1245/6167; *Annual Register, 1910* (London, 1911), 337–8.

either. Three days later the ordinary and extraordinary military budget was voted by the Chamber, and soon after Cavit left for Paris to raise a loan on the Paris Bourse.[1] On the budget Lowther commented:

The only object on which money and attention are lavished is the army . . . His budget [Şevket Paşa's], by far the largest of all [a third of the entire budget], was the only one which was passed without discussion, and, in fact, he appears to plunge his hand into the public purse exactly as he likes, leaving it to Javid Bey, the Finance Minister, to arrange the account-books afterwards. . . . It is difficult to believe that a man of Javid Bey's intelligence should contemplate the heavy military expenditure without disquietude, but he seems quite powerless in the hands of the military. . . .[2]

Such was the relationship between the military and the Committee.

The Committee's concession to Şevket Paşa regarding the military budget may be explained away by arguing that the Committee had conceded no principle. It may be argued that the Unionists in Parliament, aware that the inflated military budget would increase the deficit, nevertheless voted for it because they shared the belief in the need of a powerful army. But such arguments cannot explain away Cavit's capitulation to Şevket Paşa in a conflict which took place later in the year. This time the conflict was one of constitutional principles: whether the Ministry of War would submit its accounts to the scrutiny of the Ministry of Finance.

As a part of the programme to reorganize the financial administration, Cavit created an audit department. The function of this department was to examine the accounts of all other ministries, and to make sure that money was being spent as specified in the budget. The aim of this measure was to check corruption.[3]

---

[1] 116th Session of the Chamber of Deputies, 19 June 1910, *Takvim-i Vekayi*, viii. 2356 ff.; *Tanin* and *Stamboul* of 20 June 1910; Lowther to Grey, no. 434, very con., Therapia, 27 June, 1910, F.O. 371/993/23954; Major Tyrrell, the Military Attaché, wrote that there was a rumour that the military budget had been voted under compulsion. See Major Tyrrell to Marling, Constantinople, 21 Nov. 1910 in Marling to Grey, no. 858 con., Constantinople, 23 Nov. 1910, F.O. 371/1017/43077.

[2] Lowther to Grey, no. 434.

[3] Menteşe, *Cumhuriyet*, 18 Oct. 1946. Halil Bey, deputy for Menteşe, was elected President of the Parliamentary Party of the CUP on 27 Feb. 1910, see *Tanin*, 28 Feb. 1910—Annual Report, 1910 and *Annual Register, 1910* (op. cit., p. 71 n. 3),

There was already some tension between the military and certain Unionists, caused by the latter's demand for an investigation regarding the *Yıldız* treasure. In this demand there was a strong suggestion of embezzlement by the martial law authorities while they had been occupying the Palace after April 1909. But the matter had aroused great controversy and had been dropped at the insistence of Şevket Paşa.[1] The Finance Ministry's claim to inspect military accounts brought the conflict into the open. This conflict came to a head when Şevket Paşa asked the Finance Ministry to pay for certain war material which, he claimed, was not covered by his budget. The ministry refused on the grounds that such expenditure was provided for in the extraordinary military budget. The question came before Cavit who upheld his department's decision. But rather than abide by this decision, the Minister of War sent in his resignation.[2]

While the *Yeni İkdam* described this confrontation between Şevket Paşa and Cavit as a 'ministerial crisis', the *Tanin* dismissed it as 'differences within the cabinet'.[3] Hüseyin Cahit's editorial gave the first hint of the Committee's desire to reach a compromise with the Minister of War, rather than make this issue into a first-class crisis. He wrote that it had been obvious since the beginning of September that the subject of public accounts would lead to differences between the Ministers of War and Finance. But since such differences were not of an important character there was no need for anxiety. The Committee had summoned a special meeting to discuss this question and decided to follow a reasonable policy. Hüseyin Cahit concluded:

Knowing all this, we refuse to believe that we are faced with a ministerial crisis today. . . . Looking at the internal and external situation, we have smiled sceptically at the words 'a ministerial crisis may take place any time'. No ministry can remain in power for ever. But is the application of the above-mentioned law so urgent that ministers should disagree about it twenty or twenty-five days before the opening of Parliament? No one who trusts the judgement of our ministers can think so.[4]

[1] Menteşe, *Cumhuriyet*, 18 Oct. 1946.
[2] Ibid. and *Tanin*, 18 Oct. 1910; *Yeni İkdam*, 17 and 18 Oct. 1910 respectively; Lowther to Grey, no. 211, tel. con., Pera, 30 Sept. 1910, F.O. 371/993/35428 and no. 224, tel. pr., Constantinople, 17 Oct. 1910, F.O. 371/994/37832.
[3] 'Buhran-ı Vükelâ', *Yeni İkdam*, 17 and 18 Oct. 1910 and 'Heyet-i Vükelâda İhtilâf', *Tanin*, 18 Oct. 1910.　　　　[4] *Tanin*, 18 Oct. 1910.

In accordance with Hüseyin Cahit's prophecy a deputation consisting of Halil, Rahmi, and Dr. Nâzım visited Şevket Paşa at his residence, only to receive a rude welcome.[1] In spite of a cool reception they soon got down to discussion. Halil Bey reminded the generalissimo that though he had accomplished great deeds for the country, he had done so in collaboration with the Committee. It was still in the interests of the country that this collaboration continue and therefore the two sides should come to an understanding. An understanding was finally reached on the basis that Cavit Bey should agree not to apply the audit law to the Ministry of War, since that ministry needed absolute secrecy and security. This decision, however, was to be referred to the Chamber for its sanction.[1]

No matter how hard the Committee tried to disguise the fact, there had been a ministerial crisis and it had been resolved on Mahmud Şevket Paşa's terms.[2] The Committee's prestige suffered a setback while Şevket Paşa's prestige increased. On 24 December, going from strength to strength, the War Minister asked Parliament for authority to divert at his discretion three million liras out of a total of nine million assigned to his ministry. Though there was some opposition in the Chamber to this request, Şevket Paşa once again carried the day.[3]

The epilogue of this conflict between the Ministers of War and Finance occurred in August 1911. Cavit Bey had resigned meanwhile, but his successor, Nâil Bey, though not a Unionist, also objected to Şevket Paşa's capricious handling of finances. Again Şevket Paşa refused to reduce his estimated budget or to subject his accounts to examination by the audit department. The events of the previous year were re-enacted and a ministerial crisis was in the air.[4] But on 29 August, Grand Vezir Hakkı Paşa assured

---

[1] Menteşe, *Cumhuriyet*, 18 Oct. 1946, gives an account of the reception:
Şevket Paşa: 'Why have you come in this manner, so early in the morning?'
Halil Bey: 'To drink a cup of your morning coffee, Paşa.'
Şevket Paşa: 'Halil Bey, I can no longer work with those who want to stab me in the back.'

[2] H. Cahit, 'Buhran-ı Vükelâ, Şâyiası ve Tefsiratı', *Tanin*, 24 Oct. 1910.

[3] 'L'armée à la Chambre' and 'Chronique parlementaire', *Stamboul*, 26 Dec. 1910, 1–2; Marling to Grey, no. 937 con., Pera. 28 Dec. 1910, F.O. 371/1235/27; Tyrrell to Marling, Constantinople, 2 Jan. 1911, enclosure in Marling to Grey, no. 4 con., Constantinople, 3 Jan. 1911, F.O. 371/1242/838.

[4] *Tanin*, 29 Aug. 1911; *Stamboul*, 'Le cabinet — l'armée et le déficit', 28 Aug. 1911 and also 29 Aug. 1911. Lowther to Grey, no. 614 con., Constantinople 30 Aug. 1911, F.O. 371/1244/34689.

Lowther 'that an arrangement would easily be found . . . and that the rumours of his (Hakkı's) resignation were quite unfounded'.[1] However, no solution seemed to be forthcoming. Nâil Bey threatened to resign, Şevket Paşa took to his bed, and the Cabinet was forced to await his return before it could discuss the question.[2] In this situation, the Cabinet decided to postpone discussion until the reopening of Parliament.[3] But in the meantime events took a turn of their own and made all such discussion academic. Italy declared (29 Sep. 1911) war on the Ottoman Empire, and in time of war it became impossible to question the position of the Minister of War.

Before passing on to the growth of an opposition during 1910 and 1911, it is necessary to discuss briefly the conclusion of the loan of 1910. The implications of this loan on the internal politics of Turkey are still far from clear.

The requirements of waging the Crimean War had forced the Porte to float its first foreign loan on the money markets of London and Paris. Hereafter the issue of foreign loans became the accepted practice of meeting the financial needs of the Empire. In 1875 the Porte failed to pay the charges on a foreign debt of £200 million sterling. Six years later it was forced to permit its creditors to take charge of certain imperial revenues—salt, tobacco monopolies, silk, and fisheries—in order to redeem their money. The body set up to carry out this task was known as the Administration of the Ottoman Public Debt.[4]

The Public Debt, technically a department of the Ottoman Ministry of Finance, functioned as an independent body. Its executive members were elected by the foreign bondholders in their respective countries, and it was to them that the executive was responsible. In 1881 the Public Debt had at its disposal over 300 revenue collectors; by 1911 its total staff numbered 8,931— more than that of the Ottoman finance ministry.[5] Moreover, this body had become powerful enough to exercise great influence on the political, social, and economic life of the Empire. Such was its

---

[1] Lowther, no. 614.　　　　　　　　　　[2] *Tanin*, 31 Aug. 1911.

[3] *Tanin* and *Stamboul*, 4 Sept. 1911.

[4] On the early loans see F. S. Rodkey, 'Ottoman Concern about Western Economic Penetration in the Levant, 1849–1856', *Journal of Modern History*, xxx (1956), 348–53; Blaisdell, *Financial Control, passim*; B. Lewis, 'Düyûn-i Umumiye', *EI*² (1963).

[5] B. Lewis, *EI*² (1963).

influence that the Porte found it difficult to raise a foreign loan without the guarantee of the Public Debt.[1]

The aspiration of the Young Turks to redeem their Empire from European control has already been noted. In order to achieve this aim they considered it essential to reorganize the administration and to make it a paying concern, so that foreign loans would no longer be necessary. But they were unwilling to risk reform for the sake of financial parsimony. In the beginning the cost of reform was high. Inefficient and corrupt officials, who were entrenched in large numbers, had to be paid either a sum of money or regular pensions. But the Unionists considered this method less costly in the long run than the retention of useless functionaries.[2] There was also the cost of a renovated army to be met, and this increased year after year. Thus circumstances forced the Young Turks to continue the practice of borrowing abroad in order to make ends meet.

Hüseyin Cahit expressed the hopes and aspirations of the Unionists concerning the raising of loans abroad by the new regime.[3] He wrote of Turkey's bad reputation in European financial circles prior to the re-establishment of the constitution, when 'the Public Dept was our guarantee and financiers would not trust anything to our Sultan, our Grand Vezir or our Finance Minister, while they would give millions to the Public Debt, an institution set up by foreigners'.[3] He hoped that European financiers would show more confidence in the new regime, and allow it to float loans without imposing terms derogatory to the dignity of an independent country. He concluded that it would not be long, the Porte having settled its debts, before the Public Debt would be abolished and the Empire would be free.[3]

In the summer of 1910 Cavit went to Paris to negotiate a loan. It was natural for an Ottoman Finance Minister to go first to Paris because the Ottoman economy was irrevocably tied to France.[4] Most of the earlier loans had been negotiated through

---

[1] Hüseyin Cahit (Ottoman Representative on the Public Dept in 1910), 'İstikraz Etrafinda', *Tanin*, 9 Sept. 1909; B. Lewis, *EI*[2] (1963); Blaisdell, op. cit. 6–8.

[2] Interview with Nâzım Bey in *Pester Lloyd*, 12 May 1909, enclosure in Howard to Grey, no. 40 con., Budapest, 14 May 1909, F.O. 371/1010/19028.

[3] Cahit *Tanin*, 9 Sept. 1909.

[4] On French interests in the Ottoman Empire, see Communication du Minis-tère des Finances, Paris, 8 février 1909 in Ministère des Affaires Étrangères,

the Ottoman Bank, a French concern established in 1856. These loans had been guaranteed by the Public Debt, 55 per cent of whose bonds were held in France, while Germany held 30 per cent and Britain only 5 per cent.[1]

The French Government had been alarmed by what it saw as a tendency amongst Unionists to attack foreign financial and industrial institutions in the Ottoman Empire. As a counter-measure against this tendency, M. Pichon, the Foreign Minister suggested:

Comme cette campagne . . . de compromettre tous les intérêts étrangers en Turquie, je verrais des avantages à ce que les Gouvernements occidentaux unissent leurs efforts pour l'arrêter dès ses débuts en faisant comprendre au Gouvernement ottoman qu'au moment où il cherche à réorganiser ses finances, il a intérêt à ne pas se montrer hostile aux capitaux étrangers engagés dans l'Empire.[2]

The French naturally did not share the Committee's enthusiasm for setting up a new economic and political structure independent of Europe and more particularly France. In 1910, therefore, Pichon decided to settle the issue by making it plain to the Porte that French money would be available only if the Turks recognized the continued preponderance of French finances in the Empire. That this decision had been taken before Cavit's departure, and what French strategy was to be in the loan negotiations, are revealed in Lowther's very confidential dispatch to Grey:

. . . A suggestion had been made to me as to French policy, which seems not at all improbable. It is that the French financiers will put off Javid Bey in his negotiations with them and will leave him without money till the end of the year, by which time the financial pressure will be even more severe than now, and the amount required will be

DDF, 2ᵉ série, xi, no. 643, 1067–9. On French cultural interests, see Constans to Pichon, Pera, 1 juin 1909, ibid. 206–7; Also The Times, 17 and 24 June 1910; Blaisdell, op. cit. 5; Moukhtar Pacha, La Turquie, l'Allemagne et l'Europe, (Paris, 1924), 102–4.

[1] The Times, 17 June 1910; on the Ottoman Bank, see Boppe to de Selves, Therapia, 27 Sept. 1911; DDF, 2ᵉ série, xiv no. 370, 531–6; it is interesting to note that the Ottoman Bank's correspondence with the Ottoman Finance Ministry was conducted in French, see H. C. Yalçın, 'Meşrutiyette ilk İstikraz', YT, i. 366–7.

[2] Pichon to Ambassadors in Vienna and Berlin (strangely not London and St. Petersburg), Paris, 9 Apr. 1909, DDF, 2ᵉ série, xii, no. 164, 203. The French were most alarmed at the Unionists' desire to nationalize La Régie des Tabacs which was in French hands; for this purpose Cavit had set up a committee. See ibid. and Communication, DDF, 2ᵉ série, xi, no. 643, 1068–9.

considerably increased. They will be able to impose such terms as they like, including the grant of those concessions which they most value.[1]

Lowther's information proved to be correct. In Paris the Ottoman Bank did indeed 'put off' Cavit by offering terms which would place both Ottoman finances and the Ministry of Finance under French control.[2] Cavit offered to guarantee the loan with the customs receipts of Istanbul, but refused to have the loan underwritten by the Public Debt as was customary or to subordinate his ministry to the Ottoman Bank. Unable to accept such terms, Cavit went elsewhere and succeeded in concluding the loan on his own terms with another French syndicate.

Cavit revealed the terms of this loan at a meeting he addressed in Salonika, on his way back to Istanbul. He informed his constituents that the loan was for 11 million liras of which 6 million would mature in 1910 and 5 million in 1911. A group of four French banks—the Crédit Mobilier, the Louis Dreyfus, the Bernard–Janislowsky, and the Syndicate of Provincial Banks—had taken up the loan. The price to the Government was fixed at 86 and this would amount to about 92 to the public, including commission. The interest was 4 per cent and the only guarantee he had given was the customs receipts of the *vilâyet* of Istanbul. On these terms, he said, he was confident that the quotation of the loan on the Paris Bourse was now a mere formality.[3]

[1] Lowther to Grey, no. 434, very con., Therapia, 27 June 1910, F.O. 371/993/23945. The French Ambassador, Bompard, claimed that Cavit went to Paris with the intention of fouling up the negotiations with the Ottoman Bank, his purpose being to embarrass Laurent, his French financial adviser. Bompard claimed that Cavit was being coaxed by English financiers, represented in Istanbul by Sir Adam Block, Sir H. Babington-Smith, and Sir Ernest Cassel; Bompard to Pichon, Pera, 9 Nov. 1910, *DDF*, 2e série, xiii, no. 20, 33–6; Cambon to Pichon, Berlin, 7 Sept. 1910, ibid. 884 n. 2; see also the French Finance Ministry's brief on Cavit Bey, on his visit to Paris to discuss outstanding financial matters between the two governments. *DDF* 3e série, vi, no. 144, 182–5. René Pinon, *L'Europe et la Jeune Turquie* (Paris, 1911), 140, blames Baron von Marschall, the German Ambassador at the Porte for the failure of the loan negotiations.

[2] Y. H. Bayur, *Tarih*, i. 323; Yalçın, op. cit.; E. M. Earle, *Turkey, the Great Powers and the Baghdad Railway* (London, 1923), 244 ff.; *The Times*, 17 Aug. 1910; Bertie to Tyrrell, pr. and con., Paris, 11 Aug. 1910, F.O. 800/172 (*Bertie Papers*).

[3] Lowther to Grey, no. 599 con., Therapia, 23 Aug. 1910, F.O. 371/993/31382; *Stamboul*, 23 Aug. 1910, gives a part of Cavit's speech. Since this loan was ephemeral it does not find much space in most books.

But on 3 September, M. Pichon informed Hakkı Paşa—who was then in Paris—that the loan could not be admitted on the Bourse under the present conditions.[1] Pichon declared that the loan could only be quoted if the guarantee given by the Porte appeared to rest on solid foundations, and justified the confidence of the French investor.[2] Unable to accept any direct French control over its finances, the Porte broke off negotiations.[3]

While negotiating with Paris, Cavit had sent out feelers to London and Berlin about the possibility of floating a loan there. He was optimistic about borrowing in Britain from Sir Ernest Cassel's group. There was even a rumour in *Le Temps* of 20 September that the Turks had signed a contract with Sir Ernest's National Bank of Turkey.[4] But since Grey was co-operating with Pichon, the issue of a loan in London was out of the question. Therefore when Cassel was approached by the Turks he advised them to conclude the loan in Paris as they would not get more favourable terms in London.[5] In Istanbul Sir H. Babington-Smith, director of the National Bank, 'guided by the desire to act in conformity with the views of the British Government . . .', was also advising Cavit to be more conciliatory towards the French.[6]

In the critical political situation prevailing in the capital during the autumn of 1910, Cavit could not concede anything which would compromise the sovereignty of the Porte. Such an act would

---

[1] Bertie to Grey, no. 332, con., Paris, 4 Sept. 1910, F.O. 371/993/32248; the Foreign Office was already aware of this and was actively collaborating with France. See Grey to Bertie, nos. 225 and 380 con., Foreign Office, 30 Apr. 1910 and 18 Aug. 1910, F.O. 371/993/11472 and 29828 respectively.

[2] Bertie to Grey, no. 334, con., Paris, 4 Sept. 1910, F.O. 371/993/32407 and Bertie to Tyrrell (loc. cit., p. 78 n. 2). French terms also given in Y. H. Bayur, *Tarih*, i. 323; Blaisdell, op. cit. 215.

[3] Bertie to Nicolson, Paris, 20 Oct. 1910, F.O. 371/994/38330; Blaisdell, op. cit. 215–16; Y. H. Bayur, *Tarih*, i. 323; *The Times*, 23 and 27 Sept. 1910; *Tanin*, 9 Sept. 1910.

[4] Lowther to Grey, no. 196, tel. con., Constantinople, 20 Sept. 1910, F.O. 371/993/34141; Bertie to Grey, no. 359 con., Paris, 20 Sept. 1910, F.O. 371/993/34166.

[5] Grey to Bertie, no. 326, tel. pr., Foreign Office, 22 Sept. 1910, F.O. 371/993/34385; Earle, op. cit. 225.

[6] Sir H. Babington-Smith to Grey, London, 4 Oct. 1910, F.O. 371/993/36803; Block to Hardinge, Constantinople, 21 Sept. 1910, F.O. 371/994/38775; Earle, op. cit.; Moukhtar Pacha, 106; while Grey was supporting the French, the French, especially the Ottoman Bank, were trying to sabotage Britain's position in the Ottoman Empire. See Lowther to Grey, no. 631 con., Therapia, 6 Sept. 1910, and Block to Hardinge, 10 Sept. 1910, F.O. 371/993/33040 and 33484 respectively; Charles Hardinge, *Old Diplomacy* (1947), 165.

undermine the Committee's already shaky position.[1] In fact the *Tanin* saw this Anglo-French pressure as a means of bringing about Cavit's fall, while Block had already observed that 'by striking a blow at Djavid Bey the French are striking a blow at the party of Union and Progress and may bring about the fall of that party'.[2]

The Germans had meanwhile promised to provide the money if no one else would.[3] On 1 November representatives of the German banks arrived in Istanbul. By 7 November an arrangement was arrived at for a loan of 11 million liras, 7 million to be drawn in 1910 with an option for a further 4 million in 1911. The price was fixed at 86 with the interest at 4 per cent. Two days later the contract was officially signed.[4] Later Cavit recalled how the 'Germans handled the business with great intelligence and tact. They brought up no points which were not related directly to the loan, and they made no conditions which would have been inconsistent with the dignity of Turkey. This attitude of Germany met with great approval on the part of the Turkish Government which was then in a very difficult position.'[5]

German financial help came just in time to avert Cavit's fall. Though the Unionists were grateful to Germany, this did not, as Earle suggests, enable 'German diplomacy and the Deutsche Bank to re-establish themselves thoroughly in the good graces of the Ottoman Government.' Whatever goodwill Germany earned by this act was lost in the following year, when her ally Italy declared war on Turkey. In fact there seems to have been little change in the CUP's attitude towards Britain and France. Soon after concluding the loan with Germany, Cavit wrote to the then Turcophile, Noel-Buxton, expressing his disappointment at being let down in Britain, but adding: 'Croyez néanmoins, que cela n'a altéré en rien les sentiments d'amitié que la Jeune Turquie a à l'égard de l'Angleterre.'[6] But in internal politics Cavit's failure

[1] See above, pp. 70 ff.

[2] *Tanin*, 18 Oct. 1910; Block to Hardinge, 21 Sept. (loc. cit., p. 79. n. 6).

[3] Seymour to Grey, no. 263, secret, Berlin, 28 Sept. 1910, F.O. 371/993/35473; Earle, op. cit. 225–6; Moukhtar Pacha, *La Turquie* 106.

[4] Lowther to Grey, nos. 243, 286 con., Constantinople, 1, 7, and 10 Nov. 1910, F.O. 371/994/39840, 40350, and 41560 respectively; Earle, op. cit. 225; Y. H. Bayur, *Tarih*, i. 323.

[5] Cavit cited by Earle, op. cit. 225–6, from a memo which Cavit wrote specially for Earle, see p. 236 n. 4.   [6] Earle, op. cit. 224.

[7] T. P. Conwell-Evans, *Foreign Policy from a Back Bench, 1904–1918*, a study based on the private papers of Lord Noel-Buxton (London, 1932), 30–1.

to float the loan in Paris or London became another weapon in the hands of the anti-Unionist opposition.

By the beginning of 1910, the political climate had thawed sufficiently to permit the opposition to come out into the open. This was manifested by the formation of an opposition group calling itself the People's Party.[1] This party was formed by deputies—inside as well as outside the CUP—who were dissatisfied with the Committee on personal as well as ideological grounds. But in 1910 it was still too early for bold political activity, since all activities—the Committee's as well as the opposition's—were inhibited by the prevalence of martial law. Therefore in the beginning the People's Party confined itself to harassing the Cabinet and the Committee in the Chamber.[2]

The People's Party, however, was much more powerful and influential than its membership suggested. It had a large following in the Chamber and amongst Unionists who had not joined its ranks, but who sympathized with it and disrupted the Committee from within. The reappearance of a conservative opposition helped to bring the Committee and the military together, and it would seem that this saved the Committee from an early fall. Nevertheless the prestige and influence of the CUP declined in 1910, especially after Şevket Paşa's victory in the conflict between the Ministers of War and Finance.

The debate on the budget on 30 April gave the opposition an opportunity to embarrass the Committee. Cavit Bey, who was presenting his annual budget, proposed a small increase in the allowances of the Sultan's sons-in-law. This proposal was rejected by the Chamber. As a protest against the excessive interference by the Chamber in the workings of the government, Cavit tendered his resignation. Hakkı Paşa supported his Finance Minister and announced his intention to resign should the Chamber fail to revise its decision.[3] The Committee found itself in a crisis very similar to the one brought about by the 'Lynch Affair' in December 1909. Once again Halil Bey, President of the Committee's Parliamentary Party, rallied the Unionist parliamentary group, and on 4 May the Chamber,

[1] See above, 69 ff.
[2] Tunaya, *Partiler*, 295–6.
[3] 81st Session of the Chamber of Deputies, 30 Apr. 1910, *Takvim-i Vekayi*, viii. 1403 ff.; 'Buhran-ı Vükelâ?' *Tanin*, 1 May 1910; *Stamboul*, 2 and 3 May 1910, 'Chronique parlementaire'.

invoking Article 35, withdrew its decision, enabling Cavit to resume office.[1]

Opposition in Istanbul was one thing. Opposition in Macedonia, which had been the Committee's stronghold, another. Macedonia had so far remained loyal to the Unionist cause. When some Unionists had seceded to form the People's Party, Committee's clubs in Rumelia had been quick to shower the capital with telegrams of protest.[2] Therefore, the news that anti-Committee groups were being set up in Macedonia caused great alarm. The Committee was determined to crush this opposition before it took root. On 31 May, therefore, the premises of an opposition club at Manastır were forcibly closed, and some of its members arrested. The official pretext for this action was that the club was reactionary and had been supporting the Albanians in their recent revolt.[3]

In the capital the murder of Ahmed Samim, editor of the *Sedayı Millet* on 9 June, gave the Government the opportunity to stamp on the opposition. The similarity between this crime and the murder of Hasan Fehmi was too striking to go unnoticed.[4]

The crime of Baçhekapı [wrote Hüseyin Cahit], strongly resembles the murder committed last year on the bridge. If one remembers how this inflamed public opinion against the Committee of Union and Progress and how the reactionaries exploited it to arouse the soldiery at *Yıldız*, the repetition of a similar deed cannot but arouse the suspicion that the act was premeditated and aimed at arousing reaction against this party.[5]

The Committee was accused of the crime and a letter, alleged to have been written by Ahmed Samim to a certain Şevket Bey, was

[1] 82nd Session of the Chamber of Deputies, 4 May 1910, *Takvim-i Vekayi*, viii. 1461 ff.; *Tanin* and *Stamboul* of 5 May 1910.

[2] Tunaya, *Partiler*, 301.

[3] Vice-Consul Geary to Lowther, Monastir, 2 June 1910, enclosure in Lowther to Grey, no. 366 con., Constantinople, 7 June 1910, F.O. 371/1010/20903; also enclosure in nos. 450 and 469 con. Constantinople, 5 and 18 July 1910, F.O. 371/1010/24856 and 26779 respectively.

[4] See above, Chapter II; also *Tanin*, 10 June 1910 and Constantinople press of the same date; Y. H. Bayur, *Tarih*, i. 322; H. C. Yalçın, 'Siyasî bir Cinayete Kurban Giden Gazeteci Ahmet Samim', *YT*, i. 108; Lowther to Grey, no. 379 con., Therapia, 14 June 1910, F.O. 371/1011/21934.

[5] *Tanin*, 11 June 1910; Lowther, never partial to the Committee, cleared the Committee of both this murder and that of Hasan Fehmi, see Lowther, ibid. no. 379.

published revealing that the victim had in fact been threatened by the Committee.[1]

The lesson of 13 April had been a hard one but it had been well learned. This time the Government took no risks. Opponents of the régime were quickly arrested, and in July 1910 the authorities claimed they were on the tracks of a reactionary conspiracy, leading to the arrest of Dr. Rıza Nur, deputy for Sinop, on 19 July.[2] Next day the press published the story of the conspiracy, giving details of the organization and aims of the secret association behind the plot. This association was said to be organized into cells of four: president, secretary, and two members. The central committee consisted of a treasurer, a subscription collector, an assassin (*fedayi*), and two members. The aim of this group was to provoke an uprising by assassinating certain members of the Cabinet and some deputies. Once in power it would dissolve Parliament, hold fresh elections, end martial law, and re-employ dismissed officials. The headquarters of the movement were in Paris, where it functioned under the name of '*Osmaniye Islâhatı Esasiyei Fırkası* or Le Parti Radical Ottoman. Şerif Paşa, ex-Ottoman Ambassador to Stockholm, was its president.[3] When Major Tyrrell asked Mahmud Şevket Paşa whether he attached any importance to the reported reactionary conspiracy, the generalissimo replied: 'No; but if I did not crush these people now they would become important.'[4]

Şevket Paşa's remark sums up the nature of the conspiracy: it was a pretext to crush the opposition before it became a threat. The way in which the case fizzled out against most of those arrested confirms this view. The court martial, finding no evidence against the accused, was forced to acquit them.[5] The short-term

[1] Ahmet Samim's letter, enclosure in Lowther (loc. cit., p. 82 n. 4), no. 379; Y. H. Bayur, *Tarih*, i. 322.

[2] İsmail Hakkı, 'Bir Mebusun Tevkifi', *Tanin*, 20 July 1910; Lowther to Grey, no. 481 con., Therapia, 13 July 1910, F.O. 371/1010/25840; Tunaya, *Partiler*, 295–6; B. Lewis, *Emergence*, 215.

[3] *Tanin*, 10 and 20 July 1910; *Le Jeune Turc*, 20 July 1910, enclosure in Lowther to Grey, no. 500 con., F.O. 371/1010/26783; Tunaya, 285–94; for Şerif Paşa's denial of this charge of conspiracy, see Şerif Paşa's letter to Grey, Paris, 25 July 1910, in F.O. 371/1010/25710.

[4] Tyrrell to Lowther, Constantinople, 21 July 1910, in Lowther to Grey, no. 507 con., Constantinople, 25 July 1910, F.O. 371/1010/27811.

[5] Dr. Rıza Nur, *Cemiyeti Hafiye* (Dersaadet 1330), cited by Tunaya, *Partiler* 288; Lowther to Grey, no. 773 con., Constantinople, 25 Oct. 1910, F.O. 371/1010/39486; 'Report of the Commission appointed to enquire into the

effect of this manœuvre was to break up and cause confusion in the ranks of the opposition. But its side effects were more important: the opposition became convinced that parliamentary and legal methods would not work against a ruthless opponent.

While Şevket Paşa was dealing with the opposition, the Committee was reconsidering its policies and trying to strengthen its position. The second anniversary of the revolution was the occasion for an examination of the events of the past year and for a statement of policy.[1] In the proclamation to the nation, the Committee confessed that its measures to bring about the union of the different communities had failed, owing to the excessive zeal it had shown in the first two years of constitutional rule. It now recognized the opposition of the ethnic communities to Ottomanism, and would therefore leave them alone. The Committee would continue to pursue the cause of unity in a different way, namely, by concentrating all its energy on the material and educational development of the Empire, hoping thereby to unite all the elements through a community of interests.[1]

The administrative policy remained as firm as before. The proclamation called upon the Porte to collect taxes and enlist soldiers from places which were providing neither; to collect arms when their possession led to brigandage and to crush political and non-political bands. The proclamation ended with the words:

... the provision of soldiers and money are the foundations of a nation's sovereignty, its defense and good government. Those who give neither taxes nor military service do nothing for their country.... Sovereignty is a political and holy right which is neither given nor inherited. It is conditional on a man being worthy of it.[1]

The moderate policy towards the non-Turkish elements was no doubt intended to take the sting out of their opposition to the Committee. Talât, Cavit, and Halil Bey's tour of Macedonia in August 1910 was directed towards promoting harmony amongst the Unionist organizations, now ridden with dissension. It is in this light that we must consider the speech said to have been made

proceedings of the secret association,' a newspaper extract, enclosure in Lowther to Grey, no. 605 con., Therapia, 24 Aug. 1910, F.O. 371/1010/31388.

[1] 'Osmanlı İttihad ve Terakki Cemiyetinin Millete Beyannamesi', *Tanin*, 27 July 1910.

by Talât before a 'secret conclave' of the Salonika CUP.[1] It was in order to give confidence to demoralized Unionists that Talât spoke in harsh terms and purposely exaggerated the strength of the Committee in the capital. His claims, that 'at the present moment the reins of power are entirely in our hands . . . and the cabinet is essentially in the hands of the Committee . . .'; or that 'we have a majority in the House of Representatives and all attempts to oppose us in the House have miserably failed . . .', were not altogether justified by past events or the existing situation. Immediately after making these claims Talât contradicted himself by saying: 'In some cases Djavid Bey, myself, and other members may fail to obtain the complete success to which we aspire. . . .'[1]

The Committee's efforts to rally its Macedonian clubs and the attempt, at the 1910 Congress, to resolve the differences between the Committee and the Parliamentary Party, bear witness to the Committee's decline.[2] But these efforts met with little success and in this situation the opposition became bolder too. In spite of martial law a Salonika paper called *Turkia: Journal Démocrate* published an article on 'The Committee of Union and Progress and the Causes of its Decline.'[3] In December the British Consul in Edirne reported the formation of an opposition group of junior officers in the Second Army, which had originated in the Third Army. This movement was anti-Committee and it criticized the Government because of its policies of retrenchment, of making political appointments in the army, and for raising the loan in Germany thus losing the goodwill of France and Britain.[4]

[1] Vice-Consul Geary to Lowther, Monastir, 28 Aug. 1910, F.O. 195/2358; *BD*, ix/1. 207–9. I have been unable to find a Turkish reference for this secret speech.
[2] Resolutions of the 1910 Congress, *Tanin*, 19 Nov. 1910; Tunaya, *Partiler* 191; French translation in Marling to Grey no. 844, con., Pera, 22 Nov. 1910, F.O. 371/1017/43063.
[3] *Turkia: Journal Démocrate*, 19 Nov. 1910, enclosure in Marling, ibid. no. 844.
[4] Consul Samson to Marling, Adrianople, 2 Dec. 1910, in Marling to Grey, no. 3 con., Constantinople, 3 Jan. 1911, F.O. 371/1242/8371; Tyrrell to Marling, enclosure in same; the man behind this movement was Colonel Sadık, who was arrested, nominally on a charge of drunkenness. But on the representation of Eyüp Sabri, one of the members of the Central Committee of the CUP (Tunaya, *Partiler*, 191), he was released. See Samson to Lowther, Adrianople, 26 Dec. 1910, in Lowther to Grey, no. 71 con., Constantinople, 3 Jan. 1911, F.O. 371/1242/4280.

The failure of the Porte's repressive policy in Albania, Macedonia, and the Yemen, and the Committee's inability to contain Şevket Paşa, further weakened its position and encouraged the opposition.[1] By the beginning of 1911, opposition which had been crushed the previous summer reappeared, calling itself the 'New Party' (*Hizb-i Cedid*).[2] Like the People's Party, this party was also an offshoot of the CUP, formed under the leadership of Colonel Sadık and Abdülaziz Mecdi Bey.[3] Like the earlier opposition, this group was conservative and traditional in character, and therefore strongly opposed to the social and political ideas of the Unionists. In late January the political situation had become serious enough for the Istanbul correspondent of the *Nationale Zeitung* to report that:

Sensational rumours are current here, according to which a dissolution of Parliament is imminent. The Young Turks are even said to be disposed, in view of the revolution in Arabia and the critical situation in Albania and Macedonia, to acquiesce in the dictatorship schemes of the War Minister . . ., and after overthrowing Hakki Pasha to form a Shevket Cabinet.[4]

The situation was not as serious as rumours suggested. But it was serious enough for the Committee to sacrifice Talât to appease the opposition. Talât was the cornerstone of the Committee and as Minister of the Interior was responsible for the 'hard line' in the provinces. He resigned on 10 February and was succeeded by the more moderate Halil Bey.[5] Halil's appointment saw immediate changes in the Committee's policies. Towards the provinces and the non-Turkish elements the principle of centralization was quietly withdrawn, while the capitulations were not attacked with the same vigour as before. These changes were recorded in a circular to provincial governors in which Halil pointed out that the fundamental policy of the Porte was that all Ottomans should enjoy the benefits of liberty and justice, the object being 'to

---

[1] For the Government's policy towards Albania, Macedonia, and the Yemen, see Y. H. Bayur, *Tarih*, i. 318–22 and ii/1. 35–53.

[2] *Tanin*, 9 Jan. 1911; Tunaya, *Partiler*, 186–8; Y. H. Bayur, *Tarih*, ii/1. 55; B. Lewis, *Emergence*, 215–16.

[3] Tunaya, *Partiler*, 186; B. Lewis,

[4] *Nationale Zeitung*, 22 Jan. 1911, reported in *The Times*, 23 Jan. 1911.

[5] Talât Beyin İstifasî, *Tanin*, 11 Feb. 1911; *Stamboul*, 11 Feb. 1911; 'X', 'Les courants politiques', wrote: '. . . le Comité, s'il cédait parfois sur les questions de personnes, n'abdiquait rien de son autorité, et ne changeait rien à sa politique', *RMM*, xxi (1912), 195.

attain unity and thus efface the discord of nationalities which was the greatest wound in the State'. Governors were told to treat foreigners as guests of the state and in conformity with the capitulations.[1] Talât was taken out of the limelight and elected President of the Parliamentary Party, into which he was expected to instil discipline and harmony.[2]

After Talât's resignation the Committee tried hard to regain the initiative from the opposition. In what followed Mahmud Şevket Paşa was the key figure; but the Committee was never sure of his position. Sometimes he seemed to favour the Committee while at other times his attitude was ambivalent.[3] In this uncertainty the Committee could never act without or against him, especially as they considered him to be too popular with the people (*avam*) and the army.[4] The Committee tried to disorganize the opposition by having its leader, Colonel Sadık, posted away from the capital. Şevket Paşa refused to do this.[5] When this manœuvre failed the Committee decided to try to come to an understanding with the opposition. On 20 April, Talât went to confer with Colonel Sadık. But hours of discussion led nowhere; Sadık hurled the same old charges at the Unionists—that they were irreligious, freemasons, pro-Zionist, and self-seekers. Before he could reach an understanding, he wanted the Committee to withdraw from the Cabinet and the Chamber.[6]

When an understanding with the opposition proved impossible, a small group of Unionists discussed another plan. The Committee would confront the opposition with two alternatives: either to accept the old Unionist programme as a whole, or to assume power, form a cabinet, and accept all responsibility. If they accepted the second alternative, the Committee, which they thought could still count on about fifty loyal adherents, would retain the name of 'Union and Progress' and go into opposition.[7] But this extreme stand was not accepted by other Unionists who, while willing to appease the opposition, were determined to retain

---

[1] Translation of circular, enclosure in Lowther to Grey, no, 131 con., Pera, 20 Jan. 1911, F.O. 371/1244/7134.

[2] *Tanin*, 22 Feb. 1911; *Stamboul*, same date; Talât (Edirne) President; Seyyid Bey (İzmir), Münir Bey (Çorum), Ali Cenani Bey (Aleppo), Mansur Paşa (Bengazi) Vice-Presidents; and Gâlib Efendi (Karesi) Treasurer.

[3] Cavit's Memoirs, *Tanin*, 28 Sept. 1943; also 20, 21, and 22 Sept. 1943.

[4] Cavit, *Tanin*, 5 Oct. 1943.

[5] Ibid. 27 Sept. 1943; Y. H. Bayur, *Tarih*, ii/1. 55.

[6] Cavit, *Tanin*, 28 Sept. 1943.   [7] Ibid. 29 Sept. 1943.

power at all costs.[1] The results of these discussions was the
publication of the Committee's new ten-point programme in the
press on 23 April 1911.[2] This programme conceded all the opposition's demands on condition that they be endorsed by the next
CUP congress.

Broadly speaking and for the sake of convenience, the opposition can be divided into two groups. The traditional-religious
group whose members adhered to the old institutions and values,
and whose leader, Colonel Sadık, was appropriately a member of
the *Melâmî* Order of Dervishes.[3] Articles 6, 7, and 9 of the new
programme met their demands. Article 6 read, 'while preserving
general religious and national ethics and morals, to make use of the
advances and products of Western Civilization for the development of the Ottoman Empire': Article 7 called for 'the maintenance and safeguarding, within the framework of the constitution,
of historic Ottoman traditions'; and Article 9 required the modification of certain articles in the constitution 'so as to reinforce the
sacred rights of the Caliphate and Sultanate'.[4]

The second group may be said to consist of those motivated
by personal interest and ambition. They were either disgruntled
officials who had lost their positions after the revolution, or those
who had joined the Committee and whose high expectations were
not met by either the revolution or the CUP. Hüseyin Cahit
(Yalçın) rightly gives this group the importance it deserves.[5] The
remaining seven articles of the programme appeased this group.
Article 1 laid down that deputies should not interest themselves
in concessions or similar affairs; Article 2 stated that in future
deputies should not accept government posts; Article 3 that no
deputy could become a minister without the consent of two-
thirds of the members of the Parliamentary Party; Article 4 said

[1] Cavit, *Tanin*, 28 Sept. 1943.

[2] *Tanin*, 23 Apr. 1911; *Stamboul*, 24 Apr. 1911; Tunaya, *Partiler*, 186;
B. Lewis, *Emergence*, 216.

[3] 'Situation en Turquie', Constantinople, 13, 30 avril 1911, a memorandum
written by Count Ostrorog, soon after his resignation as judicial adviser to the
Ottoman Ministry of Justice, and communicated privately to Sir Eyre Crowe.
See F.O. 371/1247/25257. On Sadık Bey's religious background, see also Ali
Canip Yöntem, 'Hizb-i Cedid', *YT*, ii. 353–5, and Kandemir, 'Yahudiler,
Filistin ve İttihat-Terakki', *YT*, ii. 432–4; Rıza Nur, *Hürriyet*, 18 ff.; and
Y. H. Bayur, *Tarih*, ii/IV. 235.

[4] B. Lewis, 216.

[5] *Tanin*, 24 Apr. 1911; and H. C. Yalçın, 'Bizde İlk Hizipleşme', *YT*, ii.
153–4.

there must be absolute respect for the laws, and ministerial responsibility must be established; Article 5 that the Committee would work for Ottomanism . . .; Article 8, appointment and dismissal of functionaries must be regularized; and Article 10 that the establishment and working of secret societies must be brought to an end.[1]

Count Ostrorog, who until very recently had been Judicial Adviser to the Porte, saw this political confrontation as an issue between two concepts of state. On the one side there was:

le 'Rechtsstaat' de Bluntschli, un Empire constitutionnel, ayant à sa tête un monarque placé au-dessus des luttes de parti, irresponsable, et régi par un ensemble des lois qu'élaborent les membres d'un Parlement, discontant librement les questions d'intérêt général aux lumières de la raison et de l'expérience,

On the other extreme stood:

. . . la conception des conservateurs musulmans du groupe dissident, laquelle a pour idéal extrême mais logique le Dar-ul-Islam de Mawerdi ou d'Ibn-Halboun [Haldun?]. . . .[2]

Behind these ideological differences between the Committee and the opposition, Count Ostrorog saw the economic motive. Not only were the Unionists for a modern, constitutional, centralized state, they (at least Cavit and his group) had also declared themselves convinced partisans of the system of state monopoly, especially of tobacco. As a result they had become the irreconcilable enemies of those who:

par conviction, préférence ou intérêt se faisaient les défenseurs de la manufacture et la vente libre du tabac, sous réserve de la perception d'un droit d'État par l'apposition d'une banderole fiscale sur les boîtes ou les paquets mis en vente.[2]

We have already seen how alarmed the French were at the possibility of the 'tobacco *régie*', which they administered, being taken over by the Porte.[2] No doubt the establishment of French interests in the Empire over a period of fifty years and more had created an Ottoman group dependent on France. This group would be as anxious as the French to see that their interests and institutions were maintained. Thus the attacks on Cavit for not raising the 1910 loan in France, whatever the conditions. But,

[1] *Tanin*, 23 Apr. 1911.   [2] 'Situation' (loc. cit., p. 88 n. 3).

whatever the strength of this economic motive, it usually found expression in religious terms, particularly as the Committee was thought to be intimately associated with Salonika, that predominantly Jewish city.[1]

For the moment the dissidents seemed to be checkmated by the issue of the new programme. There was even a possibility that the programme and its concessions might be rejected at the congress. Meanwhile the political storm seemed to have blown over. On 27 April, Hakkı Paşa received a vote of confidence by a substantial majority of 145 to 45.[2] A few days later, Colonel Sadık, whom the Committee had been trying to remove from the capital, was transferred to Salonika.[3]

In fact all this was illusory and the Committee's situation did not improve at all. Mahmud Şevket Paşa was still in control, and with the prolongation of the state of siege indefinitely on 13 March, his mandate had been extended as well.[4] The position of the two remaining Unionists in the Cabinet, Cavit and Babanzâde İsmail Hakkı, became untenable. Both therefore resigned on 8 May.[5] Their successors Nâil Bey and Abdurrahman Efendi were chosen from the Senate, as if to meet the terms of Article 2 of the new programme. Because of the continuing dissension in the Committee, Talât resigned his post as president of the party. He was succeeded by Seyyid Bey, deputy for İzmir.[6] On 18 May the court martial suppressed *Tanin* and the defeat of the CUP now seemed complete.[7]

The opposition took advantage of its strong position and put greater pressure on the Committee. From Salonika, Colonel Sadık issued a manifesto appealing to all Unionists to make the Committee a national body embracing all Ottomans regardless of race or religion. The soldiers were asked to abstain from politics

[1] 'Situation' (loc. cit., 88 n. 3) and Fitzmaurice to Tyrrell, n.d. (received in London on 9 Mar. 1911), F.O. 800/79 (*Grey Papers*).

[2] *Tanin* and *Yeni İkdam*, 28 Apr. 1911.

[3] Cavit, *Tanin*, 5 Oct. 1943; Y. H. Bayur, *Tarih*, ii/1. 55.

[4] Lowther to Grey, no. 171 con., Pera, 15 Mar. 1911, F.O. 371/1246/10018.

[5] *Tanin*, 9 May 1911; Y. H. Bayur, *Tarih*, ii/1. 57.

[6] *Tanin*, 15 May 1911, and 'Les Unionistes à Beicos' (Beykoz), *Stamboul*, 15 May 1911.

[7] Cavit, *Tanin*, 10 and 11 Oct. 1943; *Senin*, 19 May 1911; *Stamboul*, 19 May 1911. The action of the martial Law authorities seems to have been symbolic since the editors of the suppressed paper were permitted to publish the same daily under the name *Senin*. By September *Tanin* was allowed to resume publication.

and not become tools in the hands of politicians. He concluded by announcing his intention to resign his commission in the army.[1] The end of the parliamentary session on 4 June took some of the life out of political issues. But pressure against the Committee continued.[3] Sadık Bey's efforts in Macedonia were proving effective. On 4 July the Mitrovitza branch of the CUP announced its dissolution.[3] In August, the appointment of Rifat Paşa, Minister of Foreign Affairs, as Ambassador to Paris seemed the final blow to Unionist prestige. The *Senin* is reported to have hinted that it was time for Hakkı Paşa to go.[4] In such a political situation it is only possible to guess what may have followed had Italy not declared war in late September. However detrimental the war may have proved to be for the interests of the Empire, for the CUP it came as a blessing in disguise and gave the Committee a new lease of life.

[1] *Yeni İkdam,* 21 May 1911. The manifesto was dated 19 May 1911.

[2] Lowther to Grey, no. 403 con., Therapia, 13 June 1911, F.O. 371/1250/23772.

[3] Vice-Consul Hough to Lamb (Salonika), Uskub, 4 July 1911, in Marling to Grey, no. 497 con., Constantinople, 9 July 1911, F.O. 371/1250/27808.

[4] *The Times,* 14 Aug. 1911.

V

THE DECLINE, FALL, AND RESURGENCE OF THE COMMITTEE OF UNION AND PROGRESS

ITALY declared war on the Ottoman Empire on 29 September 1911. The Italian ultimatum, delivered on the previous day, stated that as the Italian Government found that it could not obtain satisfaction from the Porte in questions relating to Italian interests in Tripoli, and in view of the dangers to which Italian subjects were exposed, it had decided to occupy the province. The Porte was instructed not to resist the invading army, and to send necessary instructions to Ottoman officials in Tripoli in this vein. The Turkish Government was given twenty-four hours to accept Italy's terms; if it did not do so war would follow.[1]

The timing of the ultimatum—the ultimatum itself was not totally unexpected—came as a surprise to Hakkı Paşa and the leeway of only twenty-four hours threw the Cabinet into a panic.[2] The Turks had been aware for some time of Italian designs on their North African province. Eight months earlier Hüseyin Cahit, writing in *Tanin*, had acknowledged the bankruptcy of Ottoman sovereignty in Tripoli and prophesied that it would 'fall of its own weight like over-ripe fruit' since the Turks could not defend it directly.[3] A little later Babanzâde İsmail Hakkı, the Unionist expert on foreign affairs, warned that the Italians, who regarded Tripoli as their private domain and who were alarmed by rumours of concessions being granted to American enterprise, would resort to arms.[4] The simultaneous replacement of Italy's Ambassador at

---

[1] Text of the ultimatum in Rodd to Grey, no. 67, tel. con., Rome, 28 Sept. 1911, F.O. 371/1251/38003; Y. H. Bayur, *Tarih*, ii/1. 93–5; text of the declaration of war in Signor de Martino to the Grand Vezir, Therapia, 29 Sept. 1911, enclosure in Lowther to Grey, no. 663 con., Therapia, 29 Sept. 1911, F.O. 371/1252/38771. See also Lowther to Grey, no. 248, Constantinople, 28 Sept. 1911; *BD*, ix/1. 282–3; Ward and Gooch, op. cit. iii. 454–6; A. Mendelssohn-Bartholdy, I. Lepsius and F. Thimme (edd.), *Die große Politik der europäischen Kabinette, 1817–1914*, 30/i (Berlin, 1926), 61–3; Jagow to Bethmann Hollweg, 28 Sept. 1911. [2] Uşaklıgil, *Saray ve Ötesi*, ii (1940), 212.
[3] *Tanin*, 21 Jan. 1911. [4] Ibid. 17 Feb. 1911; Kuran, 541–2.

Istanbul and her Consul-General in Tripoli in late July was 'regarded in Rome as indicating a definite alteration of Italian policy towards Turkey'.[1] No doubt the implications of these changes were understood in the Turkish capital for on 6 September the *Tanin* summed up the situation in no uncertain terms. 'The Italians', it complained, 'regard Tripoli as their promised land. . . . They deny us the right, not merely to defend ourselves but also to question them. They want to take from us the right to consider the future of that province.'[2] In the light of the Italian ultimatum how correct this estimate proved to be!

In spite of this awareness of their weak and hopeless situation, no Turkish cabinet could surrender Tripoli without a struggle and still hope to survive. Hüseyin Hilmi Paşa told the British Ambassador that the 'Government . . ., which is already being accused of being too Ottoman and too much inclined to neglect the interests of the other races of the Empire, especially the Arabs, could never agree to relinquish an Arab Province to a Christian Power. It would mean the rising *en masse* of all the Arab Provinces of the Empire against the Government.'[3] The inflexible conditions of the ultimatum, especially the time limit, placed the Cabinet in a predicament. It had either to capitulate or fight and the Porte knew it could do neither.

It therefore reacted in the only other way it knew how, namely, 'by showering telegrams upon its ambassadors and diplomatic notes upon the Powers. . . '.[4] Its reply to Italy was couched in the most moderate terms with the object of playing for time. Though the Italian demand to occupy Tripoli was rejected firmly, the Porte agreed to open negotiations to work out guarantees which the Italians might consider sufficient to safeguard their interests in the province. Italy was also offered special economic privileges and the only reservation that the Porte made was that Italy recognize Ottoman sovereignty in the area. Had negotiations been opened it seems likely that the Turks would have made further concessions. Only a month later Said Paşa told the French Ambassador: 'Nous demandons la "souveraineté", . . . mais si la conférence insistait pour la "suzeraineté", peut-être devrions-nous nous y

[1] Rodd to Grey, no. 117 con., Rome, 31 July 1911, F.O. 371/1251/30691.
[2] *Tanin*, 6 Sept. 1911.
[3] Lowther to Grey, no. 893 con., Pera, 4 Dec. 1911, F.O. 371/1259/49376.
[4] Moukhtar Pacha, *La Turquie*, 136.

résigner.'[1] But Italy refused to compromise and in accordance with her ultimatum declared war on the Ottoman Empire.

The outbreak of the war had immediate repercussions on the internal political situation. The anti-Unionist opposition which had been gathering strength throughout the years attacked the Committee with fresh vigour. As a result Hakkı Paşa was forced to resign, accepting full responsibility for the prevailing situation.[2] Hakkı's resignation created the problem of finding a Grand Vezir able and willing to face up to such a critical situation. Kâmil Paşa was asked to form a ministry. He refused to do so unless the Committee refrained from interfering in politics.[3] The Sultan then turned to the other veteran, Said Paşa, who accepted and was appointed Grand Vezir for the eighth time on 30 September 1911.[4] Said Paşa had some difficulty in forming a ministry. When he managed to form one a few days later, it turned out to be colourless and consisted 'of men not generally supposed to be in sympathy with extremists of the Committee, and it may be (described) as a *cabinet d'affaires*'.[5]

On party politics—particularly after Hakkı's resignation—the effect of the war was to bring about a temporary and uneasy truce. For the moment patriotism got the better of partisanship. While the Committee's prestige declined sharply the opposition were unable to exploit their advantage, and both sides concentrated on the Italian aggression. Since Italy was Germany's ally there was a resurgence of pro-British sentiment. The *Tanin* urged the Ottoman press to refrain from arousing Pan-Islamic sentiments as this

[1] Bombard to de Selves, Therapia, 29 Oct. 1911, *DDF*, 2ᵉ série, xiv, nos. 492, 722–5; significantly Said Paşa refused to be appeased by Italian recognition of the Sultan's 'spiritual sovereignty' over Tripoli. See also the Porte's reply to the Italian Ambassador, 29 Sept. 1911, in F.O. 371/1252/38347; and Danişmend, *Kronoloji*, iv. 384–6.

[2] *İkdam*, 30 Sept. 1911; Y. H. Bayur, *Tarih*, ii/1. 109; Uşaklıgil, *Saray ve Ötesi*, ii (1940), 214–27; Danişmend, *Kronoloji*, 386; İnal, op. cit. 1776; Menteşe, *Cumhuriyet*, 21 and 22 Oct. 1946; and Lowther to Grey, no. 226, tel. con., Constantinople, 1 Oct. 1911, F.O. 371/1252/38491.

[3] Kâmil's conversation with Lowther and Boppe, the French chargé d'affaires, see Lowther to Grey, no. 224, tel. con., Constantinople, 1 Oct. 1911, F.O. 371/1251/38318; and Boppe to de Selves, Therapia, 3 Oct. 1911, *DDF* 2ᵉ série, xiv, no. 391, 580.

[4] *Hatt* appointing Said Paşa in *İkdam*, 1 Oct. 1911; also İnal, op. cit. 1082–3; Y. H. Bayur, *Tarih*, ii/1. 109; Moukhtar Pacha, *La Turquie*, 139.

[5] Cabinet given in *İkdam* and *Tanin* of 5 Oct. 1911; Y. H. Bayur, *Tarih*, ii/1.109; Danişmend, *Kronoloji*; Lowther, no. 224; and also Lowther to Grey, no. 239 tel., Therapia, 5 Oct. 1911, F.O. 371/1252/39063.

would conflict with the interests of England, France, and Russia.[1] Earlier Hüseyin Cahit had rebuked the *Osmanischer Lloyd*, the German Embassy paper in Istanbul, for trying to exploit Islam as a weapon against the Triple Entente. He asked the German paper to stop this practice as it was opposed to Ottoman principles and policy.[2] Finally, on 28 September, the *Tanin* warned Germany that if she could do nothing on behalf of Turkey the Ottomans would have to reach an agreement with the Triple Entente.[3]

Consequently on the day Said Paşa assumed office he addressed a communiqué to Great Britain appealing for British intervention in the Turco-Italian conflict.[4] When this appeal did not bring a favourable response he proposed a formal alliance with either Britain alone or with the Triple Entente. The only condition he laid down was that Britain should intervene and induce Italy to accept an arrangement on the basis of recognition of the sovereign rights of the Sultan over Tripoli.[5] But an alliance was not forthcoming, and Turkey's isolation and Europe's reaction—or the lack of it—could not but make the Turks cynical about Europe's attitude towards constitutionalism in the Ottoman Empire. To Boppe, Kâmil Paşa expressed some of this disillusionment:

Nous reposions confiants dans notre maison; les portes et les fenêtres étaient grandes ouvertes . . . et voici qu'un est entré et que l'on nous a dérobé une province. Qu'est-ce donc que le droit? Qu'est-ce que la parole de l'Europe?[6]

---

[1] Hüseyin Cahit, 'İttihadı İslâm ve Matbuat-ı Osmaniye', *Tanin*, 23 Sept. 1911.

[2] *Tanin*, 28 Aug. 1911. Hüseyin Cahit wrote: 'The Sultan is the ruler of all Ottomans and Caliph of the Muslims of the entire world. It is therefore natural for Muslims . . . to turn their eyes towards Istanbul, the home of the Caliphate. But this is only a religious, moral and sentimental tie, and it would be absolutely against our principles and ideas to debase this sacred tie by exploiting it for political ends.'

[3] H. Cahit, 'İttifak ve İtilâflar Karşısında Türkiye', *Tanin*, 28 Sept. 1911. Neither the Committee nor the Porte wanted to become entangled in the dangerous web of Pan-Islam. Earlier in February 1911, Rifat Paşa, the Foreign Minister, told the Russian Ambassador: 'Ni le gouvernement ni le comité de Salonique ne cherchaient à poursuivre le panislamisme, car ils se rendaient nettement compte qu'une telle politique mènerait à des complications dangereuses avec la Russie, l'Angleterre et la France. . . .' Quoted in Moukhtar Pacha, *La Turquie*, 100.

[4] Grand Vizier to Tewfik Pasha, 30 Sept. 1911, F.O. 371/1252/38364; Y. H. Bayur, *Tarih*, ii/1. 110 ff.

[5] Turkish Minister of Foreign Affairs to the Foreign Office, 31 Oct. 1911, F.O. 371/1263/48554; Y. H. Bayur, *Tarih*, ii/1. 175–83.

[6] Boppe to de Selves, Therapia, 4 Oct. 1911, *DDF*, 2ᵉ série, xiv, nos. 394, 584.

The outbreak of hostilities coincided with the third annual congress of the Committee of Union and Progress in Salonika. Delegates from the various branches had assembled as arranged when the first session opened on 30 September. On account of the war the order of the day was abandoned and the assembly converted itself into a 'Committee of National Defence' (CND).[1] It may be recalled that one of the chief issues to be discussed and resolved at this Congress was the dissension within the CUP, and the programme which its dissident members had forced the radical wing to accept in April 1911.[2] But in the emotional climate of war the problem was not resolved and the dissidents, unable to press for a solution, had to accept a compromise. The partisan political activity which followed in the wake of the Congress suggests that the agreement reached did 'little more than paper over the cracks'.[3]

For some months past the Committee had been on the defensive. The war gave the Committee an opportunity to exploit patriotism, assume the offensive, and regain the initiative. It aroused public opinion to demand that the honour of the country be saved by a show of resistance to Italian aggression. Being unable to answer the Italians in kind, at least effectively, the Turks turned to the tried device of the boycott, which had worked against Austria, and applied it against Italian commerce. On 7 October the Ministry of Justice issued a circular unilaterally abrogating the capitulary rights of Italians in the Ottoman Empire.[4]

These measures, however, did little to elevate the Committee's

[1] Tunaya, *Partiler*, 191–2. The manifesto inaugurating the CND was issued on 5 Oct.. This body was made up of eight members and its function was to recruit volunteers for military service. Non-Muslim communities were asked to co-operate with this body through their religious heads. See *Tanin*, 6 Oct. 1911, and Lowther to Grey, no. 689 con., Therapia, 6 Oct. 1911, F.O. 371/1253/39719.   [2] See above, pp. 87 ff.

[3] B. Lewis, 216–17; the solution was not mentioned in the official decisions of the 1911 Congress, see *Tanin*, 16 Oct. 1911; French translation in 'X', 'Doctrines et programmes des partis politiques ottomans', *RMM*, xxii (1913), 152–8; nor in the 'secret decisions' sent to the Foreign Office by the British Consul in Salonika, see F.O. 371/1263/51124. It seems that the Committee dismissed this issue in a summary manner in the guise of a patriotic proclamation appealing for unity. See Tunaya, *Partiler*, 192 n. 65, who quotes a part of the proclamation from *Tanin*, 27 Sept. 1327 o.s. (10 Oct. 1911); French translation of which is found in *Le Jeune Turc*, 10 Oct. 1911, enclosure in Lowther to Grey, no. 796 con., Constantinople, 7 Nov. 1911, F.O. 371/1257/44814.

[4] Uşaklıgil, *Saray ve Ötesi*, ii (1940), 230 ff.; Moukhtar Pacha, *La Turquie*, 138; the circular enclosed in Lowther to Grey, no. 737 con., Therapia, 12 Oct. 1911, F.O. 371/1255/41663.

position and prestige in the long run. Cavit Bey writes how during 'Said Paşa's first days they had nourished a great secret hope . . . and how it had proved empty.'[1] The Committee was still thought to be powerful but every day it found itself face to face with a new crisis. It was thought that the Committee had brought Said to power and formed the Cabinet. But this 'was not true . . .; we did not even have the power to criticise this body [and] every sign of moderation [itidal], concession [sükût], and compromise [itilâf] came from our side'.[1] Finding their position difficult, on 16 October some members of the inner circle of the CUP—Talât, Cahit, Cavit, Dr. Nâzım—discussed the possiblity of setting up a coalition government, which they considered 'a seductive idea for the present'.[2]

In moments of crisis politicians tend to be guided by intuition and the general good as well as by calculated cunning and self-interest. The Unionists were no exception and saw in a coalition government the end of political strife and animosity especially while the country faced a crisis. They had discussed this idea earlier while Said Paşa had been forming his ministry. But because some members had refused to enter the Cabinet at that point—particularly Hüseyin Cahit—the idea had been dropped.[3] A coalition, they reasoned, would mollify the opposition in all parts of the country and smooth over all political and ideological differences.[4] Once the Unionists had agreed about the practicability of their scheme, Talât and Halil Bey were chosen for the delicate task of negotiating with the opposition and persuading them to join a coalition. Talât and Halil first called upon the ideologue of the opposition, Prince Sabaheddin, at his villa in Kuruçeşme. They offered him a post in the government which he turned down, and without his active co-operation the coalition scheme was doomed to fail.[5]

[1] Cavit, Tanin, 16 Oct. 1943, and 15 Oct. 1911.

[2] Ibid. 17 Oct. 1943.

[3] Ibid.; Talât was to become Minister of Post and Telegraph, and Cavit, Finance.

[4] Menteşe, Cumhuriyet, 20 Oct. 1946.

[5] Ibid.; Dr. Nihad Reşad, a confidant of Sabaheddin's, answering Halil Bey's memoirs, wrote that during this period he and the Prince were in Paris and that the meeting took place a year later during the Balkan War. This, according to Dr. Reşad, was the last meeting between Sabaheddin and the CUP. See Dr. Nihad Reşad, 'İttihad ve Terakkinin Muhaliflerle Temasları', Cumhuriyet, 22 Nov. 1946.

It would have been a grave tactical error for the opposition to have formed a coalition with the Committee. A coalition government would have maintained the CUP in power, forced the opposition to share the blame for the declining situation, while conferring no real advantage upon them. As it was, the Committee was fast waning, and given a little more time it was sure to be eclipsed by itself. The opposition had only to bide their time and the government would be theirs. Consul Samson reported that the Committee's influence was eroding in the *vilâyet* of Edirne, and Kâmil Paşa was convinced that the Committee would collapse at the fourth session of Parliament when the majority of the deputies would come out in opposition.[1] Parliament convened for the fourth session on 14 October, and Said Paşa came before the Chamber to seek a vote of confidence. This would have been a difficult undertaking under normal circumstances, and even during such critical times the parties had to meet and discuss before consenting to give the Cabinet their mandate. The parties met on 17 October and next day Said's Cabinet received a vote of 125 for and 6 against.[2] For the moment the political atmosphere had been cleared by the vote. The opposition had to temporize until the war—not yet a month old—had reached a deadlock and emotions had calmed before going into the offensive.

By November the war had been reduced to a stalemate. The Italians, because of their naval supremacy, made it virtually impossible for the Turks to send troops and munitions in large quantities. The Porte and the Committee had sent a token force of officers (including Enver and Mustafa Kemal) who organized the local Bedouins and harassed the Italian troops from the inaccessible desert. In this kind of warfare neither side could be defeated quickly. In the spring of 1912, therefore, the Italians tried to force the pace by occupying some Turkish islands, bombarding coastal towns like Beirut and İzmir, and even trying to force the Straits. But these measures had international implica-

---

[1] Samson to Lowther, Adrianople, 20 Oct., 3 Nov., and 31 Dec. 1911, F.O. 195/2364; and Ryan's interview with Kâmil Paşa, in Lowther to Grey, no. 236, tel. con., Therapia, 4 Oct. 1911, F.O. 371/1252/39009; also Tunaya, *Partiler*, 192 n. 66.

[2] On the opening of Parliament, see *Tanin* and *Yeni İkdam*, 15 Oct. 1911; on the meeting of the parties, see 'Fırkaların Dünkü İçtima'i, *Yeni İkdam*, 18 Oct. 1911; on the vote of confidence, see *Tanin* and *Yeni İkdam*, 19 Oct. 1911; also Lowther to Grey, no. 714 con., Therapia, 20 Oct. 1911, F.O. 371/1255/41858.

tions and were opposed by the other Great Powers whose commerce they endangered.[1]

The stalemate was reflected politically by the formation of the
Liberal Union (*Hürriyet ve İtilâf Fırkası*) on 21 November. This
party was formed under the auspices of ex-Colonel Sadık, *Damad*
Ferid, İsmail Hakkı Paşa, Lütfi Fikri, Rıza Tevfik, Dr. Rıza Nur,
and others, men who had only one thing in common: they were
all bitterly opposed to the CUP. Otherwise the Liberal Union was
a mass of contrasts and confusions where 'liberals mingled with
conservatives, clericals with free-thinkers, and constitutionalists
with absolutists'.[2] The strength of this party lay in its ability to
unite all those elements which had been long hostile to one another. Greeks, Bulgars, Armenians, Arabs, and Turks now worked
together, though only with the limited aim of overthrowing the
CUP.[3] The founding of the Liberal Union coincided with Kâmil
Paşa's meeting with King Edward VII at Port Said, an event
which the opposition press exploited to further its own political
ends. One outcome of all this activity was what Baron von Marschall
described as a 'remarkable mania of enthusiasm for England'.[4]
Internal politics were now irrevocably intermingled with foreign
affairs.

The Liberals chalked up their first success after only twenty
days of formal existence. This was marked by the victory of
Tahir Hayrettin, the son of the famous Grand Vezir of Tunis,
Hayrettin Paşa, over the Unionist candidate and Minister of the
Interior, Memduh Bey, in the Istanbul by-election on 11 December,

[1] For accounts of the Tripoli war, see Y. H. Bayur, *Tarih*, ii/1. 99–440
passim; Kuran, 541 ff.; Danişmend, *Kronoloji*, iv. 384–6; G. F. Abbott, *The
Holy War in Tripoli* (1912); and W. C. Askew, *Europe and Italy's Acquisition of
Libya* (1942), which has an extensive bibliography.

[2] 'X', 'Les courants politiques', *RMM*, xxi. 207 and 218–19; The fullest
treatment of this party is found in Tunaya, *Partiler*, 315–44; and Nur,
op. cit. also see Kuran, 552–3; Y. H. Bayur, *Tarih*, ii/1. 233–4; B. Lewis,
217; D. A. Rustow, Damad Ferid Pasha, *EI²*; accounts in the press of the day,
especially *Yeni İkdam* and *Tanin* of 22 and 23 Nov. 1911; and Lowther to Grey,
no. 864 con., Constantinople, 25 Nov. 1911, F.O. 371/1263/48319.

[3] Nur, op. cit., quoted by Menteşe, *Cumhuriyet*, 23 Oct. 1946; Tunaya,
Partiler, 318–19; Y. H. Bayur, *Tarih*, ii/1 233–4; B. Lewis, 217.

[4] Marschall to the German Foreign Office, Constantinople, 30 Nov. 1911,
GDD, iv. 65–6. Cavit complained to Marschall that 'Bompard as well as Low-
ther have been agitating against the Committee and so, indirectly in favour of
Kiamil Pasha', see same to same, Constantinople, 31 Oct. 1911, ibid. 64. See
also 'İngiltere Kralı — Kâmil Paşa, Bir Hatıra', *Yeni İkdam*, 23 Nov. 1911;
R. Storrs, *Orientations*, 125–6.

1911. The by-election was fought for the seat which had fallen vacant when Rifat Paşa was appointed Ottoman Ambassador to Paris. The Liberal victory by a mere one vote proved to have great significance in the politics of the day.[1] On the day of the election Mahmed Cavit wrote in his diary:

To-day the Istanbul by-election took place and in spite of all our hopes the nominee of the Liberal Union won. . . . This may be counted as the Committee of Union and Progress's first defeat. For some days past something within me made me sense this reverse, but I did not want to believe it. I thought they were pulling my leg. I do not think I know of anything which has affected me so much since 31 *Mart*.[2]

The opposition made great capital out of their 'triumph'. They spoke of the CUP as a force which had passed into the pages of history. Having destroyed it they thought they had also laid the foundations of another institution to replace it.[3] This election set the mood for the future political activities of both parties. To the Liberals it seemed as if the tide had finally turned immutably in their favour. The Unionists saw it as the sign of their impending fall and therefore the signal for immediate action.

The Committee's first move in this direction was to try to have some Unionists—particularly Talât, Cavit, and Babanzâde İsmail Hakkı—appointed to the Cabinet. But this move was effectively blocked by Mahmud Şevket Paşa and Hayri Bey, Minister of Justice and *Evkaf*.[4] After much endeavour the Unionists succeeded in having Hacı Âdil Bey appointed Minister of the Interior. But there was an immediate reaction from the opposition. Hurşid Paşa, who was Minister of Marine, sent in his resignation, refusing to work with a member of the CUP, and Hacı Âdil had to step down.[5] Finding themselves in this impasse the Committee were forced to turn in another direction. Already in August 1910 Talât had told the 'secret conclave' of the CUP in Salonika that 'should we ever observe the smallest possibility of a vote of no confidence . . ., we are prepared to secure the immediate dissolu-

---

[1] The Istanbul press of 12 Dec. 1911; Tunaya, *MEA* (Apr. 1954), 117–18; and its Turkish original in *Cumhuriyet*, 18 Feb. 1954; Tunaya, *Partiler*, 322; Y. H. Bayur, *Tarih*, ii/1. 236; Kuran, 553 and B. Lewis, 217.

[2] Cavit, *Tanin*, 30 Oct. 1943.

[3] Ibid.; *Yeni İkdam*, 12 Dec. 1911; Tunaya, *Partiler*, 322 n. 31; the *Tanin* played down the Committee's defeat representing it as a triumph of reaction. See H. Cahit, 'Istanbul İntihabı', *Tanin*, 13 Dec. 1911.

[4] Cavit, *Tanin*, 4 Nov. 1943.   [5] Ibid. 5 Nov. 1943.

tion [of the Chamber]'.[1] Though the circumstances were not as Talât had speculated, the situation had now arisen where these tactics were required.

The dissolution of the Chamber of Deputies would force both parties to go to the country where the Committee thought it could win comfortably. Though the Committee was on the decline in the Empire, its hold on the provincial administration was still secure. This was a great asset in an electoral campaign held in a country such as the Ottoman Empire, where democratic habits and values had still to take root, and where the electoral system was indirect, providing for the election of a local electoral college which then voted for a candidate for Parliament. The Committee also enjoyed the added advantage of having an Empire-wide organization and experience of many years. All these points would score heavily especially if elections were held before the Liberals could set up their own organization or break up that of the Committee.

The vehicle for bringing about the dissolution of the Chamber was the modification of Article 35 of the constitution. This article had been amended in 1909 depriving the Sultan of many of his prerogatives, and giving the last word to the Chamber of Deputies in case of disagreement between the Chamber and the Cabinet.[2] Said Paşa wanted to remodify this article to its original form thereby restoring to the sovereign the power to dissolve the Chamber without consulting the Senate. He introduced the Bill on 16 December explaining to his audience the need for a strong and stable government to direct a war or negotiate a peace with Italy. He also pointed out that his Bill conformed with the demands of the opposition, who stated that the restoration to the Sultan of some of his former powers was one of the fundamental principles of their programme.[3]

The opposition could not refute Said Paşa's arguments especially after having called for the restoration of the Sultan

---

[1] See above, p. 85 n. 1.
[2] See above, p. 60.
[3] On the amendment of 'Article 35' see 'Yine Kanunu Esasi', *Yeni İkdam*, 14 Dec. 1911; H. Cahit, 'Kanunu Esasinin Tebdili', *Tanin*, 15 Dec. 1911; Cavit, *Tanin*, 1, 2, and 3 Nov. 1943; Y. H. Bayur, *Tarih*, ii/1. 237 ff.; Kuran, 553-4. Text of Said Paşa's speech of 16 Dec. in *Takvim-i Vekayi*, 20 Dec. 1911. See also Lowther to Grey, no. 934 con., Pera, 18 Dec. 1911, F.O. 371/1263/51583, with extract from *Liberté* of 18 Dec. 1911.

to his former position time and again.[1] Though thoroughly out-manœuvred by Said Paşa, the Chamber refused to surrender its recently acquired privileges voluntarily. Therefore Said Paşa resigned on 30 December, only to be reappointed the following day.[2] Said's 'new ministry', in which there were no important changes, received the Sultan's sanction on 3 January 1912.[3] Next day the debate on Article 35 was resumed and it continued until 13 January when the matter was finally put to the vote. The Bill to remodify Article 35 was defeated because it failed to obtain the two-thirds majority necessary to carry a constitutional amendment.[4] Two days later the Sultan dissolved the Chamber and ordered fresh elections, and in accordance with the requirements of the constitution this decision was sanctioned by the Senate on 17 January.[5]

With the Chamber dissolved both parties began campaigning feverishly for the coming election. Some of the Committee's advantages over the opposition have already been noted. The Committee further strengthened its position by having its members appointed to the Cabinet and to other positions of influence. Âdil Bey gave up his post as Secretary-General of the CUP and became Minister of the Interior. Talât became Minister of Post and Telegraph, Ahmed Rıza went to the Senate, Said Halim Paşa was made President of the Council of State, and finally on 18 February Cavit Bey entered the Cabinet as Minister of Public Works.[6]

[1] See above, p. 88 nn. 2 and 4. See also Ferid Paşa's speech before the Senate, in *Tanin* and *Stamboul*, 23 Feb. 1910 and enclosure in Lowther to Grey, no. 109 con., Constantinople, 23 Feb. 1910, F.O. 371/1000/6989; and his letter to *Stamboul*, 19 Feb. 1910. Ferid Paşa argued that the constitutional amendments of 1909 had constituted a total break with the past and marked an end of the Sultan's prerogatives. The Empire, he said, would have done better to emulate the British rather than the example of the French Revolution. In a country like Turkey the application of the theory of the sovereignty of the people would lead to the dismemberment of the Empire since the Turkish element was in a minority. Consequently the 1909 amendments must be undone.

[2] *Tanin* and *Yeni İkdam*, 31 Dec. 1911, and 1 and 2 Jan. 1912. İnal, op. cit. 1086–7; Y. H. Bayur, *Tarih*, ii/1. 240; Danişmend, *Kronoloji*, iv. 386–7.

[3] *Yeni İkdam*, 4 Jan. 1912.

[4] 'Yine 35[inci] Madde', *Tanin*, 5 Jan. 1912. The measure received 125 votes for, 105 against, with 4 abstentions. See *Tanin* and *Yeni İkdam*, 14 Jan. 1912, and 'X', 'Les courants politiques', *RMM*, xxi. 199–200.

[5] The Sultan's *Hatt* and the Senate's decree in *Tanin* and *Yeni İkdam*, 16 and 18 Jan. 1912. Also see Y. H. Bayur, *Tarih*, ii/1. 242; İnal, op. cit. 1087; Kuran, 554; and Lowther to Grey, nos. 52 and 66 con., Pera, 17 and 24 Jan. 1912, F.O. 371/1487/2877 and 3939 respectively.

[6] *Tanin*, 23, 24, and 25 Jan. 1912, and *Yeni İkdam*, 19 Feb. 1912.

The 1912 election is known in Turkish history as the 'big-stick election' (*Sopalı Seçim* or *Dayaklı Seçim*).[1] Though there was some violence this aspect of the campaign has been exaggerated. The belabouring of Rıza Tevfik at the hustings at Gümülcine has even been immortalized in the poem 'The Star of Truth' (*Hakikatin Yıldızı*), in which Tevfik Fikret is said to have evoked the image of Christ before his tormentors:[2]

> All those feverish gangs armed with stones
> Attacked justice in the name of 'justice'.
> But every blow restored and every curse refreshed
> And from that holy face blood trickled as stones flew.

The Committee's methods, however, were more sophisticated than simply the use of the stick. While both sides canvassed, the Committee was in a position to offer some positive reward in return for votes. Hacı Âdil's object in touring Macedonia and Albania was to appease the disgruntled elements by promises and concessions and thus win their support.[3] On the other hand, the Government was also able to pass restrictive legislation against the press and the holding of public meetings, measures which hindered the opposition's electioneering campaign.[4]

The opposition could muster nothing as powerful against the Committee's big guns. In February 1912 they tried to damage the Committee's position by publishing Kâmil Paşa's letter to the Sultan, which amounted to nothing less than an indictment of the CUP and its policies. Kâmil had written the letter from Egypt on 20 December 1911, flushed with prestige from his meeting with

[1] B. Lewis, 218; R. E. Koçu, 'Türkiye'de Seçimin Tarihi, 1876–1950', *Tarih Dünyası*, i/v–vii. 1950; Tunaya, *Partiler*, 322; Kuran, *Osmanlı* 496–7.
[2] Quoted by Mustafa Ragıp, 'Meşrutiyet Devrinde İntihab Mücadeleleri', *Akşam*, 18 Mar. 1943. See also Mehmet Kaplan, *Tevfik Fikret ve Şiiri*, 120.

> Ve bütün kâfile taşlarla mücehhez mahmum,
> Ettiler 'hak' diyerek hakka hücûm.
> Ona her darbe şifa, her acı söz bir müjde;
> Taşlar indikçe sızan kanlar o kudsî yüzde.

[3] Lamb to Lowther, Salonica, 22 Feb. 1912, enclosure in Lowther to Grey, no. 170 con., Pera, 27 Feb. 1912, F.O. 371/1487/9316; and 'Hacı Âdil Bey ile Mülâkat', *Tanin*, 25 Feb. 1912.
[4] The Press Laws are in *Tanin*, *İktiham* (*İkdam*), and *Le Jeune Turc* of 19 Mar. 1912, the latter being an enclosure in Lowther to Grey, no. 230 con., Constantinople, 20 Mar. 1912, F.O. 371/1493/12552; Server İskit, 'Tahlil ve Tarihçe Kısmı', *Türkiyede Matbuat Rejimleri* (1939), 104–5. The İrade on Public Meetings is in *Tanin* and *İktiham*, 19 Mar. 1912; and enclosure in same to same, no. 235 con., Constantinople, 20 Mar. 1912, F.O. 371/1493/12557.

the English monarch. 'He blamed the Unionists for the mis-
fortunes of the Empire, and demanded the raising of the state of
siege and the dissolution of the Committee of Union and Progress. At the same time he proposed an alliance with England as
the best means of preventing further disaster.' This feeble attack,
dismissed by Hüseyin Cahit as 'A voice from the grave', had
no noticeable effect on the fortunes of the Liberals.[1] In March
Damad Ferid Paşa resigned as President of the Liberal Union,
making way for Marshal Fuad Paşa, presumably with the idea
of arousing more active support from the army.[2] The result of
the election, however, was a landslide for the CUP. Out of 284
deputies only a small minority belonged to the Liberal Union.
Writing about the election in the *vilâyet* of Manastır where nine
out of the ten deputies elected were Unionists, Acting Vice-
Consul Morgan wrote: 'I have no need to say that all legal and
illegal means were used to secure this result.'[3] This verdict is just
as applicable to the elections throughout the Empire.

Parliament was opened officially on 18 April 1912. But because
there was no quorum the first meeting could not be held until 15
May. Halil Bey, who had recently been elected President of the
Parliamentary Party of the CUP, was elected President of the
Chamber of Deputies.[4] Within a few days Nâil Bey, finding that
he was unable to cope with the financial situation during wartime,
resigned. He was replaced by Cavit Bey, whose post at the Ministry of Public Works was filled by Halaçyan Efendi.[5] The Cabinet
now took on a decidedly Unionist colouring. On 5 June Hacı Âdil,
who had made an extensive tour of Macedonia and Albania
before the elections, made an important statement in Parliament.
He described the situation prevailing in the areas he had visited as
explosive, and proposed measures he intended to take to amelio-
rate the situation. The point of departure in his proposals was the

[1] B. Lewis, 217–18. The text of Kâmil's letter was published in *Tanin*, 16
Feb. 1912 along with Hüseyin Cahit's counter-attack, and in Hilmi Kâmil
Bayur (Kâmil's grandson), op. cit. 308–12. A French translation was enclosed
in Lowther to Grey, no. 152 con., Pera, 19 Feb. 1912, F.O. 371/1486/8187.
[2] *İktiham*, 20 Mar. 1912.
[3] Morgan to Lowther, Monastir, 18 May 1912, enclosure in Lowther to
Grey, no. 435 con., Constantinople, 24 May 1912, F.O. 371/1495/23463;
B. Lewis, 218.
[4] *Tanin* and *İktiham*, 19 Apr. 1912, and ibid. 15 and 16 May 1912; also
Y. H. Bayur, *Tarih*, ii/1. 244.
[5] *Tanin* and *İktiham*, 23 May 1912.

abandonment of coercion as a means of bringing about centralization for a policy of concessions and conciliation, carrying with
it the implication of decentralization. This important change was
welcomed by all and Hüseyin Cahit, in particular, expressed his
impatience to see reform introduced as soon as possible.[1]

The amendment of Article 35 was still very much on the cards.
This should have been easy to carry out with their huge majority
in the Chamber. But in spite of this majority, Unionists were
most uncertain about being able to carry this measure through,
because of opposition from within the ranks of the party. This
problem was discussed at Cavit Bey's house by Said Paşa, Emrullah, Midhat, Nesimi, Ziya, Hayri, and Dr. Nâzım, and they all
agreed that it would not be possible to have Article 35 amended at
the moment. They thought that if the Cabinet insisted upon it, it
would fall.[2] The Chamber was divided on this issue and to bring
about unity seemed an impossible task. 'In the Chamber even our
best friends, Halaçyan for example, [were] canvassing against our
proposal.'[2] The situation seemed a repeat performance. As in
1908 the Chamber was packed with deputies elected under the
auspices of the CUP, but who refused to subscribe to all its
policies. It was to remedy this state of affairs that the Committee
was determined to revise the constitution and dispossess the
Chamber of its power. The Committee of Union and Progress
had come a full circle: in 1908 the Committee had invested all the
hopes of the revolution in the legislature; after four short years it
was reverting to the old situation by handing back the power to
the executive. It was on 11 June that the Committee's Parliamentary Party finally agreed to remodify some of those articles which
had been amended in 1909, and taken away the Sultan's prerogatives.[3] The Bill to remodify Articles 7 and 35 came before the
Chamber on 22 June, and after some discussion it was voted by the
Chamber 210 votes to 13.[4]

The Government's manipulation of the Chamber and its
disregard for the opposition showed again the futility of trying
to bring about change peacefully and according to the law. The
measures which the Government had taken—the dissolution of

[1] Hacı Âdil's speech in the Chamber, and H. Cahit's editorial, 'Hacı Âdil
Beyin Beyanatı', *Tanin*, 6 June 1912; Y. H. Bayur, *Tarih*, ii/1. 262-5.
[2] Cavit, *Tanin*, 2 Jan. 1944.
[3] See above, pp. 58-9 and *Tanin*, 12 June 1912; Tunaya, *Partiler*, 323 ff.
[4] *Tanin* and *İktiham*, 23 June 1912.

Parliament, the elections and the constitutional amendments, though absolutely legal—did much to discredit constitutionalism and its practitioners, the politicians, and more particularly the Unionists. Their acts revealed a total lack of direction and ideology, and led to a mood of cynicism and disillusionment. In the circumstances there seemed no other way out but for the junior officers, who had long been in the background, to step on to the stage of politics.

A group of officers had formed an association in Istanbul in May–June 1912 known as the Group of Saviour Officers (*Halâskar Zabitân Grubu*). This group had connections with both the rebellious troops in Macedonia and the Liberal Union in the capital.[1] Their objective was to destroy the power of the CUP and restore 'legal government'. They also demanded the withdrawal of the armed forces from politics, and wanted the government to be left to politicians and officials. Having ousted the Committee from power in July, they remained faithful to this principle and did not permit their members to accept governmental posts.[2]

Faced with a revolution reminiscent of the movement of 1908, the Porte's first reaction, like that of Abdülhamid, was to take repressive action. A Bill forbidding officers to take part in politics and laying down heavy penalties for those who disobeyed was drafted by Şevket Paşa. While presenting his Bill in Parliament the Minister of War declared that he had always regretted the interference of the military in politics. Even as *vali* of Üsküb in 1908 and subsequently, he said he had tried to check such activity, and events in Macedonia had finally forced him to take stern measures which he hoped the Chamber would pass.[3]

Şevket Paşa's legislation came too late in the day to save the situation. Meanwhile, the Unionists were negotiating with Nâzım Paşa, offering him the War Ministry as a means of placating the rebellious troops and saving Said Paşa's Cabinet at the same time. Nâzım, a shrewd politician and not 'the honest, easily deceived, and clean soldier that history knows him to be . . .', continued to toy with the Committee and refused to commit

---

[1] Tunaya, *Partiler*, 354 ff.; Major Tyrrell to Lowther, Constantinople, 27 Apr. 1912, enclosure in Lowther to Grey, no. 371 con., Constantinople, 1 May 1912, F.O. 371/1486/19065.

[2] Y. H. Bayur, *Tarih*, ii/1. 253–8; Tunaya, *Partiler*, 347; B. Lewis, 219.

[3] *Tanin*, 2 July 1912; Cavit, *Tanin*, 14–20 Jan. 1944.

himself. The rebellion continued unabated and on 9 July Mahmud Şevket resigned making the final concession to the rebels.[1]

Şevket Paşa's resignation, rather than solving the problem, created a new one; that of leaving vacant a vital Cabinet post at such a critical moment. The War Ministry was again offered to Nâzım Paşa but he turned it down by putting forward demands the Committee could not accept. In the prevailing chaos no one responsible or with any political acumen was willing to become War Minister, and this only discredited the Cabinet which the CUP was desperately trying to save. Mahmud Muhtar Paşa was approached but he too declined as did other prospective candidates.[2] But in spite of the crisis and the Cabinet's precarious position, Said Paşa was given an almost unanimous vote of confidence (194 to 4) on 15 July.[3]

The vote confirmed the opposition's charge that the Chamber was not independent but merely echoed the Committee's opinions. 'The Saviour Officers' now went into action. 'A manifesto in the press, a declaration sent through the Army Council to the Sultan and, above all, certain ominous military movements and preparations, brought swift results.'[4] The situation deteriorated rapidly. Said Paşa lost heart and resigned on 17 July. When the Sultan asked 'Why did you resign? They still have confidence in you.' Said Paşa replied, 'they have confidence in me, but I have no confidence in them'.[5] The Committee had also lost the will to continue and finally seemed resigned to its fall. Talât is reported to have told Halil Bey:

My dear friend, we go through one crisis after another without ever overcoming it. I keep asking myself the question are *we* ruining the country? Therefore let others come, they are also sons of the country, are they not? Perhaps they will do better than us. We will help them. The purpose is service to the country, is it not?[6]

[1] *Tanin*, and *İktiham* 10 July 1912; İnal, op. cit. 1871–3; Cavit, *Tanin*, 14-15 Jan. 1944; Y. H. Bayur, *Tarih*, ii/1. 258–9. The quotation is from Y. H. Bayur, *Tarih*, ii/iv. 212.

[2] M. Ragıp, *İttihat ve Terakki Tarihinde Esrar Perdesi*, 96–100; Cavit, *Tanin*, 14 and 15 Jan. 1944; Moukhtar Pacha, *La Turquie*, 159.

[3] *Tanin* and *İktiham*, 16 July 1912; İnal, op. cit. 1089; Ragıp, *Esrar Perdesi*, 102.

[4] B. Lewis, 219; Tunaya, *Partiler*, 349; Ragıp, *Esrer Perdesi*, 101.

[5] Türkgeldi, op. cit. 55 and İnal, op. cit. 1089 give the same quotation, İnal using slightly older language; B. Lewis, 219.

[6] Menteşe, *Cumhuriyet*, 23 Oct. 1946; Ragıp, *Esrar Perdesi*, 103; Y. H. Bayur, *Tarih*, ii/iv. 210–11.

The Empire was without a government and it was left to the Sultan to take charge. One of his first acts was to issue a proclamation to the army. He rebuked in it those soldiers who had sent the declaration to him a few days earlier, and asked the army to refrain from interfering in politics. He announced that he had consulted the Presidents of both Chambers and decided that, at a time such as this, it was desirable and necessary to have a new Cabinet made up of personalities with great experience in the affairs of state, independent views, and free from external political influences. Therefore he had invited Tevfik Paşa, his Ambassador in London, to come and lead the new Government. Until it was formed he expected his troops to remain loyal to the constitution and to the sacred rights of the Caliphate and the Sultanate.[1]

Tevfik Paşa, who had formed the caretaker Government on 13 April 1909, rejected the Sultan's appeal by placing too many conditions, and the problem of finding a suitable Grand Vezir remained. Kâmil Paşa, Ferid Paşa, and Hüseyin Hilmi Paşa were considered possible candidates but were dismissed as being too controversial. In the case of Kâmil Paşa, Talât Bey even asked Hâlid Ziya to use his influence with the Sultan to prevent Kâmil's appointment since this would lead to civil war.[2]

Gazi Ahmed Muhtar Paşa was the most suitable choice in the circumstances and he was appointed Grand Vezir on 21 July 1912. He was known to stand above politics and also possessed a military reputation sufficient to win and command the respect of the rebellious army. His Cabinet—known as the 'father and son Cabinet' (Baba-Oğul Kabinesi) because of the presence of his son Mahmud Muhtar, or as the 'Great Cabinet' (Büyük Kabine) because of the array of three ex-Grand Vezirs in its ranks—contained 'personalities with great experience in the affairs of state . . .' as the Sultan had desired. Only a few of its members were free of outside political influence; the majority was determined to destroy the Committee as a political force.[3] In the

---

[1] Royal proclamation in Tanin, 20 July 1912, with French translation enclosed in Marling to Grey, no. 622 con., Constantinople, 23 July 1912, F.O. 371/1496/31978; also İnal, op. cit. 1713–14.

[2] Uşaklıgil, Saray ve Ötesi, iii (1941), 47; Türkgeldi, op. cit. 49; Y. H. Bayur, Tarih, ii/1. 279–80; Ragıp, Esrar Perdesi, 104–6.

[3] Hatt appointing Ahmet Muhtar Paşa in Tanin, 22 July 1912; İnal, op. cit. 1812–15; Türkgeldi, op. cit. 49; Moukhtar Pacha, La Turquie, 159; Uşaklıgil, Saray ve Ötesi, iii (1941), 47–8.

Cabinet Kâmil Paşa was President of the Council of State, Ferid Paşa — Minister of the Interior, Hüseyin Hilmi Paşa — Minister of Justice, Nâzım Paşa — Minister of War, and Mahmud Muhtar — Minister of Marine. The *İktiham* which called this line-up the 'Muhtar Paşa–Kâmil Paşa Cabinet' was proclaiming an open secret: once the political storm had blown, Ahmed Muhtar would make way for Kâmil Paşa.[1]

The Committee had been formally ousted from power and the new Government immediately set about digging up its roots. At the first meeting of the Cabinet the Grand Vezir told Nâzım Paşa that the Committee 'had only three or four days more to live'.[2] On 23 July, fittingly, the fourth anniversary of the revolution, the state of siege was lifted though only to be re-established on 6 August 1912.[3] Hereafter, it was the Government's policy to crush the Committee and replace officials associated with the CUP with ones who were hostile to it. Being opposed to this policy because it accentuated the differences rather than brought about harmony, Hilmi Paşa resigned in August.[4]

The 'Saviour Officers', who had only partially achieved their objective, went into action again on 24 July. They sent an ultimatum to the President of the Chamber demanding the dissolution of Parliament within forty-eight hours.[5] The Committee, still a force to be reckoned with in the Chamber, decided to meet the challenge. Halil Bey had the ultimatum read and amid an uproar the Unionists clamoured for an explanation from the Government for the overt role which the military was being permitted to play in politics. Ömer Naci, himself an ex-soldier, refused to believe that the ultimatum had come from the military who, he said, were not capable of such action. He implied that it was purely a political act inspired by opponents of the Committee.[6]

[1] List of Cabinet in *İktiham*, 22 July 1912; İnal, op. cit. 1812–15; and Tewfik Pasha to Grey, 23 July 1912, F.O. 371/1496/31368.

[2] Uşaklıgil, *Saray ve Ötesi*, iii (1941), 52.

[3] *Takvim-i Vekayi*, 24 July 1912; İnal, op. cit. 1816; B. Lewis, 220; Ragıp, *Esrar Perdesi*, 118.

[4] İnal, op. cit. 1617; Türkgeldi, op. cit. 56; *İkdam*, 15 Aug. 1912; Cavit, *Tanin*, 23 Jan. 1944; and Marling to Grey, no. 647 con., Constantinople, 30 July 1912, F.O. 371/1496/32942; also same to same, no. 352, tel. pr., 14 Aug. 1912, F.O. 371/1509/36732.

[5] Menteşe, *Cumhuriyet*, 29 Oct. 1946; Cavit, *Tanin*, 18 and 19 Jan. 1944; Tunaya, *Partiler*, 229.

[6] Debate in *Tanin*, 26 July 1912; see also Babanzâde İsmail Hakkı, 'Meclis-i Mebusanda Tarihi bir Gün', ibid.; Kuran, 565–7; Ragıp, *Esrar Perdesi*, 109.

The War Minister was held responsible and summoned to give an explanation. Nâzım Paşa, however, dismissed the ultimatum as a bluff but said he would take action against papers which had published the ultimatum.[1] But it was actually he who was bluffing; the Group of Saviour Officers was in fact the military extension of the Liberal Union and both Nâzım and Prince Sabaheddin were connected with it.[2]

After this debate it became evident that so long as the Committee continued to dominate the Chamber the Cabinet's position would be insecure. The dissolution of the Chamber—constitutionally—became the aim of the Government. On 30 July, following a sharp debate, the Cabinet received a vote of confidence of 167 votes to 45 with 9 abstentions.[3] The Government, now more secure, submitted to the Senate Article 35, which had already been passed by the Chamber. Ahmet Muhtar Paşa, who had been President of the Senate and who had great influence with Senators, many of whom were ex-officers, had no difficulty in persuading the Upper House. Article 35 was sanctioned on 4 August, and in the same session the Senate sanctioned the modified form of Article 43, which stipulated that in the event of dissolution, the session of the new Chamber would be in an extraordinary session lasting two months, and which could be prolonged for another term. The *Tanin* described this measure as the 'final blow' against the Committee and the constitution.[4] Knowing that the Chamber would be dissolved next day, the Unionist deputies met early in the morning, passed a motion of censure against the Government, and adjourned *sine die*.[5] Immediately after, the Sultan issued an *irade* declaring the Chamber's action illegal and a *Hatt-ı Hümayun* dissolving the Chamber and ordering new elections.[6]

The Unionists had felt their way carefully after the formation of the 'Great Cabinet'. The editorial in the *Tanin* of 23 July had

---

[1] Debate in *Tanin*, 26 July 1912.

[2] Menteşe, *Cumhuriyet*, 23 Oct. 1912, and Tyrrell to Marling, Constantinople, 29 July 1912, enclosure in Marling to Grey, no. 657 con., 4 Aug. 1912, F.O. 371/1495/33863; Tunaya, *Partiler*, 346–7.

[3] *Tanin* and *İktiham*, 31 July 1912; Y. H. Bayur, *Tarih*, ii/1. 290–3; Ragıp, *Esrar Perdesi*, 110–11.

[4] Babanzâde İsmail Hakkı, 'Son Darbe', *Tanin*, 5 Aug. 1912; Ragıp, *Esrar Perdesi*, 111–12.   [5] *Tanin*, 6 Aug. 1912.

[6] Ibid.; İnal, op. cit. 1817–18; translations of the *irade* and *hatt* enclosed in Marling to Grey, no. 663 con., Constantinople, 6 Aug. 1912, F.O. 371/1496/33869.

been most moderate and they were hoping to function as an active opposition in the Chamber.[1] But the dissolution dispelled these hopes, and fearing there were harder times ahead the Unionists began to shift their activities from the capital to Salonika.[2] But the Government, fearing a resurgence of Unionist power in Macedonia, proclaimed martial law on 8 August.[3] The Government's measures against the Committee became more repressive, and the fortunes of the *Tanin* reflect their harshness and the Committee's decline. The *Tanin* suspended publication 'voluntarily' on 11 August under government pressure, reappearing on 21 August and continuing publication until it was suspended on 3 September. Next day it appeared as *Cenin* and was immediately suspended. The following day it emerged as *Senin* and appeared until 12 September. It was then suspended and came out next day as *Hak*. This game of hide and seek continued into November when *Tanin* suspended publication until more favourable times.[4]

Yet the Committee did not lose heart; the 1912 Congress bears testimony to this. It was the first Congress to be held outside Salonika, meeting in the capital under police surveillance. It denounced the Government's action of dissolving Parliament, which had been sanctioned by the Sultan, as unconstitutional.[5] But having denounced unanimously the dissolution as illegal, the delegates disagreed over participation in the coming elections. The extremists maintained that participation would be inconsistent with the denunciation and when it was put to the vote it was defeated. But Talât, always the realist, argued that refusal to participate would bring the Committee into open conflict with the Government, enabling it to crush the Committee legally. After much heated discussion it was again put to the vote and those in favour of participation won by eighty-five votes.[6]

---

[1] İsmail Hakkı, '10 Temmuz ve Yeni Kabine'.

[2] Cavit, *Tanin*, 22 Jan. 1944.

[3] *İktiham*, 9 Aug. 1912; 'X', 'Les courants politiques', *RMM*, xxi. 205; circular proclaiming martial law enclosed in Marling to Grey, no. 695 con., Constantinople, 10 Aug. 1912, F.O. 371/1482/35852.

[4] *Cenin*, 4 Sept. 1912; *Senin*, 5 Sept. 1912; *Hak*, 13 Sept. 1912; Cavit, *Tanin*, 24 Jan. 1944; and L. Bouvat, 'La Guerre balkanique dans la presse ottomane', *RMM*, xxi. 234 and 226–7.

[5] Resolutions of the 1912 Congress enclosed in Marling to Grey, no. 788 con., Constantinople, 16 Sept. 1912, F.O. 371/1486/39742; Tunaya, *Partiler*, 192–3; Ragıp, *Esrar Perdesi*, 208 ff.

[6] Resolution, Marling to Grey, no. 788; Ragıp, *Esrar Perdesi*, 214–16.

The impending war with the Balkan states made all political debate academic. For the moment political activity went into the background, elections were postponed, and political factions concluded a spontaneous and informal truce to meet the challenge. Mobilization in the Balkans on 30 September was followed next day by the Turkish mobilization decree. On 2 October the allies presented their minimum demands. The Porte was asked to nominate with the consent of the Powers a Swiss or Belgian Governor-General for Macedonia; set up local legislative assemblies; create local gendarmeries; and lastly, carry out reform under the supervision of the Ambassadors of the Great Powers and the representatives of the four Balkan states. The French Minister of Foreign Affairs commented that after ordering mobilization these demands were virtually an ultimatum.[1]

The Porte agreed to carry out the necessary reform in accordance with the proposals of the Eastern Rumelian International Commission of 1880. But it refused to give any guarantees until Parliament met and gave its sanction.[2] No cabinet could have leaned back further to meet the demands of the allies. Public opinion as expressed in the press agreed that reform was necessary, but only to prevent European intervention. Reform must not take the form of autonomy or decentralization.[3] The Committee warned that no cabinet should take upon itself a guarantee to carry out reform under the mandate of the Powers, or recognize Europe's right to exercise direct or indirect control over Ottoman affairs.[4] Once war was declared opinion against concessions hardened and 'all sections of the native press took up a hostile attitude towards the acceptance by the Porte of any intervention. . . . They were unanimous in declaring that war would be preferable to such an humiliation.'[5]

The new situation called for certain changes. The first need was to end the war with Italy, and peace was signed at Lausanne on 17 October, the day before war broke out in the Balkans.

---

[1] Bertie to Grey, no. 145, tel. con., Paris, 2 Oct. 1912, F.O. 371/1499/41350; Ragıp, *Esrar Perdesi*, 120.

[2] The Sublime Porte's official note to the Powers is in F.O. 371/1501/43420.

[3] *Tanin* and *İkdam*, 8 Oct. 1912; Bouvat (loc. cit., p. 111 n. 4), 225; Moukhtar Pacha, *La Turquie*, 170–1.

[4] H. Cahit, 'Devletlerin Teşebbüsü', *Tanin*, 10 Oct. 1912; İsmail Hakkı, 'Harp ve Diplomasi', *Tanin*, 22 Oct. 1912.

[5] Lowther to Grey, no. 875 con., Constantinople, 18 Oct. 1912, F.O. 371/1502/44676.

Italy retained Tripoli but allowed the Porte to save face by permitting the Sultan-Caliph to retain his right of appointing the *Kadı* of Tripoli. His representative was also permitted to act as the religious liason between the Caliph and his Libyan followers.[1] In order to assume the offensive on the diplomatic front, the experienced Anglophile former Grand Vezir, Kâmil Paşa was recalled on 29 October.[2] On 3 November the Foreign Minister 'considered the moment opportune for the intervention and mediation of the Powers'.[3] Four days later Kâmil wrote a personal letter to Sir Edward Grey appealing to Britain 'to induce Russia, her ally, to prevent this war, the sole object of which is to weaken Turkey'.[4]

Externally Kâmil's appointment did not have the desired effect of winning the sympathy of Britain or the Triple Entente. Internally, however, it had the unfortunate effect of ending the political truce brought about spontaneously by the threat of war. The Committee's opponents welcomed Kâmil's appointment; the Unionists denounced it as a direct threat and challenge to the Committee of which Kâmil was described as being the arch-enemy.[5]

The outbreak of war proved disastrous for Ottoman arms. The Turkish army, which had been at war with Italy, took time to mobilize. War against new adversaries in a new theatre of war caught the army unprepared for fresh mobilization and concentration. Any preconceived plans which might have been used in Macedonia were upset by political changes at the War Ministry. Nâzım Paşa, when asked if war plans were ready, replied: 'There is a set of plans prepared during the time of Mahmud Şevket Paşa, I am going to obtain and examine them.'[6] But they were never used. Fighting with the minimum of organization, Turkish troops were routed everywhere. By early November they had

---

[1] Karl Strupp, *Aktenstücke zur Orientalischen Frage* (1916), 256–61; Danişmend, *Kronoloji* iv. 395–6.

[2] *İkdam*, 30 Oct. 1912; İnal, op. cit. 1410; Türkgeldi, op. cit. 67–8.

[3] Lowther to Grey, no. 576, tel. con., Constantinople, 3 Nov. 1912, F.O. 371/1513/46564.

[4] Kâmil Paşa to Grey, 7 Nov. 1912, F.O. 800/79 (*Grey Papers*). While Kâmil's appeal to Grey was official, Cavit wrote to Churchill on behalf of the CUP, begging him 'to join our efforts using your influence in bringing out this friendship'. See Winston S. Churchill, *The World Crisis* (1923), i. 523–5.

[5] *Tanin* and *İkdam*, 30 Oct. 1912.

[6] Türkgeldi, op. cit. 60; Ragıp, *Esrar Perdesi*, 118–20 and 129 ff.; for accounts of the Balkan Wars see Kuran, *Osmanli* 573–85; R. Rankin, *The Inner History of the Balkan War* (1914), *passim*.

been driven back to the Çatalca line of defence, about forty miles from the capital. Total defeat seemed imminent and the Cabinet, having no stomach for a fight, sought the best possible terms from the enemy.

On the evening of 6 November, when the Ottoman armies were in full retreat, Kâmil summoned a Council of Ministers. Such was their state of despair that they agreed to allow the Powers to dispatch one warship each to the Bosphorus to safeguard their interests in Istanbul. This was an open confession that the Porte no longer considered itself capable of maintaining law and order. This was severely criticized and exploited in the *Renin* the following day.[1] Some days later Kâmil saw Fitzmaurice and confided that since the Powers had rejected his request for mediation he was now seeking to communicate directly with the King of Bulgaria. He said that he had also given his War Minister discretionary powers to ask for an armistice if he found that the position at Çatalca was untenable.[2] Talking to Kâmil, Fitzmaurice could not fail to get the impression 'that the Turks have no real stomach for further fighting with the Bulgars'.[3]

While Kâmil was working for an early peace, the Committee was advocating resistance. Turkey, wrote Hüseyin Cahit, had nothing to gain from a conference. If the Porte could obtain the cessation of hostilities either by the recognition of the *status quo ante bellum* or by some small sacrifice, it should do so. But to place Turkey unconditionally into the hands of Europe would be disastrous.[4] Later in November, however, the Bulgarian advance was halted at Çatalca. Hereafter Turkish arms regained their confidence and made a recovery while the Bulgars with their extended lines of supply fought at a disadvantage.[5] This placed the Porte in a better position to negotiate an armistice though it raised a clamour amongst the Unionists. Kâmil, who thought that the CUP should go along with Salonika which had fallen to the Greeks on 8 November, took strong measures against the Committee. Unionists were arrested in large numbers and either

[1] *Renin (Tanin)*, 7 Nov. 1912.
[2] Lowther to Grey, no. 611, tel. con., Constantinople, 11 Nov. 1912, F.O. 371/1513/48125.
[3] Fitzmaurice to Tyrrell, pr., Constantinople, 6 Jan. 1913, F.O. 800/79 (*Grey Papers*),   [4] *Tanin*, 9 Nov. 1912.
[5] George Pilcher, 'In the Chatalja Lines During the November Battle', *NC*, lxxiii (1913), 624–43; Ragıp, *Esrar Perdesi*, 130.

imprisoned or exiled to Anatolia, while others escaped to Europe.[1] With the vocal elements of the CUP out of the way, the Porte was able to sign an armistice on 3 December on condition that the belligerents open negotiations within a week.[2]

For the moment the initiative had passed from the battlefield to the conference table and the issue of war and peace now hinged on the besieged town of Edirne. Both parties met in London in December–January to discuss the terms of peace. But the Turkish delegation had already stated in Paris that they could conclude peace only on honourable terms. Reşid Paşa pointed out that Turkey's military strength was increasing daily and that fighting would break out if one of the two parties attempted to impose onerous terms on the other.[3] On 1 January 1913, the Turkish peace proposals were stated at the conference.[4]

(i) All occupied territories to the west of the *vilâyet* of Edirne would be ceded, but the determination of the boundaries and status of autonomous Albania must be submitted to the decision of the Great Powers.

(ii) The *vilâyet* of Edirne would remain in direct possession of the Ottoman Empire, and Turkey and Bulgaria would negotiate any rectification of the frontier recognized by them as necessary.

(iii) Turkey would not cede any of the Aegean islands, but would discuss with the Great Powers questions relating to them.

(iv) Turkey would consent to any resolution that the protecting powers may come to regarding Crete.

(v) The four points above form an indivisible whole.

The Turkish proposals were not accepted by the allies, and though the Porte made other minor concessions a deadlock was soon reached. But for Grey's patience and perseverance the conference would have broken up. He intervened personally and decided to settle the dispute by imposing the will of the Powers on both parties. On Monday, 13 January, he summoned a meeting of Ambassadors of the Powers. The meeting drafted a Collective

---

[1] 'Tevkifata Dair — İdarei Örfiye Beyannamesi', *İkdam*, 26 Nov. 1912; Cavit, *Tanin*, 12, 14, and 18 Feb. 1944. After the fall of Salonika Kâmil is reported to have said: 'Now they have no future; they were a revolutionary party and their centre was Salonika, Salonika has gone; they should clear out too.' See Türkgeldi, op. cit. 76.

[2] *İkdam*, 4 Dec. 1912. [3] Reported in *The Times*, 14 Dec. 1912.
[4] *İkdam* and *The Times*, 2 Jan. 1913.

Note asking the Porte to cede Edirne to Bulgaria and to leave the question of the islands to the Powers. If the Porte failed to accept their 'advice', the note warned that there would be a renewal of war which would expose Turkey to grave perils. In the final conclusion of peace the Porte would require the moral and material support of the Powers, but this would depend upon how she took their advice. This note was communicated to the Porte on 17 January.[1] Faced with what was virtually an order from the Powers, the Porte found itself in a difficult situation. There seemed no way out but to give in. On 23 January the Unionists, assuming that Kâmil was about to surrender Edirne, carried out a *coup d'état*, forced Kâmil to resign, and formed a government of their own.

The *coup*, known as 'the Attack on the Sublime Porte' (*Babıâli Baskını*), was not an act of desperation made in the simple belief that Edirne was about to be surrendered. Much thought and organization went into the *coup* and its seed is to be found in Kâmil's appointment as Grand Vezir.

We may recall how, at the outbreak of the war with Italy, the Committee attempted and failed to reach an understanding with the opposition by proposing a coalition. With the threat of war in the Balkans, the Committee, now in opposition, again endeavoured to have a non-partisan government in power. When the allies put forward their demands, the Committee responded at once with a declaration stating their solidarity with the Government, offering their co-operation and showing a willingness to let bygones be bygones. But Kâmil's appointment ended the goodwill and reintroduced animosity and suspicion on the political scene.[2]

But in spite of this change—adverse from the Committee's point of view—the Committee tried to come to an understanding with Kâmil, though with no success. They wanted a more representative Cabinet with Şevket Paşa as War Minister. He had held that office for two and a half years and had prepared the war plans, and was therefore better equipped to deal with the situation. Nâzım Paşa's name was linked with the Liberals and he was known

[1] Grey to Lowther, London, 17 Jan. 1913, *BD*, ix/ii. 417; Bombard to Poincaré, Pera, 17 Jan. 1913, *DDF*, 3ᵉ Série, v, nos. 230, 290–1; *The Times*, 14 and 17 Jan. 1913; and G. F. Abbott, 'Peace?', *NC*, lxxiii (1913), 41–52.

[2] See above, p. 97, n. 5; and Ragıp, *Esrar Perdesi*, 96–100.

to be an opponent of the CUP. Furthermore, he had been *vali* of Baghdad, and had been out of touch with the military situation. Talât and Said Halim Paşa saw Kâmil on 6 November in order to discuss the situation, but Kâmil refused to co-operate. He dismissed them with 'a short dry statement' that reports from the front revealed extremely low morale among the troops. Since fighting was out of the question he was seeking mediation and carrying out negotiations.[1] Talât also saw Şevket Paşa and the latter complained of ill health, declaring that he was unable to accept any position.[2] On 8 November the *Tanin* published the news that Şevket Paşa was to be appointed Inspector-General. This news caused confusion in government circles and '*Damads*, Kâmil Paşa and the *Şeyhülislâm* went to the Sultan to prevent this appointment',[3] and the *Tanin* was immediately suppressed.[4] What appears to have been the last meeting between the Committee and Kâmil took place on 9 November. This encounter did not prove to be fruitful either. In Kâmil's words, 'since their situation and opinions did not reveal any good intentions the matter was dropped after suitable advice (on both sides)'.[5] Kâmil's policy became more repressive and the Committee also turned from words to conspiracy.[6]

Having failed to move Kâmil, the Committee turned to Nâzım Paşa. In a letter to Unionist exiles in Brussels, Talât wrote of how they finally decided to stage a *coup*.[7] He described how they approached Nâzım Paşa first and encouraged him to continue fighting, and to use experienced men like İzzet Paşa, the Chief of General Staff, as well as Unionist officers like Enver, Fethi, and Cemal. But Nâzım did not respond to their overtures either, and after some time, having done all they could, they gave up trying to win him over. They then turned to Mahmud Şevket Paşa,

[1] H. K. Bayur, op. cit. 390; Cavit, *Tanin*, 7 and 9 Feb. 1944.
[2] Ibid. Cavit, 7 Feb. 1944.   [3] Ibid. 8 Feb. 1944.
[4] Ibid. 10 Feb. 1944; also see above, 111 ff.
[5] H. K. Bayur, op. cit. 390; Y. H. Bayur, *Tarih*, ii/iv. 258–63.
[6] See above, pp. 111 ff., Cavit, *Tanin*, 12, 14, and 18 Feb. 1944, and *The Times*, 11, 18, and 20 Nov. 1912.
[7] Talât's letter was reproduced by H. C. Yalçın in *Tanin*, 24 Feb. 1944 as an annex to Cavit's memoirs. This letter of 444 words and dated 14 Jan. 1913 (1 *Kânunisâni*, 1328 o.s.) described Unionist activity over a period of about two months, from mid November to mid January. Throughout Talât gives no dates and it is therefore never clear when the meetings he mentions took place, or, more important, when the Committee changed its plan of action. Nevertheless it is a most valuable document.

İzzet Paşa, and their own officers and discussed the possibility of overthrowing the Government and taking over.[1] At a special meeting (no date) all eventualities were discussed and plans made, all top secret. But it was decided that since they (the Turks) did not possess the means to wage war—especially to take the offensive and to break out of the Çatalca lines—a *coup* would only demoralize the people (*efrad*) further. Therefore, for the time being all plans for the *coup* were shelved. A little later (it is difficult to say when), they found that some members of the Cabinet were arguing that since the existing Cabinet was committed to retaining Edirne—though it lacked the means to do so—it ought to resign and the ministry that followed would be able to cede the town and save the country from a difficult situation.[2]

Kâmil Paşa was meanwhile proposing to convene a consultative council (*meclisi meşveret*), though some ministers thought that this would lower the Cabinet's prestige further and bring the country nearer to calamity.[2] The Unionists decided not to interfere while the Cabinet was negotiating. But if the Cabinet resigned they resolved that they would:

. . . prevent harmful characters like Albanian Ferid (Paşa) or Reşid from coming to power. If Nâzım were asked to form a ministry they would [remain neutral] neither commit themselves not enter his cabinet. . . . In any peace which resulted the army would certainly wish to punish those responsible for this situation, namely the cabinet; and this, too, had been prepared. After that our plan would be brought into operation. The cabinet would be overthrown and as Cavit and Cahit had proposed, we would come to power and try to bring the country back to life, if this were destined. For this eventuality we must prepare from now.[2]

Talât's letter suggests that the Committee wanted to assume power and responsibility only after someone else had made peace and borne the odium for doing so. Their only condition was that peace must not be made at the cost of Edirne. But after the Collective Note of 17 January this condition was impossible. Kâmil,

---

[1] Yalçın *Tanin*, 24 Feb. 1944; on 12 Jan., two days before the date of Talât's letter, a 'Lieutenant Zeki Bey . . . the most influential leader after Enver Bey, of the Unionist Officers', visited the German Ambassador and told him that 'his comrades condemned Kiamil Pacha's vacillating attitude in the peace question and wished to overthrow the cabinet in order to go on with the war'. See Baron von Wangenheim to the German Foreign Office, 12 Jan. 1913, *GDD*, iv. 156.

[2] Yalçın, *Tanin*, 24 Feb. 1944.

who had been pessimistic from the start, was aware of this. But he was too shrewd and experienced a politician to accept the reprobation for surrendering Edirne. His way out of this impasse was to summon a Grand Council, composed of important and responsible people in the Empire, which would shoulder collectively the responsibility for ceding the town to the Bulgarians.

The Grand Council was summoned and met at Dolmabahçe on 22 January and almost unanimously supported the Cabinet's policy of peace.[1] Next day the Cabinet met at the Sublime Porte in order to draft the reply to the Collective Note. But before the Cabinet had drafted the reply, the Unionists launched their attack. Enver and a small group burst into the Cabinet chamber and at gun-point forced Kâmil to write out his resignation.[2] Nâzım Paşa who confronted them at the door of the chamber was shot. His remark, 'You have deceived me: is this what you promised?' suggests complicity between him and the Committee.[3] His assassination, on the other hand, seems to have been the punishment which the army would want to inflict on 'those responsible for the situation'.[4]

One can only speculate on whether Kâmil would have surrendered Edirne; though there is some evidence which suggests that he would have ceded the town. The very summoning of the Grand Council was for the purpose of having a consensus on war and peace. Twelve days after his fall Kâmil expressed to Fitzmaurice, who was escorting him to the Khedival liner departing for Egypt, 'his fears that the refusal of his successors to accept the friendly counsels of Europe would eventually entail greater territorial and financial losses on Turkey. He said he had hoped to save the guns and military equipment . . . which would cost about T. £2,000,000 and which would have been required for the fortification of Chatalja. . . .'[5] The implication is clear: Kâmil was prepared to give up Edirne.

[1] İkdam, 22 and 23 Jan. 1913; H. K. Bayur, op. cit. 384–6; Bompard to Jonnart, Constantinople, 23 Jan. 1913, DDF, 3ᵉ série, v, nos. 242, 300.
[2] On the coup d'état, see Ragıp, Esrar Perdesi, passim; Kuran, 586 ff.; Danişmend, iv. 397–401; Y. H. Bayur, Tarih ii/1. 254 ff.; H. K. Bayur, op. cit. 386 ff.; İnal, op. cit. 1411 ff. and 1874 ff.; Türkgeldi, op. cit. 78–9; Edib, Memoirs, 342.
[3] Nâzım Paşa's remark quoted in Türkgeldi, op. cit. 79–80 and Kuran, 588; on the complicity between Nâzım and the Unionists, see H. K. Bayur, op. cit.
[4] Talât's letter (op. cit., p. 117 n. 7).
[5] Fitzmaurice's Report, 5 Feb. 1913, F.O. 195/2451/340.

Whether the Committee made a mistake in thinking that Kâmil had already ceded Edirne is of no importance. They had decided on overthrowing the Government long before. The question of Edirne, which had become an emotional factor in current politics, provided them with the psychological moment and with ample justification for staging their *coup*. The Unionists were also aware of the difficulties of holding the town. But once in power they could not surrender the town without loss of face or indeed their very position. Edirne fell to a joint Serbo-Bulgar assault after a long and brave resistance on 26 March 1913. But when the allies began bickering among themselves over the spoils of war, the Committee took advantage, recaptured Edirne in July, and vindicated their claim as saviours of Edirne.

VI

THE CONSOLIDATION OF POWER

DURING the six months the Unionists were out of power, the Ottoman Empire had undergone great physical change. Virtually the entire European portion of the Empire had been lost to the Balkan powers. Edirne was under siege and it was the salvation of the town which provided the Unionists with the rationale for overthrowing Kâmil's Cabinet. In the six months that followed, the role of Edirne in Turkish politics was paramount. But in fact the centre of gravity had shifted to the Arab provinces.

The *coup d'état* of 23 January was a bold and reckless step for the Unionists to take, yet one that was necessary if they were to make a come-back. Talât's faction in the CUP had already stated their preference for assuming power after Edirne had been ceded to Bulgaria and the Liberals had borne the odium for its surrender.[1] Judging from all available evidence, Kâmil would have ceded the town. But to have waited would have meant missing the psychological moment when excitement and patriotism were high and the act appeared spontaneous. Kâmil, armed with the consensus of the National Assembly, would have benefited from any delay to legitimize his position. The decision for peace would have been popular and generally acceptable, and in circumstances of greater stability the Unionists lacked the force necessary to carry out the *coup*. Six months of repression had weakened the Committee and only timing and tactics could make up this shortcoming.

Back in power the CUP was far from being secure. The internecine political struggles of the past five years had reduced the Committee to a shadow of its former self and the Liberals, too, were better organized. And although the Liberal Government had been overthrown, a Liberal organization continued to exist and pose the threat of a *contre-coup*. This threat was potent while Turkey retained Edirne and the tension was high; its fall or

[1] See above, p. 118.

surrender would provide another psychological moment for a *coup*. The Unionists, aware of this, waited in anguish.

In this tense and critical situation the Committee acted with remarkable maturity. Instead of wreaking vengeance on the opposition and widening the existing political gulf, they adopted a moderate line thereby hoping to mobilize the country behind the new Government. This policy was manifest in the proclamation which Cemal Bey (Paşa), Commandant of the Istanbul garrison, issued a few days after the *coup*. The tone of the proclamation was conciliatory and Cemal appealed for co-operation, promising that there would be no arbitrary arrests and that political associations would be permitted so long as they remained within the law.[1] Meanwhile members of the opposition who had been detained after the *coup* were being released, with the caution to 'abandon all ideas of untimely opposition'. Prominent Liberals such as Ali Kemal of the *Ikdam* and Dr. Rıza Nur were bought off and sent into comfortable exile to Europe.[2] The Law of General Amnesty appeared in the press on 14 February granting a free pardon to all those who had committed political crimes until the date of the law. Only 'those responsible for the military reverses and those who had aided the enemy, materially or morally, during the war' were exluded from the amnesty.[3] The vague and ambiguous nature of this law made it plain that while the Unionists were willing to allow an opposition to exist, it must be loyal and neither bark not bite.

In the formation of the new Cabinet too, the Committee showed a combination of good sense and caution. There was no attempt to set up a Unionist regime and this was in keeping with Talât's claim that Kâmil had been overthrown for no other reason than to preserve 'the sacred rights of the nation'.[4] Mahmud Şevket Paşa, who was not a Unionist as past events had shown, was appointed Grand Vezir and War Minister. The other members of the Cabinet were non-partisan, and there were only three Unionists—Said Halim Paşa, Hacı Âdil, and Hayri Bey—all of whom

[1] *Stamboul*, 28 Jan. 1913.
[2] Djemal Pasha, *Memories of a Turkish Statesman, 1913–1919*, 16; Turkish edition, 23.
[3] *Takvim-i Vekayi* and Istanbul press of 14 Feb. 1913. French translation of amnesty law enclosed in Lowther to Grey, no. 135 con., Constantinople, 19 Feb. 1913, F.O. 371/1788/8666.
[4] *Stamboul*, 24 Jan. 1913.

were moderates. Once again the aim was to have a non-partisan Cabinet which would end party politics and rally all elements in a patriotic alliance.

Any regime in power during this critical period faced certain built-in problems. The treasury was empty, the army demoralized, and the Turks diplomatically isolated. Kâmil's solution to these problems had been peace at any price. His overthrow, rather than improving the situation, aggravated it. At the London Conference there was confusion, and the delegates decided to suspend action until they had received fresh instructions from their respective governments. On 26 January they agreed to address a joint note to the Turkish delegation announcing the rupture of the peace negotiations. This note was delivered to Reşid Paşa on 29 January, and on the following day the Balkan states denounced the armistice which was to expire on 3 February at 7 p.m.[1]

In Istanbul, the new Government's problem was clear-cut: to wage war. But first it had to formulate a reply to the Collective Note. This, too, posed no real problem because the contents of the note were dictated by prevailing circumstances. Edirne could no longer be surrendered and at the same time the note had to be conciliatory, making concessions which the Balkan states would not accept. But perhaps the support of the Great Powers could be won over!

The Turkish reply was drafted and presented to the ambassadors of the Powers on 30 January. The Porte agreed to cede only that part of Edirne situated on the right bank of the Maritza, retaining the left bank where the mosques, tombs, and other places of historical and religious association were situated. To cede this area would provoke 'un sentiment de réprobation dans tout le pays et une effervescence telle qu'elle a amené la démission du précédent Cabinet.'[2] With regard to the Aegean islands, the Porte accepted the suggestion made in the Collective Note that the Powers should determine the status of these islands. But it pointed out that while some were essential for the defence of the Dardanelles, others formed an integral part of Anatolia and were therefore necessary for its security. Finally, the note urged the

[1] *The Times*, 25–31 Jan. 1913; Colonel Lamouche, *Quinze Ans d'histoire balkanique* (Paris, 1928), 133–5.
[2] Texts of the Collective Note and the Porte's reply in Lowther to Grey, no. 81 con., Constantinople, 1 Feb. 1913, F.O. 371/1788/5501; also in *Stamboul* and Turkish press of 31 Jan. and *The Times*.

Powers to show goodwill towards Turkey and recognize her rights to establish an autonomous customs tariff, to tax foreigners on the same terms as Ottoman subjects, to agree to the Porte's increasing custom dues by 4 per cent and eventually to abolish the capitulations.[1]

That the reply would be rejected and hostilities resumed was a foregone conclusion. The armistice expired on 3 February and the bombardment of Edirne commenced once more. Military successes would have aided the new regime at home, but they were not forthcoming. The Turks continued to hold Edirne but towns like Üsküdar and Yanina fell to the enemy. The Porte appealed to Europe for intervention and mediation only to be told that Edirne must be surrendered first. Apart from the firm hold the Turks had on the Çatalca line their military position continued to decline. This had serious consequences on the internal political situation.

In spite of this deteriorating military situation, the mood of the country had changed. Cavid, returning from his three-month exile in Europe, felt that 'there [was] something different about the country. There [was] a glimmer of hope. As in the past it [did not] feel as if one [was] living in a dying country. This time they think the army, especially with young and courageous officers in command, will be able to do something.'[2] In the spirit of this new optimism the CUP, on Talât's initiative, formed the Committee of National Defence on 1 February. This was a quasi-official organization whose aim was to mobilize the entire country behind the war effort and thereby help the Government conduct the war. Raising funds was one of its main activities.[3] A few days later a 'Provisional Law concerning Military Supplies in case of War' was promulgated, placing the country on a war footing and extending military over civil authority.[4]

This newly found optimism and sense of unity proved ephemeral. Military defeat shattered all illusions and very soon even Şevket Paşa and his Cabinet were totally demoralized. Talât and Halil saw Şevket Paşa on 15 February and pointed out the need for military and political successes so as to prevent the Cabinet from falling into the situation of its predecessor. Şevket Paşa lost

[1] See p. 123, n. 2.   [2] Cavid, *Tanin*, 25 Feb. 1944.
[3] *Stamboul*, 3 Feb. 1913; resolutions of CND in *Stamboul*, 4 Feb.
[4] Ibid. 7 Feb. 1913.

his temper, claiming that though he favoured war even if Edirne fell, he was more anxious about Anatolia. If the Bulgars and Greeks should combine and land troops there it would be impossible to defend Anatolia. Furthermore, there was the financial problem and there was no money to be found anywhere.[1] At a later meeting, on 22 February, the Grand Vezir reported that

the army had lost the will to fight . . . and İzzet Paşa, the Commander-in-Chief, had even proposed resigning. Edirne was expected to fall on 18 February [o.s., 3 March N.s.], and four days earlier the Commander had discussed the necessity to surrender. Thereafter the enemy with all his force would advance to Çatalca, break through and enter Istanbul. Mahmud Şevket proposed making peace so as not to bring the country to ruin. If we [the Unionists] did not decide to put forward new peace proposals before the Powers, he said he would resign immediately.[2]

Talât, to say the least, was furious with Mahmud Şevket Paşa.[3]
    Edirne did not fall on 3 March and Şevket Paşa did not resign. But the situation throughout February and March remained precarious. On 26 February Lowther reported dissatisfaction in the army, the arrest of dissident officers, and the fortification of *Babıâli* to prevent a *coup*. The *Tanin* too, he wrote, had lost hope of retaining Edirne and was preparing the population for the fall.[4] Mahmud Şevket's despondency over Edirne has already been noted, but his entire Cabinet was split over the issue. To prevent any public leakage or discussion of this demoralizing disunity Cemal issued a secret circular to the vernacular and foreign language press on 12 March. The press was forbidden to publish, under penalty of suppression and expulsion of editors, any references to reported differences in the Cabinet or rumours of its resignation. This, suggested Fitzmaurice, was because of the differences between the Grand Vezir and the militant members in the Cabinet.[5] Two weeks later the fall of Edirne (26 March) healed the split in the Cabinet; but it also left the anti-Unionist forces free to take the offensive in internal politics.
    Ever since 23 January a *contre-coup* had always been on the

[1] Cavid, *Tanin*, 7 Mar. 1944.   [2] Ibid. 9 Mar. 1944.
[3] Ibid. 19 Mar. 1944.
[4] Lowther to Grey, no. 111, tel. con., Constantinople, 26 Feb. 1913, F.O. 371/1788/9253. See also the extract of *Tanin* in *Stamboul* of 26 Feb.
[5] Fitzmaurice to Lowther, Pera, 12 Mar. 1913, F.O. 195/2451/340.

cards. By late February the situation seemed ripe for such action and it was then that the police uncovered a conspiracy against the Government and the CUP. The organizer of this plot was Saffet Lütfi Bey, secretary to Prince Sabaheddin. But many others were implicated including some officers of the Çatalca army, among whom was Abuk Ahmed Paşa, commander of the Çatalca forces and Sabaheddin's uncle.[1] Perhaps 'the plot [was] manufactured by the Committee Cabinet as a handle for dealing with its political adversaries, and judging by the . . . version which the Grand Vizier gave me [wrote Lowther], the plot would not so far seem to be serious.'[2] It resembled in many ways the plot of 1910 (see above, p. 82 ff.) and it fizzled out in a similar manner. Sabaheddin was cautioned by Cemal and challenged to produce his secretary and prove his innocence. Saffet Lütfi, however, had taken refuge in the home of an Austrian diplomat, where he enjoyed immunity. This was violated on 16 March and Lütfi Bey was arrested. But he was a Bosnian and had an Austrian passport. Therefore, under Austrian pressure he was released and allowed to leave the country.[3]

However spurious this conspiracy may have been, far more important opposition activity was taking place abroad; and as far apart as Paris and Cairo. Both cities had played important roles in opposition activities against Istanbul during the period of despotism and after. In 1913 Paris was the headquarters of Şerif Paşa's Parti Radical Ottoman, while Cairo provided refuge for Kâmil, Şeyhülislâm Cemalettin and, after June, Sadık Bey. But it is to Cairo we must turn in order to examine anti-Unionist intrigue.

Kâmil left for Cairo on 4 February whence he continued to intrigue against the CUP. Cairo offered certain operational advantages: its proximity to Istanbul and Kâmil's familiarity with the terrain, the Khedive's hostility to the Porte and his support for anti-Unionists. Perhaps most important of all from Kâmil's point of view was that, in Egypt under British occupation, Kâmil—that incorrigible Anglophile—could still find British support for his

[1] Djemal Pasha, op. cit. 23–4; Turkish edition, 29–32.

[2] Lowther to Grey, no. 181 con., Constantinople, 3 Mar. 1913, F.O. 371/1798/10822.

[3] Djemal Pasha, op. cit., 23–4; Stamboul, 24 Mar. 1913; Lowther to Grey, nos. 149 and 154, tel. con., Constantinople, 17 and 19 Mar. 1913, F.O. 371/1798/12423 and 12849; and Fitzmaurice to Lowther, Pera, 3 and 26 Mar. 1913, F.O. 195/2451/340.

activities. Commenting on Kâmil's sojourn in Cairo in 1910 Storrs, the Oriental Secretary to the British Resident, noted that

the aged Cypriot . . ., four times Grand Vizier of the Ottoman Empire, tried and convinced defender of the traditional friendship between Turkey and Great Britain, . . . received no recognition from the Egyptian Government but was immediately visited by Lord Kitchener at the Semiramis Hotel.

In 1913 Storrs

was amused to note the difference in his reception . . ., when he may at any moment become Grand Vizier. The Royal waiting-room had been opened and a red carpet laid down: the Governor, Prince Haidar and the Ottoman High Commissioner all pawing the platform.[1]

Not that Storrs's words are indicative of either the British or the Egyptian Government's intention of becoming kingmaker; rather they reveal the belief in certain quarters that the life of the Istanbul Government would be short. There were many who wished to hasten this process.

Early in March when the situation in Istanbul was desperate Kâmil told Kitchener that 'he did not expect the present Turkish Government to last very long, and that information had reached him as to the probability of another revolution in the very near future'.[2] Kâmil also related how he had been approached by the Greek chargé d'affaires who, speaking on behalf of his Prime Minister, had told Kâmil that

the Balkan allies could not reopen peace negotiations with the Government at present in power at Constantinople, as the latter were not representative either of the Sultan or the nation. He then went on to sound Kiamil Pasha as to whether he would be willing, with a view to the conclusion of peace, to return to Turkey and form a government with whom the allies could negotiate. The Pasha [continues Kitchener] objected that such a task would be impossible unless he could count on the support of the Entente Powers, and more especially of England. He added that the situation should be laid before you [Grey].

When informing me of the above, his Highness expressed the wish that you might give your consideration to the question whether some adequate foreign control might not be established in regard to administration in Turkey. Such a course was, in his opinion, the only means of

[1] Storrs, op. cit. 125–6; quotation from a contemporary letter.
[2] Viscount Kitchener to Grey, no. 21, tel. con., Cairo, 5 Mar. 1913, F.O. 371/1798/10407.

preserving Turkey from extinction, and he would be very glad to undertake the task. He added that it would of course be necessary for England and the Powers of the Entente to impose proper foreign control, as he could not undertake to introduce it himself. Were they, however, to adopt such a policy he would gladly carry it out.[1]

Foreign control of the Turkish administration seems to have been a consistent theme in Kâmil's political ideas. This does not find a place in his biographies by İnal and H. K. Bayur, possibly because he never expressed this sentiment in public or in writing. Perhaps his biographers, in the older tradition of biography writing, omit details which might tarnish their hero's image. Kâmil did, however, relate similar views to Ali Haydar Midhat in 1908–9 and to Fitzmaurice in 1913.[2]

The Foreign Office's reaction to Kitchener's dispatch remains unknown. But from other dispatches of this period it is clear that Britain was unwilling to assume responsibility that any active interference might entail. In 1913 she did not want to endanger the accord she was on the verge of reaching with Germany by introducing an element of suspicion with regard to Turkey. If a pro-British government ruled Turkey well and good; the Foreign Office would not actively foster it.[3]

Kitchener now turned to Lowther on Kâmil's behalf and asked 'whether you think that he Kâmil had better return to Istanbul or not as he fears this might precipitate revolution against present Government and wishes to be guided by your advice . . .'.[4] Lowther's reply was diplomatic and non-commital. No wonder Kâmil had earlier complained 'bitterly of Lowther, whom he accused of laziness, slackness, and love of comfort, and exclaimed: "Alas, where is White, where is Currie?" '[5] Lowther answered: 'I cannot possibly give advice on such an important matter directly concerning the internal affairs of the country. But the general situation is very uncertain until after peace which the present cabinet are apparently desirous of concluding.'[6]

---

[1] Kitchener to Grey (op. cit., p. 127, n. 2).

[2] Midhat, *Hatıralarım*, 199; Fitzmaurice's report, 5 Feb. 1913, F.O. 195/2451/340.

[3] Feroz Ahmad, 'Great Britain's Relations with the Young Turks, 1908–1914', *MES*, ii/IV (July 1966), 302–29.

[4] Kitchener to Lowther, tel., Cairo, 7 Apr. 1913, F.O. 195/2452/1574.

[5] Türkgeldi, op. cit. 75; and Bernard Lewis's translation in *BSOAS*, v/23 (1960), 147.

[6] Lowther to Kitchener, tel., Pera, 8 Apr. 1913, F.O. 195/2452/1574.

It may be of interest to note that Lowther's reply in draft included a second section which would have made the position clearer to Kâmil. It read: 'But the general situation is very uncertain until after the conclusion of peace, and those who bear the responsibility of making it will have to bear the odium. Matters having advanced as far as they have I should say that the common-sense view w[oul]d be to leave matter alone.'[1] Why Lowther did not send this draft is pure speculation. Perhaps he considered it a risk to let the Unionists conclude peace and then await their fall. There was a chance that they might not fall even after peace with dishonour. And just as the same problem seems to have worried the Unionists in January, forcing them to act, so Lowther may have considered it expedient to have Kâmil come to Istanbul even against his own common sense.

Kâmil's impending visit to Istanbul became an open secret and the authorities forbade his return. The Reuter's agent was told by the authorities that this action had been taken because they had intercepted telegraphic correspondence showing that the Khedive and Kitchener were trying to bring about Kâmil's restoration as Grand Vezir.[2] By early May Kâmil was in Cyprus where he was expected to stay a few days, prior to his departure for London where he was to be the guest of the Queen of England.[3] He arrived in Istanbul on 28 May only to be placed under house arrest and all communications with him prohibited. Had Cemal had his way Kâmil would have been packed off without ceremony. He knew that Kâmil's arrival was the signal for a *coup* against the CUP.[4] Lowther, finding Cemal's behaviour 'a glaring instance of the suppression of constitutional and personal liberties', made representations on Kâmil's behalf. As a result the British Embassy was allowed to communicate with him and he was permitted to stay in the capital for three days before leaving for İzmir.[5]

Cemal's timely action probably aborted the planned *coup* and forced the conspirators to take more hasty action. On 11 June Mahmud Şevket Paşa was assassinated while on his way to the Sublime Porte. Cemal reacted immediately and prevented the breakdown of law and order. Members of the opposition were

[1] Ibid.   [2] Ibid. 22 Apr. 1913.
[3] The *Alemdar*, 8 May 1913, quoted in the *Stamboul*, same date.
[4] Djemal Pasha, op. cit. 29–34; Turkish edition, 42–6.
[5] Ibid.; also Lowther to Grey, no. 488 con., Constantinople, 31 May 1913, F.O. 371/1822/25440; and *İkdam*, 29 May and *Stamboul*, 31 May 1913.

rounded up and exiled to Sinop. The capital was placed under a 10 p.m. curfew, and a court martial was set up to try those implicated in the plot. Twelve men were sentenced to death and executed on 24 June; among these was *Damad* Salih Paşa, nephew-in-law of the Sultan and Tahir Hayrettin's brother. Members of the opposition such as Şerif Paşa in Paris, Prince Sabaheddin, Reşid Bey, Kâmil Paşa's Minister of the Interior, and İsmail Hakkı, deputy for Gümülcine, were sentenced to death *in absentia*.[1] The assassination continued to provide the CUP with an excuse to crush the opposition. As late as 12 February 1914 the court-martial sentenced Sadık Bey—then in Cairo—to death.[2] His party, the 'Freedom and Accord', however, had neither been banned nor dissolved. This fact enabled the Committee to maintain the fiction of a multi-party system and representative government in the years to follow.

In Paris, on the day before assassination, Kâmil's son Said Paşa was discussing with Cavid 'the establishment of a Unionist cabinet under his father in order to save the country'. He explained that Kâmil's Cabinets had always been ineffective because Kâmil had never relied on the CUP, the only power in the land. But if the Paşa were restored he could immediately set out for Europe, presumably to negotiate peace, leaving behind Mahmud Şevket as his deputy. Internally this would unite the country and those who remained in opposition would be silenced by public opinion.[3] Had this proposal been more timely and sincere the Unionists would surely have accepted it. On the day they forced Kâmil to resign, Ömer Naci is said to have lamented: 'Kâmil Paşa, if you had joined us and not opposed us, you would have remained Grand Vezir until the end; why did you do it?'[4] Ever since 1908 the CUP had sought a Grand Vezir such as Kâmil who could give their movement respectability and legitimacy.

Mehmed Said Halim Paşa, a grandson of Mehmed Ali of Egypt, succeeded Şevket Paşa. His Cabinet was distinctly Unionist. It included such prominent Committeemen as the Grand Vezir himself, Talât, Halil, and Hayri Beys. In time the other ministers, too, were replaced by members of the CUP.

---

[1] Türkgeldi, op. cit. 103–5; İnal, op. cit. 1895; *İkdam*, 12 June 1913; *Stamboul*, 12, 13, 21, 22, and 24 June 1913; and Djemal Pasha, op. cit. 34–9; Turkish edition, 47–53.

[2] *The Times*, 13 Feb. 1914.   [3] Cavit, *Tanin*, 16 May 1944.

[4] Türkgeldi, op. cit. 79; Kâmil's reply: 'Get away!'

The military situation in the Balkans was slowly changing in Turkey's favour during these months. This was brought about by division among the allies over the spoils of war, and it was only a matter of time before they began fighting. The Unionists waited patiently to exploit this situation, even though they had already signed the peace Treaty of London on 30 May. Anticipating military action in the near future, the *Tanin* of 18 June advised the Porte 'not to be caught unprepared even though the cost of maintaining a mobilised army which was not fighting was very great'. A week later Babanzâde İsmail Hakkı wrote that 'in the prevailing situation in the Balkans Turkey must retain total freedom of action. Even if war between the allies does not break out, our military position is superior at the moment. . . . This does not mean that we must go to war; but it constitutes a good reason why our immediate and essential right should be quickly recognized.'[1] Fighting among the allies broke out in earnest on 30 June, and Turkey began to prepare, quickly and unobtrusively, for the reoccupation of territory she had claimed during the negotiations. But the Porte feared a diplomatic reaction and on 7 July Said Halim assured the British chargé d'affaires that Turkey did not intend to attack Bulgaria. She only wanted Bulgaria to vacate Turkish territory in accordance with the new frontier, and military preparations were being made only to show Bulgaria that force was available. Newspaper articles ascribing more aggressive intentions to Turkey were without foundation.[2]

The Unionists supported an offensive to recapture Edirne but the Cabinet was divided and uncertain of the outcome. Their chief concern was the reaction of the Powers, and the financial situation which was still critical and did not warrant an offensive. The War Minister, İzzet Paşa, wanted satisfaction on two accounts: would the political complications be too dangerous for the regime, and was there sufficient money in the treasury for the project?[3] In spite of all assurances the Cabinet remained unconvinced. It was explained to them that Edirne had been the sole reason for overthrowing Kâmil and unless they attempted to recapture it they would lose their moral right to lead the country.

---

[1] 'Bulgaristan Siyaseti', *Tanin*, 26 June 1913.
[2] Marling to Grey, no. 323, tel. con., Constantinople, 7 July 1913, F.O. 371/1834/31281.
[3] Djemal Pasha, op. cit. 46; Turkish edition, 58.

However, no consensus was reached and in the end it was Talât and Said Halim who took the decision to advance.[1]

Mr. Nachevich, the Bulgarian plenipotentiary, arrived in Istanbul on 10 July to open negotiations. They were immediately suspended on the baseless grounds that there was a change of government in Sofia.[2] On the 13th an Imperial *İrade* directed the Commander-in-Chief to reoccupy Turkish territory, but without specifying the straight line running from Enoz to Midya.[3] The press clamoured for the recapture of Edirne. But the Grand Vezir, fearing Europe's and particularly Britain's reaction, explained that the Turks would only reoccupy Edirne out of fear 'that the Greeks flushed with their successes against Bulgaria, might have designs on Edirne, which had very few troops'.[4] But the military threw caution to the winds. On 17 July at Çerkesköy, Enver declared that 'no one could, nor had the right to stop the march of the Turkish troops on the Enoz–Midya line, and that even should the Turkish Government obey the Powers, he himself would order the troops to advance on Edirne and beyond'.[5] The advance continued and Edirne was reoccupied on the fifth anniversary of the revolution.

Turkey's problems did not end here for there was still the acquiescence of the Powers to be won. Once again the Cabinet was divided over the question of retaining Edirne, thereby violating the Treaty of London and challenging the Powers. But Talât, as spokesman for the CUP, was explicit about not surrendering the town; it was, after all, his home town. To the press he declared:

It is possible that partisans of the evacuation of Edirne exist. In that case it is impossible for persons holding such views to remain in the cabinet. The ministers are all in accord about retaining Edirne. . . . Therefore in the name of all the members of the government I authorise you to publish a denial of rumours to the contrary. Ottoman patriotism is not for sale for the price of an increase in customs duties. . . . Edirne

[1] Djemal Pasha, op. cit. 46 ff.; Turkish edition 58 ff.; Menteşe, *Cumhuriyet*, 29 Oct. 1946; Türkgeldi, op. cit. 106.

[2] *Stamboul* and *Tanin*, 11 and 12 July 1913; Marling to Grey, no. 331, tel. con., Constantinople, 12 July 1913, F.O. 371/1834/32161.

[3] *Stamboul* and *The Times*, 14 July 1913.

[4] Marling to Grey, no. 336, tel. con., Constantinople, 14 July 1913, F.O. 371/1834/32474.

[5] Military Attaché Cooper to Marling, Constantinople, 25 July 1913, in ibid., no. 664, con. Constantinople, 26 July 1913, F.O. 371/1834/35300.

can only be bought at the price of the blood of our devoted and courageous army, prepared to sacrifice itself in order to defend the town.[1]

On 7 August, the Powers presented a note summoning the Porte 'most categorically' to respect the principles of the Treaty of London, and this was rejected firmly but politely by the Porte on the 11th. Fortunately for the Turks the Powers were not united, and as in the past (and future) found it impossible to act in unison. There followed a stalemate though by the end of August Bulgaria agreed to open direct negotiations with Turkey. The Bulgarian delegation arrived in Istanbul on 3 September and after protracted negotiations the peace treaty was signed on 29 September. The Porte was finally free to pursue other pressing matters, even though the treaty with Serbia was not signed until 15 March 1914, and Turco-Greek tension continued to play an important role in the politics of the country.

The effect of five years of war in Albania, Yemen, Libya, and the Balkans was enormous in all spheres of life. It was natural that the amputation of these areas would have serious consequences, and not necessarily only harmful ones. It made the Empire much more homogeneous and therefore forced the Turks to rethink their entire policy of Ottomanism and decentralization.

While the predominantly non-Muslim areas of the Balkans formed part of the Empire, the Islamic element in the Ottoman ideology had to be diluted. The centralization of education, the army, and economy seemed the only way to knit together such a heterogeneous Empire. Both the ideology and the administrative policy had to undergo change if the only non-Turkish element of any importance—the Arabs—were to remain within the Empire. The Arab question therefore came into the foreground.[2]

Earlier in July 1912 when the CUP had been ousted from power, the Arab provinces had hoped for a change of policy from the Cabinets of Muhtar and Kâmil Paşas. Both men were familiar with the Arab provinces and sympathetic to their aspiration, and indeed Kâmil did issue a protocol containing proposals to modify

[1] *Stamboul*, 4 Aug. 1913.
[2] There were, of course, other non-Turkish communities within the Empire, Armenians, Greeks, Kurds, and Circassians. But unlike the Arab they lived as minorities in Turkish areas. The role of the Armenians and Greeks is discussed below. On the Arab question, see Y. H. Bayur, *Tarih*, ii/III (1951), 218–31, and Zeine N. Zeine, *Arab-Turkish Relations and the Emergence of Arab Nationalism* (Beirut, 1958).

the Organic Law for the Lebanon, in operation since 1864.[1] Soon after the Sublime Porte Incident, a committee to consider reforms in the administration of the Arab provinces on principles of decentralization was set up in Istanbul. The British Consul in Beirut noted that '. . . the people were suspicious of this and the Committee of Union and Progress were playing for time. There was much more sympathy in the Arab world for Kiamil Pasha. . . .'[2]

The Unionists, while willing to make concessions, had no intention of granting complete autonomy as the Arabs hoped. This became clear with the promulgation of two provisional laws on 9 and 26 March 1913. The law of 9 March separated the provincial from Imperial finance and stated that in future revenues would be collected by a special machinery—to be set up —for the provinces. Payments for local services were to be made out of a special provincial account made up of local revenues, and the budget of each province would be drawn up by its General Assembly.[3]

The law of 26 March on provincial administration was designed to establish quasi-autonomous administration with the *vali* appointed from Istanbul at the head of a locally elected council. Though the *vali* was to be the chief executive authority, in matters of finance and other important matters outside everyday administrative routine, he was dependent on the decisions of the General Council. Members of the council were elected under virtually the same laws as deputies for Parliament. Soldiers on active service, senators, deputies, judges, government officials, and contractors were excluded from being elected. Councillors were to be paid and were to be elected in the first instance by a joint electoral college composed of secondary electors, chosen for the purpose of the 1912 elections.[4] The aim of the Unionists in introducing this legislation was clear: to decentralize, and at the same time preserve the national authority of the central Government through the *vali* and the Ministry of the Interior; in short, to reconcile the

[1] *The Times*, 1 Jan. 1913. See also B. Lewis, *Emergence*, 384–5.

[2] Consul-General Cumberbatch (Beirut) to Lowther, in Lowther to Grey, no. 104, con. Constantinople, 7 Feb. 1913, F.O. 371/788/7281.

[3] *Takvim-i Vekayi*, 11 Mar. 1913. See also Lowther to Grey, no. 228 con., Constantinople, 22 Mar. 1913, F.O. 371/1801/13761.

[4] *Takvim-i Vekayi*, 28 Mar. 1913; İ. H. Göreli, *İl İdaresi* (Ankara, 1952), 17 and 21–3; Lowther to Grey, no. 300, con. Constantinople, 12 Apr. 1913, F.O. 371/1801/17400; Y. H. Bayur, *Tarih*, ii/III (1951), 220–1, and ii/IV (1951), 304–7; B. Lewis, *Emergence*, 385.

claims of provincial autonomy with national unity. And while local elements had a greater say in their administration, the elections of the local councils would tend to favour the more forward-looking people at the expense of the traditional leaders of Arab society. The traditional element resented this foray into their domain and rose in defence of their interests.

The reaction of the Arab notables in Iraq to this new administrative scheme was unfavourable, to say the least. The notables and deputies of Basra sent telegrams of protest directly to the Ministry of the Interior. Seyyid Talib, one of the more important Iraqi notables, told the British Consul that 'there were some good points in the new laws and much that was bad; on the whole it was inacceptable in its present form, and the Arab notables oppose its execution as it stands'.[1] The Arabs took exception principally to those clauses which conferred upon the *vali* the right to interfere in the deliberations of the General Council, to eliminate from its debates any subject he disapproved of, and to suspend its sittings or dissolve the body if he so desired. While martial law prevailed he also had the right to deal with any recalcitrant member without reference to the courts. In the main, however, much would depend on the attitude and personality of the *vali*.

The Arab notables led by Seyyid Talib Bey declared that they would neither accept nor tolerate such arbitrary conditions. Protests to Istanbul drew the reply that the law in its present form would be put into operation, and the elections for the General Council under the prescribed conditions would proceed forthwith. The Porte's negative response exasperated the notables and Talib Bey warned Crow that

they would not hesitate to resort to methods of violence in order to attain their ends. . . . They were already organized and prepared for this development, and that serious disturbances would undoubtedly occur if the new vali . . . insisted on resorting to arbitrary measures in order to carry out the provisions of the law in its present form.[1]

The Porte's attitude remained firm but moderate and major incidents were averted. Such was the situation at the outbreak of war in the following year, and then events took a turn of their own.

---

[1] Crow to Lowther, Basra, 29 Apr. 1913, in Lowther to Grey, no. 490 con., Constantinople, 31 May 1913, F.O. 371/1801/26188.

The Porte's change of policy with regard to the language question coincided with introduction of these administrative reforms. Henceforth Arabic was permitted to be used as the medium of instruction in schools and as the administrative language in certain departments. While this change met a major Arab demand its real significance lies in that it marked a turning-point in ideology from 'secular' Ottomanism to 'Islamist' Ottomanism; a change prescribed by historical reality. *Tanin*, the chief exponent of national unity and modernization, echoed this change when it asked:

> How could it be that Turkey, a Muslim state, ever had an aversion to Arabic, its religious language? Was it not realised that hostility to Arabic meant hostility to Islam? We love Arabic as the language of the Quran and of the Prophet. We love it because Muslim civilisation and Arabic are inseparable, and to turn away from Arabic is to turn away from thirteen hundred years of learning and civilisation. One thing is clear: Arabic is more widespread and has more vitality than any other Islamic language. In denying this claim a Turk . . . wipes out his own civilisation and his own past.
>
> It is true that the Ottoman Government has not exerted itself in order to spread Arabic; but it is guilty of the same charge with regard to Turkish. . . . The disease is general. It must be admitted that the whole Ottoman and Muslim organism is affected by this disease and is responsible for it.
>
> The Ottoman Government has taken a step in the right direction, but this step must be followed by others. Greater attention must be paid to Arabic not only in Arabic-speaking areas but everywhere else. The Government should do this, not as the ruler of a few million Arabs, but as a Muslim state.[1]

Had this article appeared in some Islamist journal, it would have caused no surprise. But its appearance in the foremost Unionist journal was indicative. In 1909 the *Tanin* had written in the strongest terms on behalf of the Government's language policy, and on its right to centralize education and inspect all schools. Admittedly these articles were written against the Greek reaction to the Government's centralizing measures, but the same measures were applied to the Arabs.[2]

In May 1913 there were rumours that Hüseyin Hilmi, ambassador in Vienna, had been appointed Inspector-General for reform

[1] Babanzâde İsmail Hakkı, 'Arapça ve İslâhat', *Tanin*, 21 Apr. 1913.
[2] See *Tanin*, 13 and 21 June 1909 and others during this period.

in Syria. Such an appointment was bound to be popular among the Arabs for Hilmi Paşa had established a reputation for honesty and efficiency, and furthermore he was familiar with the problems of the Arab provinces, having spent the earlier part of his administrative career there.[1] This rumour was never substantiated. In the following month, however, an Arab, Said Halim Paşa, was appointed Grand Vezir. Whatever interpretation one may care to give to this appointment, it would be fair to conclude that it was designed *inter alia* to placate Arab opinion. It turned out to be the longest grand vezirate of the Young Turk period, and, significantly, terminated only after the outbreak of the Arab revolt. It was no accident that 'at a time when the Turkish Government was accused of pursuing a policy of Turkification, its Sadrazam was an ardent Islamist who wrote only in French and Arabic'.[2] Nor was he the figurehead as he is sometimes described. He seems to have been responsible for the Unionist Arab policy, and it was because of his personal intervention that the break between the Amir of Mecca and the Unionists did not take place earlier.[3] In retrospect, it is easy to conclude that the seed of Turkish nationalism had been sown; contemporary evidence reveals that it had yet to take root.

Further concessions were made to Şerif Hüseyin and the idea of restricting his authority or extending railways in the Hejaz was abandoned. By March 1914 the Porte had virtually repudiated the application of the law of provincial administration. In return for the completion of the railway network in this area Hüseyin was guaranteed the emirate in his lifetime and then hereditary in his family. Furthermore he would receive money in order to buy off the tribes, he would control one-third of all revenues derived from the railway, and have total command over the force necessary to complete the project.[4]

Even after the introduction of decentralized administration in the provinces, agitation for local autonomy continued in Syria and

[1] *Sabah* and *Stamboul*, 27 May 1913; İnal, op. cit. 1654 ff.; and Ḥusayn Hilmi in *EI*².

[2] Niyazi Berkes, *The Development of Secularism in Turkey*, 349 n. 5 and passim; B. Lewis, *Emergence*, 221 and 352, and İnal, op. cit. 1893 ff.

[3] C. E. Dawn, 'The Amir of Mecca Al-Husayn ibn-Ali and the Origin of the Arab Revolt', *Proceedings of the American Philosophical Society*, 104/i (1960), 18; Djemal Pasha, op. cit. 227–8; Turkish edition, 278.

[4] Dawn, loc. cit., 17–19.

Iraq, culminating in an Arab Congress which convened in Paris in June 1913. As far as the Unionists were concerned they had already met this demand for local autonomy. They did not take the Congress too seriously though they feared that one outcome of Arab agitation on French soil could be French intervention in Syria. To prevent this eventuality they sent a delegation to Paris, headed by the party secretary Midhat Şükrü [Bleda], to negotiate with the Congress.[1] Negotiations were continued in Istanbul and again the Unionists reiterated the concessions they had already made— administrative decentralization, the use of Arabic in schools— along with the promise of appointing more Arabs to the Senate and other high offices. One author suggests that the 'early Arab societies seem to have been founded rather as a reaction to Turkish failure to take Arab leaders as equal members in their own organisations than to carry out a well-defined programme of action'.[2] To appease the Arabs five Arab senators were appointed, one of them being Abdülhamid Zehrawi, Deputy for Hama and President of the Arab Congress. He, it appears, coveted the office of şeyhülislâm. The other four senators, according to Antonius, were 'strangers to the Arab national movement'.[3] This reflected the Unionist policy of appointing, or having elected to Parliament, only those Arabs, Armenians, Greeks, or indeed Turks, who would support or at least acquiesce in the policies of the Committee of Union and Progress.

The arrest of Aziz Ali Mısrı on 9 February 1914, revealed that the Arab Question was still far from solution. Aziz Ali was an Arab officer in the Ottoman army who had played a role of some importance in the CUP until 1909. Later he joined Arab secret societies working for autonomy within the Empire, and prior to his arrest he had founded a new society, al-Ahd or the Covenant. The British Ambassador described him as 'one of the leading spirits in the group of young Arabs . . . who were dissatisfied with the present Turkish Government'.[4] To say the least the

---

[1] Djemal Pasha, op. cit. 59; Turkish edition, 69; Y. H. Bayur, *Tarih*, ii/IV. 314–25; George Antonius, *The Arab Awakening* (Capricorn, ed. New York, 1965), 116. See also Y. H. Bayur, *Tarih*, ii/III. 224 ff.

[2] Majid Khadduri, 'Aziz Ali Misri and the Arab Nationalist Movement', *St. Antony's Papers*, no. 17, *MEA*, iv (1965), 141.

[3] Djemal Pasha, op. cit. 59; Turkish edition, 71; Antonius, op. cit. 117.

[4] Mallet to Grey, no. 117 con., Constantinople, 24 Feb. 1914, F.O. 371/ 2131/9033; Antonius, op. cit. 110 and 118–21; Djemal Pasha, op. cit. 60–4; Turkish edition, 71–6; Khadduri loc. cit.

Porte was suspicious of Aziz Ali's activities. From the Grand
Vezir Mallet learned that Aziz Ali was in the pay of the Khedive
who wanted the latter to persuade the Sanussi to make peace with
the Italians. The Turks, being at peace with Italy, could not
object openly to such action on the part of Aziz Ali but they
resented the Khedive's intrigues. The Porte, wrote Mallet, also
'Suspect His Majesty's Government, or, at any rate, the Egyptian
Government, were privy to His Highness's Khedive's activities,
which they may regard as a further indication of British interference in Arab politics.'[1]

Turkish suspicions regarding Aziz Ali's conspiratorial activities
were confirmed by his own friends who informed Mallet that
'they were planning an insurrection in Iraq which would involve
Kuwait and even Ibn Saud'.[2] But as these activities could not be
publicly reviewed Aziz Ali was charged with having embezzled
£T20,000 during the Tripoli War. The frivolous nature of this
charge convinced the Arabs that the only reason for Aziz Ali's
arrest and humiliation was Enver Paşa's constant hostility towards
him. Aziz Ali was tried *in camera* and condemned to death. His
sentence was commuted to one of fifteen years' hard labour, and on
21 April he was dramatically pardoned, leaving for Egypt the next
day.[3]

The motive for Aziz Ali's arrest and trial is still not clear. Its
only result was to discredit the Porte in the eyes of Arab nationalists. But if Talât's words are any guide the Turks were satisfied
with the situation. In a conversation held on 24 March, Talât told
Mallet that Arab-Turkish accord had been established on a firm
footing:

Talib was now on good terms with the Government, and that Sheikh
Khazal and Sheikh Mubarak were also friendly and would help them
settle matters with Ibn Saud. . . . The Porte had come to a satisfactory
arrangement with the Arabs about their representation in Parliament . . .,
and that the Arabs were now quite satisfied. A new Arab Senator had
been appointed that day, which had given satisfaction. . . . The Porte
[concluded Talât] was nowadays very wise and prudent, and that they

---

[1] Mallet to Grey, no. 335 con. Constantinople, 12 May 1914, F.O. 371/
2124/22042; and no. 153, tel. con. 9 Mar. 1914, F.O. 371/2131/10697; *BD*, x/II.
833.
[2] Ibid. Aziz Ali's love of conspiracy and adventure remained with him all
his life. See Khadduri (loc. cit., 138 n. 2).
[3] Antonius, op. cit. 120–1; Khadduri (ibid., 144–5).

meant to settle their differences peacefully in future and not by the sword.[1]

By the middle of 1913 the Porte had achieved political equilibrium. The worst of the Second Balkan War was over and Edirne was in Turkish hands. All overt political opposition had been demolished for all intents and purposes, and the CUP was truly in power. Said Halim's appointment seems a repetition of the old gambit of putting up a socially acceptable personality—the Prince Sabaheddin of the CUP—as Grand Vezir. This undoubtedly is part of the explanation. But primarily Halim Paşa's appointment reflects the change to an Islamist policy and the Unionist desire to appease the Arabs and to come to an understanding with them. Being a cultured and educated gentleman, Said Halim, in his capacity as Grand Vezir and Foreign Minister, was well qualified to deal with ambassadors. Throughout this period diplomacy was and continued to be one of the main occupations of the Porte.[2]

Reviewing the post-war situation—but prior to the recapture of Edirne—Hüseyin Cahit wrote that 'the disease of apathy is worse than war. War is an examination, an examination our nation took and failed, proving that it has been a lazy student, one who has not acquired the knowledge necessary to graduate. We now have before us two goals: to repair the ravages of war and to reform our administration.'[3]

In spite of all the reverses the Unionists retained their optimism and determination to face the future. There was no note of despair or any inclination to invite a foreign power (or Powers) to take charge and put things right. The belief in reform and modernization remained unshaken and even during critical periods the Unionists introduced reform. Immediately after coming to power Şevket Paşa's Government entered into negotiations with the Powers in order to obtain their consent to an increase of 4 per cent in the customs and duties and the revision of tariff dues, the application of certain taxes to foreigners, the abolition of foreign post offices in Ottoman territories, and the eventual abolition of the capitulations. But it was only in September that the Unionists

[1] Mallet to Grey, no. 205, very con., Constantinople, 25 Mar. 1914, F.O. 371/2128/13883.
[2] On Said Halim and his Cabinet see Babanzâde İsmail Hakkı's editorial in *Tanin*, 19 June 1913.   [3] Ibid. 26 Apr. 1913.

were able to devote themselves fully to the problem of internal reform.

The question of reforming the administration of the country and of the CUP, as well as the new ideological basis of the Empire, was discussed at the 1913 Congress of the Committee of Union and Progress. The fifth annual Congress opened in Istanbul on Saturday, 20 September and Ali Fethi (Okyar) read the opening speech. His report covered the events of the past year when the Committee had been faced with a 'vindictive government'. One of his charges against anti-Unionists was that they were 'above all, the enemies of government by the young'. But the real importance of the speech lay in that it put forward the agenda to be discussed at the Congress. Fethi Bey pointed out the need for new legislation which would lead to economic revival in the Empire, the need to develop commerce and industry by setting up agricultural co-operatives, banks, and other institutions of this nature. He called for an expansion in education and appealed to the delegates to work to bring Islam in line with the modern world 'in order to preserve it from decay'. With regard to the language issue, he declared that

as the Ottoman Government aspired to see the progress and develop-ment of all the diverse elements which constitute its population, it must adopt as the basis of its internal policy the use of the local lan-guages of the predominant element as the medium of instruction in schools, in the tribunals and in the bureaucracy, and to choose from among those functionaries who knew the language of the area to which they were being sent.[1]

But, he continued, that while this principle would be applied to all elements in the Empire, Ottomanism would constitute the force binding all ethnic groups, forming a unified and solid block cemented through having common aspirations. Finally, the CUP was to be converted from a society to a political party (not for the first time!) and its internal structure was to be completely re-organized.

Ali Fethi's proposals were discussed during the Congress and found expression in the political programme and party regulations of the CUP.[2] The political programme approved at the Congress

[1] *Stamboul*, 22 Sept. 1913.
[2] Ibid, 15, 16, 17, and 24 Oct. 1913; Tunaya, *Partiler*, 214–25.

was divided into four sections: political (Articles 1–17), economic (Articles 18–33), administrative (Articles 34–41), and educational (Articles 42–8). Essentially the programme was a reiteration of the policy of modernizing and rationalizing the entire political socio-economic and administrative structure of the Empire. The difference was that the Committee had decided to do this in a quasi-federalist, multi-national framework, not unlike that put forward by Sabaheddin and the Liberals. . . .[1] The party regulations defined the powers and functions of the Committee's hierarchical organization, beginning with the General Assembly at the very top and coming down to the local club.[2] Prior to this reform, the Central Committee (*merkez-i umumî*), a small secret body, had guided the destinies of the CUP and the Empire from its headquarters in Salonika. This had led the opposition to accuse the Committee of being an irresponsible secret body interfering in politics. In the Unionist organization itself, it had led to an anomaly: while there was a Unionist Parliamentary Party, its powers and functions were never clear because of the undefined powers of the Central Committee. The new regulations attempted to resolve this situation once and for all.

The regulations declared that henceforth the Committee of Union and Progress would constitute a political party with its headquarters in Istanbul. (The Committee was forced to move to Istanbul at the outbreak of the Balkan wars.) The party was organized as a General Assembly (*meclis-i umumî*) consisting of twenty members and chaired by the President (*reis-i umumî*), a Central Committee (*merkez-i umumî*) of ten members under the General Secretary (*kâtib-i umumî*), and a General Secretariat (*kalem-i umumî*) of about half a dozen members headed by the Vice-President (*vekil-i umumî*). The function of the General Assembly was to co-ordinate the work of the Central Committee, which dealt with all the Unionist organizations outside Parliament, and the General Secretariat, which handled the Unionists in Parliament. In this way the power to make decisions was no longer restricted to one body which could be monopolized by a clique. Power now resided in the General Assembly, where all shades of opinion could be represented. Furthermore there would be greater cohesion and unity of action between all elements in the

---

[1] *Stamboul*, 15, 16, and 17 Oct. 1913; Tunaya, *Partiler*, 214–18.
[2] *Stamboul*, 24 Oct. 1913; Tunaya, *Partiler*, 218–25.

CUP. The Central Committee still remained the most powerful single body, but this more flexible system introduced by the 1913 regulations linked it to the other two bodies and restricted its freedom. But the success of this new system depended on favourable political circumstances. The outbreak of war in 1914 and the events leading up to it made the operation of competitve politics difficult. Under these circumstances the CUP Congress, which was scheduled to meet annually, did not assemble again until 1916 and the Central Committee regained its old power.

The end of war in the Balkans and the return to everyday life called for the return to normal politics. For the Unionists, this meant the restoration of Parliament and a parliamentary regime. In the autumn of 1913 the Porte announced that a general election for Parliament would be held in the Empire. This election was held during the winter of 1913/14 and the third Ottoman Parliament met in Istanbul on 14 May 1914.

One is tempted to ask why, being as firmly established as the Unionists seemed to be, they thought it necessary to have a Parliament at all. They could conceivably have ruled without one. It is easy to be cynical and to answer as the British Ambassador did:

... that having the ability to make it [Parliament] an entirely obedient machine they [Unionists] have nothing to lose and something to gain by an outward respect for constitutional principles, the assertion of which, as against Abdul Hamid's tyranny, was their own original *raison d'être*. Rather than stultify the revolution they have chosen to reconcile constitutional form with the only kind of Government suited to an Oriental country, and especially composed of mixed elements, i.e., a more or less intelligent despotism.[1]

If one discounts Mallet's rather over-confident liberalism, his penetrating analysis contains more than a grain of truth. But his basic assumption that the new Parliament would necessarily be an 'entirely obedient machine' is false, or at best unproven. If earlier Turkish parliaments—from the first one in 1877–8 to those following 1908—are any criteria to go by, they all proved to be less obedient than expected, especially the Parliaments dominated by the CUP. The 1914 Parliament functioned under

---

[1] Mallet to Grey, no. 363 con., Constantinople, 21 May 1914, F.O. 371/2134/23213.

rather extraordinary circumstances and therefore never proved its mettle. But a review of the way in which the Unionists arrived at a consensus in the election suggests that the new Parliament would not have been entirely malleable.

It is true that the only organized political party to contest the 1913–14 elections was the Committee of Union and Progress. The other political party, the Party of Freedom and Accord, had ceased to exist though it had neither been officially dissolved nor outlawed. However, the all-embracing ideological character of the CUP continued to be decisive and the non-Turkish groups— Armenians, Greeks, and Arabs—were still vocal and demanded representation in Parliament in proportion to their numbers in the constituencies.

On 30 October the Armenian community of Istanbul held a meeting and decided to fight the coming elections as a united group.[1] Soon after, the Armenian Patriarch presented to the Ministry of Justice a *takrir* proposing that his community be given proportional representation in Parliament, assessed at about twenty deputies for a population of two million.[2] The Porte dismissed this proposal by claiming that it was not competent to deal with an issue which required revising the constitution. But it pointed out that a matter relating to the right of all Ottomans was not in the competence of the Armenian Patriarchate either.[2] The *Tanin* of 24 November warned that the Armenians were making a serious mistake in wanting to give the deputies who represent the nation the quality of ethnic representatives. In this way the Armenians would always remain a minority without the strength to achieve their aims.

The Greek community also pressed similar demands for proportional representation only to have them rejected.[3] The *Tanin* (11 December) lamented that if each community in the Empire chose its own representatives for Parliament, the constitution would lose its point. The country would become a confederation and it would be necessary to set up different chambers for the Armenians, Greeks, Turks, and Arabs, with each community having its own programme.

The Armenians and Greeks continued to press for their demand, and though the Unionists could not capitulate, they did

[1] *Stamboul*, 31 Oct. 1913.   [2] *Tanin*, 19 Nov. 1913.
[3] *Stamboul*, 10 Dec. 1913.

open negotiations in order to try to reach a compromise. After long and protracted discussions the compromise reached was that the CUP would concede to the quantitative demands of both communities. But the Committee insisted that Greek and Armenian representatives should not be ardent communalists, and that they should be screened by the Committee before they stood for elections. The matter did not end here and bickering continued, but finally the Armenians agreed to being represented by sixteen deputies, and the Greeks who wanted three deputies from Istanbul also had their demands met.[1] Though the matter was resolved behind the scene, not all the deputies elected were Unionist nominees. Besides there was no indication of how even the nominees would behave in Parliament if certain issues were raised.

Early in 1914 the CUP turned its attention to the problem of administrative reform. The first institution on the list was the old Ottoman army whose reputation and pride lay supine on the battlefields of Rumelia. To carry out the organizational side of the reform the Porte had called in a high-powered military mission from Germany, and this arrived in December under the command of General O. V. K. Liman von Sanders.[2] More important than the reorganization of the army was the need to purge many of its old officers. Their defeatist attitude during the wars has already been mentioned, and this could not have failed to arouse a feeling of revulsion among the more patriotic junior officers. Furthermore, it was they who, ignoring the advice of the timid and cautious generals, recaptured Edirne. Thereafter it was only a question of time before the military institution was purged.

The need to rejuvenate the army had been discussed even while İzzet Paşa was Minister of War. İzzet had agreed that a purge of the old officer corps was essential but had refused to carry it out, claiming that 'all those to be purged are my friends . . .'. Talât tried to persuade him to undertake the task but to no avail. In the end they decided that İzzet would resign temporarily, Enver would replace him, carry out the process of rejuvenation and then

[1] *The Times*, 26 Feb. 1914, and *Stamboul*, 10 Dec. 1913 and 2 Mar. 1914. For the Greek and Armenian point of view in this election, see *Stamboul*, 9, 12, 13, 14, and 15 Dec. 1913 and other contemporary papers. On the Armenian question see folio 2116 in F.O. 371 (1914).

[2] On the work and problems of this mission, see Liman von Sanders's own account, *Five Years in Turkey* (Annapolis, 1927).

resign and make way for İzzet Paşa once more.[1] Enver, who had
been made a brigadier-general and a Paşa, was appointed War
Minister on 4 January 1914. Three days later an Imperial *İrade*
promulgated changes in military appointments and 'the comman-
ders responsible for the dreary series of defeats in Macedonia,
along with most generals over fifty-five, were placed on the retired
list . . .'.[2]

The effects of the purge were felt in all branches of the administration, but its greatest impact was probably on the process of
modernization. The old officers—if one accepts Şevket Paşa as
typical—were patriotic but conservative. Their understanding of
the process of modernization was limited to the modernization of
the army and therefore they tended to slow down the pace of the
process as a whole. To them the army was the most important
institution in their society and therefore one whose needs must be
satisfied no matter the cost. They abhorred the idea of the politicization of the army under civilian control and did their best to keep
it isolated. The politicization of the army was perhaps the major
charge effected by the reform, making for greater co-operation
between the military and the civilians.

The financial problem continued to trouble the Porte. But
this problem was virtually impossible to solve while the foreign-
controlled *dette publique* consumed a large proportion of Turkish
taxation and while the military refused to curb its expenditure.
The Committee could do very little about the *dette publique* and
the capitulary rights enjoyed by foreigners in Turkey, but it was
determined to limit military spending. It was not surprising, therefore, that in his first statement to the press Enver declared his
intention to cut down the military budget.

I always thought [he said] that it would be possible to reduce the
budget of the Ministry of War. I am of the opinion that to ask the
country to make sacrifices above its capacity and to resort to onerous

[1] Menteşe, *Cumhuriyet*, 3 Nov. 1946, Y. H. Bayur, *Tarih*, ii/IV. 316. Bayur,
(317) dismisses the Unionist claim that İzzet would be brought back after
the purge. But it seems that this was the intention of the Unionists and Said
Halim Paşa informed the Russian Ambassador that Enver's appointment was
temporary. See Mallet to Grey, no. 17, tel. con., Constantinople, 8 Jan. 1914,
F.O. 371/2111/1068.

[2] This quotation is taken from a draft on the Young Turks which Professor
Dankwart A. Rustow was kind enough to let me read. The *irade* is in *Stamboul*
and the press of 8 Jan. 1914 and for Enver's appointment, see Menteşe, *Cumhuriyet*, 3 Nov. 1946, and *Stamboul* and *Tanin*, 3, 4, and 5 Jan. 1914.

loans in order to carry out reform only ruins the country. We will begin modestly, attaching more importance to quality than to quantity and I strongly believe that God will help us in our task.[1]

Commenting on the military purge Enver said that in the past the Ottoman army had consisted of officers suitable for peacetime activity and officers suitable for war; he was going to retain only the latter. He had no use for officers who had spent years in the war college and were well versed in the theory of war. In future only officers with ability would be given the opportunity to advance. 'The function of an officer is not merely to wear a colourful uniform. Being a soldier means exercise and education, science and art, and above all bravery and hard-work. It is only the young who possess these virtues and are capable of learning and hard-work.'[1]

The authority of the Ministry of Finance increased during this period. In March the powers of the Commission of Financial Reform, which had been formed in July 1911, were augmented. This body consisted of five members—the majority being foreign financial specialists—and was chaired by the Minister of Finance. In future all financial measures were to be controlled by the Ministry of Finance, and the budgets of the various ministries could not be submitted without a prior examination by the Commission. It would also draw up a scheme for reforming the financial administration and to examine claims and disputes as well as the financial clauses in government contracts and concessions.[2] The War Ministry agreed to subordinate its finances to this scheme, whose over-all aim was to rationalize the financial administration and provide an agency through which an effective control could be secured over expenditure.

If the size of the military budget is an index of the power and prestige of the military institution, then in 1914 the army no longer dominated politics as it had done during the past few years. Mehmed Cavid presented the 1914/15 budget on 30 May— the first budget to be voted for over two years—and it showed a decrease of approximately 30 per cent in military expenditure. It went before the Chamber on 4 July and was passed without much

[1] *Tanin*, 10 Jan. 1914.
[2] Mallet to Grey, no. 153 con., Constantinople, 9 Mar. 1914, F.O. 371/2132/11482. Mallet's informant was Sir Richard Crawford, who was financial adviser to the Porte and the architect of this whole scheme.

debate.[1] Parenthetically it may be noted that during this period when there was friction with Greece, the Porte was building up its navy with voluntary subscriptions and not with budgetary grants.

Ever since the Sublime Porte Incident of 23 Jan. 1913 the Unionists had been consolidating their position in the Cabinet. This was undertaken with caution and in Şevket Paşa's Cabinet they remained in the background, content with having Said Halim as President of the Council of State, Hacı Âdil as Minister of the Interior, and Hayri Bey as Minister of *Evkâf*. After the assassination the new Cabinet was positively Unionist. Nevertheless important posts such as the Ministries of War, Finance, Public Works, and the *Şeyhülislâmate* remained in non-Unionist hands. In time this too was rectified and Cemal became Minister of Public Works, Enver took over the War Ministry, Cavid returned to Finance, and Hayri, was made *Şeyhülislâm*.

The first three changes were straightforward and logical; the fourth was not and it requires comment. The appointment of Ürgüplü Mustafa Hayri Bey was a radical departure from Islamic tradition, and seems all the more strange as it was made at a time when the Unionists had adopted an Islamist policy, and when they were appeasing the Arabs, who it seems, cherished this very office.[2]

Traditionally, the *Şeyhülislâmate* was reserved for someone from among the *ûlema* who was well versed in Islamic theology and law. The *Şeyhülislâm* was, after all, the chief religious dignitary in the land. Hayri Bey had once belonged to this religious élite but he had long ceased to identify himself with it, having given up wearing the turban, the symbol of this élite. Furthermore he had been taking part in politics and serving on secular tribunals. After the revolution he was elected deputy for Niğde, his home district, and served on various cabinets as Minister of Justice and Minister of *Evkâf*.

In a developing society, the *Şeyhülislâm* was far too important

---

[1] *Stamboul*, 1 June and 6 July 1914; Mallet to Grey, nos. 417 and 496 con., Pera and Therapia, 3 June and 11 July 1914, F.O. 371/2114 and 2135/25475 and 32683 respectively.

[2] Djemal Pasha, op. cit. 59; Turkish edition, 71, In Jan. 1913, Şevket Paşa had asked the Sultan to appoint Ali Şerif Haydar *Şeyhülislâm* but the Sultan had rejected him on the grounds that he was not sufficiently well versed in Islamic law and jurisprudence. See İnal, op. cit. 1877.

a figure to be appointed from among the traditional-conservative element. Apart from his religious importance, he enjoyed a privileged position in the Cabinet as he was appointed directly by the Sultan. Consequently he almost stood outside the authority of Parliament, and on occasions the *Şeyhülislâm*, and even the Minister of *Evkâf* had questioned the competence of the Chamber to interpellate them. A conservative and unco-operative *Şeyhülislâm* could always obstruct reform. In 1914 the Unionists were in a position to remove this obstacle from the path of reform by having one of their nominees appointed. Hayri's appointment aroused no conservative reaction and in the press it was favourably received.[1] The Unionists, determined to modernize, were exploiting a traditional institution and symbol to further the process of social and political modernization.

Another institution which had posed a problem for the political modernization of the Empire was the Palace. After the revolution the Committee thought that *Yıldız* had been tamed, only to find that the Palace had played a role of great importance in the insurrection of April 1909. Immediately after the insurrection, the CUP placed Halid Ziya [Uşaklıgil] in *Yıldız* to keep a watchful eye on affairs within. But the Palace always remained outside the Committee's reach and it was here that anti-Unionist elements could find a symbol around which to rally. Significantly *damads* and royal princes played a role completely out of proportion to their numbers in the politics of the day, especially in the politics of the opposition. It was only natural, therefore, that the Committee should want to bring the Palace and all those connected with the Imperial Family under their control.

In January 1914 Mallet learned from a 'confidential source' that a secret commission had been formed at the Palace for regulating and defining the conduct of the Imperial family. It was said to consist of the *Şeyhülislâm*, Enver Paşa, who was soon to become a *damad*, and Said Halim Paşa, 'with the heir-apparent as nominal, but not effective, president'.[2]

The commission drew up a set of regulations which received the Sultan's sanction. Members of the Imperial family were no longer

---

[1] *Stamboul*, 17 Mar. 1914, quotes the reactions of other papers.
[2] Mallet to Grey, no. 47, secret, Constantinople, 25 Jan. 1914, F.O. 371/2128/4586. Unfortunately I have come across no Turkish source for these events.

permitted to take part in politics or to identify themselves with any political party. Furthermore, they could not travel without the authorization of the commission and the sanction of the Sultan. The regulations also laid down that Princesses of the Blood who were married to persons outside the Imperial family could be separated or divorced from their husbands, should the latter be considered *personae non gratae* by the commission or the Government. At the same time as these regulations were being framed, many members from the entourage of the Sultan, the heir-apparent, and other princes were changed. They were replaced by adherents of the Committee of Union and Progress, which now had the Imperial family under its complete control.[1]

When Parliament reconvened on 14 May all the strings of political power were in the hands of the CUP. The opposition parties were no more, the Committee had a majority in Parliament, the military was under control, and all sources of internal conflict and friction seem to have been removed. Ever since the conclusion of the Balkan wars the country had made considerable progress. Revenue figures for 1913/14 showed that the loss of territory had affected finances less than had been expected. In comparison with the figures for 1912/13 there was an increase of £T945,000, and this had been brought about by efficient collection, increased taxation, and a greater yield of old taxes in Anatolia and Istanbul.[2] More significant than all this for the future of the Empire was the atmosphere of hope and the feeling of optimism which prevailed in the country and found expression in the various speeches delivered at the opening of Parliament.[3] Reformism had taken a hold in the country and the Unionists after six years of mixed experiences were more realistic about their problems. Mallet predicted that 'unless some such convulsion as the Albanian movement which drove them from power in July 1912 should again occur, the present Committee Government may hope for a long lease of life'.[4]

[1] Mallet to Grey, no. 47 (loc. cit., p. 149 n. 2). See also a fuller report on this subject, with an enclosure of the regulations drawn up by the commission in ibid., no. 124 con., Constantinople, 24 Feb. 1914, F.O. 371/2128/9040.

[2] Ibid., no. 322 con., Pera, 12 May 1914, F.O. 371/2114/22029.

[3] The Speech from the Throne in *Stamboul*, 15 May 1914, the President's speech, ibid. 20 May; the Chamber's speech, ibid. 24 May; and the Senate's speech, ibid. 26 May.

[4] Mallet to Grey, no. 363 con., Constantinople, 21 May 1914, F.O. 371/2134/23213.

Valid as this prediction was on the basis of an analysis of the internal situation, Mallet had overlooked the factors of European diplomacy in which Turkey was inextricably involved. For Turkey one problem remained: the problem of her isolation. Neutrality seemed the most obvious and logical solution; though it is doubtful if she would have been permitted to remain neutral after the outbreak of war. Besides, in the climate prevailing in Istanbul after the Balkan wars, the policy of neutrality was psychologically impossible to follow.[1] The Unionists were convinced that if Turkey remained neutral and isolated it would be partitioned between the Great Powers. There were ample historical precedents for holding this belief. Therefore an alliance with the *Entente* Powers was sought but with no success. Finally, and almost in panic, the Unionists turned to Germany and gladly accepted her offer of an alliance. It was a desperate gamble, one which events did not justify.

[1] Djemal Pasha, op. cit. 108, Turkish edition, 121; Türkgeldi, op. cit. 114.

THE POLITICS OF UNION
AND PROGRESS

IF the story appears to come to an abrupt end in 1914, it is
because this study is intended as the first part of a larger work
dealing with the Young Turks at war. However, even in the
six years (1908–14) under review, the Ottoman Empire underwent
a radical transformation in almost every sphere of life. In this
brief period of time, much occurred to make the Empire of 1908
hardly recognizable in 1914. The process of change continued even
more rapidly after 1914, so that in the wake of defeat in World
War I the Empire had passed into history. The year 1914, therefore,
seems a fitting date to stop at and take stock of the situation.

The most striking change of these years was the loss of territory
the Porte suffered at the hands of a number of powers. This
factor influenced all other developments, as was only natural. The
process commenced with Bulgaria's declaration of independence
and Austria-Hungary's annexation of Bosnia and Herzegovina.
The cause of both events was the fear that the new regime in
Turkey would try to reassert its authority in these territories, over
which the Porte still had nominal sovereignty. Far more damaging
to the Porte's prestige and the fortune of the Young Turks was
the war with Italy in 1911 and with the Balkan powers the following year. The Italians captured Libya and the Balkan states
conquered virtually the whole of Turkey in Europe, leaving the
Turks only the hinterland extending from Istanbul to Edirne.

The significance of these losses is difficult to exaggerate. In
terms of territory and population alone, the Turks lost about
424,000 square miles out of a total area of about 1,153,000 square
miles, and approximately 5,000,000 souls from a population of
about 24 million.[1] These losses, substantial by themselves, were

[1] The figures have been taken from the *New International Yearbook 1908*
(New York, 1909), 703. The area of Libya was about 405,800 square miles with
a population of approximately 1 million. European Turkey consisted of about
65,000 square miles with 6,130,000. Out of all this the Porte retained the
vilâyet of Istanbul, the *mutasarrifate* of Çatalca, and the *vilâyet* of Edirne in a
truncated form. The area of these three together was about 4,750 square miles
with a population of around 2,300,000. (These figures have all been rounded.)

all the more important because Rumelia was involved. For centuries Rumelia had been the heart of the Empire, its provinces being by far the most advanced and the most productive. They had always provided much of the Empire's wealth and had long been the recruiting ground for the army and the bureaucracy. Rumelia had given the Empire its multi-national character and its loss had an immediate effect on the ideology of the Young Turks: the centre of gravity began to shift to Anatolia. In view of the over-all importance of Macedonia it is surprising that irredentism was not stronger among the Unionists, many of whom were from Macedonia and whose movement had flourished in these regions.

The loss of Libya could be dismissed as a blessing in disguise since Libya was a material liability to the Turks. But, for ideological reasons, the Porte regarded the retention of its African provinces as being essential for maintaining the integrity of the rest of the Empire, especially the Arab lands. Soon after the outbreak of war with Italy, Hilmi Paşa warned Lowther that the surrender of Libya to a Christian power would mean a mass rising of the Arabs against the Turks.[1] The Porte's failure to defend Libya weakened its position in Arab eyes and destroyed much of the faith the Arabs had in a revived Empire. One of the aims of the newly formed Arab Decentralization Party was 'to create concord among the potentates of the Arabian Peninsula, in order to bring strong pressure on the Turks on behalf of the Arabs and to provide for the defense of the Arabs against foreign ambitions, should the Ottoman Empire fall to pieces. The latter seemed likely, after Ottoman defeats in Tripoli and during the Balkan Wars.'[2]

The Unionists entertained the fear—and with good reason— that France had designs on Syria. This fear seemed to be substantiated when the Arab nationalists convened in Paris in the summer of 1913 to hold their congress. The Young Turks in exile had sometimes considered inviting foreign intervention against Abdülhamid; the Arabs now seemed to be turning to the same source against the Committee. So in order to retain Arab loyalty the Unionists made some concessions to the nationalists, and supported the local resistance movement in Libya, even after the provinces had been ceded to Italy. The organization of a local

[1] See above, p. 93.
[2] Sylvia G. Haim (ed.), *Arab Nationalism* (California, 1964), 25.

guerilla movement in Libya became one of the functions of the *Teşkilât-ı Mahsusa*, a para-military organization set up by the CUP in 1914.

It is generally agreed that the policy of Ottomanism was scuttled after the Balkan wars and replaced by Pan-Islam and nationalism, nationalism of the Turanist and not the Turkish kind though the distinction is not clear-cut. But the change was one of emphasis and not the introduction of a new ideological formulation. The Albanians, Greeks, and Slavs had no longer to be appeased; only the Armenians and Arabs remained. The three ingredients—Ottomanism, Islam, and nationalism, all undefined —continued to constitute the recipe for the ideological cake; only the proportions had changed. Since the Turks had now become the numerically most important element in the Empire more emphasis had to be given to nationalism. At the same time, there were also the Arabs to be reconciled and this was to be achieved by Islam. The Sultan and the dynasty would still provide the focus of loyalty for Muslims and non-Muslims, Turks and non-Turks alike. Ottomanism would continue to resolve the contradiction between the three elements.

Islam had always been one of the principal strands in the ideology of the Empire and the Turks were deeply attached to their religion. The prevalence of national feeling among Albanian Muslims (as well as the Arabs) and their secession from the Empire in 1912 struck a fatal blow at Islamic unity and Ottomanism. The Albanians had long been one of the pillars of the state and had usually received preferential treatment in the Empire. After the role they had played in the Empire their rebellion and secession came as a great shock to the Turks.

The Turks reacted to these changes by becoming more ethnocentric, and they began to give a more definite form to their own nationalism. At first this was of the Pan-Turanian variety, partly because Pan-Turanism was sufficiently vague to be easily reconciled with Pan-Islam and partly because of the fact that Turks from Russia were influential in the Committee. Furthermore, Pan-Turanism, like Pan-Islam, was an expansionist ideology which suited the mood of the Young Turks, then in full retreat at the opposite front. The outbreak of war with Russia on the one hand, and England and France on the other, gave a stimulus to both ideological strands. Both aimed at the liberation of their co-religionists from the yoke of Christian powers. The Unionists did not mind which particular element of the ideology was emphasized because leadership remained always in the hands of the Turks. Turkish nationalism, centred around the Turks in Anatolia, was in the process of development in 1914. It was to emerge out of the defeats in World War I, only after Pan-Turanism and Pan-Islam had proved to be mere dreams.[1]

The political significance of these ideological positions is clearly reflected in the representation of the various communities in the Parliaments of 1908, 1912, and 1914:[2]

Year	Total	Turks	Arabs	Albanians	Greeks	Armenians	Jews	Slavs
1908	288	147	60	27	26	14	4	10
1912	284	157	68	18	15	13	4	9
1914	259	144	84	—	13	14	4	—

The figures for 1908 may be taken as the index for 'normal politics' before the latent tensions came out into the open. The ethnic communities were represented in proportion to their numerical strength and everyone, except the Greeks, had expressed their satisfaction. The Committee had negotiated with each community and had tried to arrive at a consensus on the politics of each deputy. No one hostile to the general programme of the CUP was to be elected. In this way the Committee was expected to dominate Parliament. But things did not turn out according to plan and the Unionists decided to manipulate the 1912 elections more ruthlessly in order to guarantee a majority in the House.

The Albanians and Greeks had been the most vocal and obstreperous anti-Unionists both in Parliament and in Macedonia. Their representation, therefore, dropped very substantially. Comparing the Greek figures for 1912 and 1914 it seems as though their representation from Rumelia was almost totally excluded in 1912. There was not any marked difference in the number of Armenian and Slav deputies, though it is worth noting that some of the more vocal anti-Unionists amongst them were replaced. The Turks and Arabs increased their strength in Parliament; the

---

[1] Niyazi Berkes (trans., ed.), *Turkish Nationalism and Western Civilization: Selected Essays of Ziya Gökalp* (London, 1959). Professor Berkes's introductory essay is particularly useful for studying the ideological shifts.

[2] Unpublished study by Rustow and Ahmad, see above Chapter II.

Turks in order to make up the Albanian and Greek losses and the Arabs possibly because of the war in Libya.

In the 1914 elections the most notable change is in the representation of the Arabs. In 1912 there had been 59 deputies from the Arab provinces, 9 deputies were from Libya. In 1914 there was an increase of 25. The Arabs no longer had any cause to complain on this score because their 84 deputies represented a population of 5,338,000 while a Turkish population of about 12,500,000 was represented by 144 deputies. These concessions, it was hoped, would serve to placate Arab dissidents and to give substance to the Islamic policies of the CUP in Arab eyes. The first hope was dashed when Seyyid Talib, Arab notable and leader of a group of dissident deputies, resigned on 3 June 1914. The second hope proved as empty!

Almost all the problems which faced the Unionists during these years were the direct outcome of their modernizing policy, a policy they pursued with uncompromising determination. The complete modernization of the entire structure of the Empire was their answer to the problem of saving the state. They did not want only to save the state in its existing form; Abdülhamid had accomplished this in a masterly way. The Unionists wanted to revive it and make it a going concern in the modern world. In a sense they were gamblers: they wanted all or nothing. Their programme of reform was destined to alienate all those whose privileged positions were based on the traditional order. Muslim Turks, Arabs, and Albanians protested as vigorously as the Christian Greeks, Slavs, and Armenians against the rationalization of life. But the CUP found the idea of a Muslim and Christian, both citizens of the same state, being governed by different laws an anachronism opposed to the most fundamental principles of modernization. On such an issue they refused to compromise. This policy proved disastrous for the Empire though it laid the foundations for the future Turkish state.

The quest for modernity also clashed head-on with the interests of the foreign powers. A sovereign state was unlikely to tolerate the privileged position enjoyed by foreigners in Turkey. Not only did it violate the principle of the unity of law but it made the task of modernization impossible. Until 1914 the Unionists attempted to abrogate the capitulations through negotiations with the powers concerned and by reforming the administration and making their application unnecessary. Their methods were of little avail. Finally they abrogated the capitulations unilaterally on 9 September 1914 when the Great Powers were busy waging war. The Powers protested in the strongest terms but there was little they could do at the time.

The quest for equality was an important element in the signing of the Turco-German Alliance of 2 August 1914. Turkey had been accepted as an 'equal' partner by a European Power after having received innumerable snubs. The capitulations were not even mentioned in the alliance, but during the war Germany negotiated a treaty with the Porte, giving the latter the status of equality. The Unionist had learned that national sovereignty without economic sovereignty was meaningless. This depended not only on being free of foreign control but on the establishment and development of a national economy supported by the state. This emphasis on *étatisme* was merely a reflection of the traditional role of the state in the Ottoman Empire and in Islamic society generally. The political foundations for such economic activity had been laid by 1914 and the CUP set about the task of establishing a national economy during the war.

The character of post-revolution politics in Turkey was very largely determined by the diffuse nature of Unionist ideology and organization. In July 1908 the CUP emerged, not as a political party representing limited socio-economic interests, but as a society which conceived itself the agent of the general will. This was the legacy of the secret society struggling against absolutism and it remained a part of the Committee's psychological personality after the revolution. During the period of struggle all kinds of conflicting interests—Turkish and non-Turkish, Muslim and non-Muslim—had united against Abdülhamid and the notion of plurality of interests had been obscured. Everyone save Unionists saw consensus as a temporary phase which would end when the constitution was restored. The Committee looked upon it as something to be maintained until the Empire had been saved through modernization and reform. While the CUP would permit other interests to exist, the latter must recognize their obligations to this single purpose and to society at large.

The Unionists did not concern themselves very much with political ideas and their formulations were usually simplistic and naïve. They were tough-minded, stubborn men unimpressed with

precedents except those they themselves created. They had no
guiding principle for future action save an opaque notion of
constitutionalism. Their values were those of a small disparaged
group which placed collective discipline above individualism, and
favoured a centralized and oligarchical control over politics. They
were conscious of being innovators and they felt they owed no
debt to earlier movements; their one desire was to cleanse the
Young Turk movement of the contamination of liberalism, which
they regarded as both outmoded and corrupting. But continuity
being as much a part of the historical process as change, they took
much more from their past then they cared to acknowledge!

The CUP faced the problem all successful movements came up
against when they have accomplished their goal, namely, how to
adapt themselves to changed circumstances? Ideally such a movement ought to be dissolved. But this would lead to a political
vacuum in which the old régime could return to power, or there
could be chaos. The Committee resolved this dilemma by keeping
their organization secret and setting themselves up as watchdogs
over the constitutional regime. This 'exercise of power without
responsibility' became one of the causes of political strife. The
tactics of the CUP forced their opponents to take the initiative and
enabled the Committee to make the calculated moves. By 1914 the
political game had been played out in favour of the Committee.
Dissidents in the society had kept joining the opposition so that
in time the CUP became much more unified. Yet, even in 1914
the Unionist organization remained vague and undefined and
leadership had still not polarized. To be sure, the situation, both
internal and external, favoured the CUP, otherwise survival against
such overwhelming odds as the Committee faced would have
been well-nigh impossible. The army saved the Committee in
1909 and later the Balkan wars saved it from military domination. For their part the Unionists strengthened their position by
infiltrating the provincial administration and by consolidating
their organization.

It is indicative of the Committee's organization that in 1908 no
identifiable leaders emerged save for Adjutant-Major Niyazi and
Major Enver. The former played no further political role and the
latter, possessing a charismatic personality most suitable for
leadership, was prevented from doing so because of his youth and
because he chose to remain engaged in full-time military duties.

Enver emerged as a Unionist leader only after he had led the Sublime Porte *coup* in January 1913, and thereafter the changing situation and his own personality enhanced his position.

Leadership in the Committee was always a collectivized process and it is an over-simplification to talk of the rule of the triumvirs (Enver, Talât, and Cemal) after 1914. This is not to deny the importance of Talât as a political figure throughout the decade, of Cemal in the military and civil administration after 1909, and of Enver after mid 1913. Talât comes closest to the position of the leader, but even he did no more than head an important faction. His position became increasingly important as the Committee's hold on the provincial administration became stronger. As Minister of the Interior he was able to exploit this to increase his support in the Committee. Cemal, as the senior member of the trio, also had a following. But he was efficient and ruthless, and the Committee used him in situations requiring these qualities; in Adana after the 1909 reaction, in Baghdad where there was much opposition to the CUP, in Istanbul after the Sublime Porte *coup*, and finally in Syria after the outbreak of war. The inner workings of the Committee remain a mystery because the records were lost during that chaotic decade, having been distributed to a number of scholars who were entrusted with the writing of a history of the CUP.[1] But the organization of the Committee was infinitely more complex than it appears at first sight.

Immediately after the restoration of the constitution a number of Unionists came into prominence. They included Talât, Enver, Dr. Nâzım, Dr. Bahaeddin Şakir, Rahmi Bey, and Emanuel Karasu, better known in Europe as 'Carasso, the Jewish lawyer from Salonika'. This small group was soon joined by Ahmed Rıza who returned from Paris in late September. But this was an *ad hoc* group which had no official position and represented the CUP to foreign embassies unofficially. In October at the first Congress of the CUP a body of eight members (Talât, Hüseyin Kadri, Midhat Şükrü, Hayri, Ahmed Rıza, Enver, Habib, and *İpekli* Hafız İbrahim) known as the Central Committee *merkez-i umumî* was elected in a secret session.[2] For the moment power resided in this small group. The men who formed this clique were those who had organized and led the secret struggle within the Empire, and Ahmed Rıza was included because of his role in the

---

[1] Yalçîn, *Talât Paşa*, 8.   [2] Tunaya, *Partiler*, 199.

Unionist movement in exile. But their monopoly of power was only temporary for as soon as Parliament convened, the Unionist parliamentary group began to compete for power.

The competition for power was resolved by decentralizing the power structure of the CUP. The Unionists in Parliament were conceded the right to form an 'autonomous' parliamentary party. In practice the autonomy of this group was restricted because someone from the inner group, like Talât, became its president. Yet there were times when the deputies disregarded the Committee's wishes and followed their own independent line. The local party bosses like Kara Kemal were accommodated into the structure by enlarging the Central Committee from seven or eight to twelve. This was done in 1911.[1] The change of headquarters from Salonika to Istanbul in 1912 also facilitated decision-making among the various bodies of the CUP. At the 1913 Congress, the process of decentralization was carried a step further and it seemed as though the Unionists had resolved many of their inner tensions.

But the dissolution of organized opposition in 1913 also marked the end of the CUP as a unified group. The Committee, like most political organizations, had always been plagued by factionalism. The existence of an opposition had forced the Unionists to maintain some semblance of unity. Even in 1912, however, when the Committee was out of power and its position was precarious, factionalism was evident. At the Congress the factions were divided on the issue of participating in the coming elections. The extremists were against participation and succeeded in having the Congress vote this. Talât had this vote annulled, rallied the other factions to his opinion, and in the second vote the Congress voted for participation.[2]

It is characteristic of this organizational decentralization that a balance was maintained between the Central Committee and the Cabinet. Members of the Central Committee beyond a certain proportion were not permitted to hold public office. This explains why important figures like Mithat Şükrü and Dr. Bahaeddin Şakir never became ministers and Kara Kemal and Dr. Nâzım were only brought into the Cabinet at a critical moment. While these bodies were balanced, abuse of power by one could be checked by the other and neither could become dominant. In

---

[1] Tunaya, *Partiler*, 192.   [2] See above, p. 111.

1918 when Kara Kemal and Dr. Nâzım were called upon to take up the posts of Minister of Food and Minister of Public Instruction respectively, there was much debate before the CUP changed the regulation. Right up to the very end the Committee of Union and Progress had primacy over all else.

The most consequential changes the Unionists introduced in the six years before the war were in the political structure of the Ottoman Empire. The July *coup* put an end to court politics and the rule of a Palace cabal. Power passed into the hands of the administrative élite in the Sublime Porte. The liberals in the CUP hoped that the revolution would stop at this juncture and when it did not they broke away from the Committee and formed the *Ahrar Fırkası* or the Liberal Union. The Liberals believed in the élitist concept of change. They visualized reform as a process which should be carried out by a small group of educated and cultured individuals well versed in the ways of Europe. They naturally thought that they were the epitome of this type. They had opposed Abdülhamid only because he refused to share power with them and thereby made his sytem static and corrupt. They believed that once they were in power, the rule of law and rationality would be established, corruption and stagnation would cease to exist, and the state would be saved. The Liberals were Europeanizers rather than modernizers and some of them even believed that it was necessary to invite a European power, or a group of powers, to accomplish this task. They were cosmopolitans and not nationalists and it was on this point that they clashed with the Unionists most bitterly.

The Unionists were part of a purely indigenous movement which contained very few cosmopolitan elements. Ahmed Rıza shared the élitist concept with Sabaheddin and the Liberals but he was a fervent nationalist and this alienated him from the latter. It was this quality which reconciled him with the Unionists. Even so Ahmed Rıza was dropped from the Central Committee in 1910 and never obtained any other important post. After 1912 he was relegated to the Senate, where he became the chief critic of Unionist policies.

The Committee had too broad a social base and too heterogeneous a class structure to be élitist. Therefore it could not function in the old political framework and had to change the focus of political rivalry from the historical plane of socio-economic interests and parties to something less tangible. The first was replaced by a contrived identity of Ottomanism and later religious and national unity; the parties were replaced by the all-embracing CUP. The Unionists saw themselves as the representatives of the evolving Ottoman nation and the agents of change. Their movement was essentially urban though it had filtered into the countryside through the administrative machinery and by means of their alliance with the landowning 'aristocracy'. Parliament provided the meeting-place for all the diverse elements. Though the Unionists were committed to the principles of constitutionalism, they undermined its very basis by their emphasis on consensus and by not allowing independently established groups to support a constitutional balance. Yet the search for consensus forced them to dilute their own programme in order to satisfy the alliances they had made.

The Committee was the first political organization in the Empire to have a mass following and this gave the politics of the day a populist basis. The Unionists used the urban crowd with consumate skill in their political manœuvres. They held mass meetings and brought out the crowd on their behalf whenever necessary. When organized, as in the case of the boycott of Austrian goods, the people were very effective and they were used against both Greece and Italy in the same way. The very idea of mobilizing the masses was revolutionary for the politics of the Empire. Yet the Committee never had any intentions of broadening the power structure to include or even serve the urban workers or the peasants.

The Committee of National Defence—possibly the first explicit official use of the term national—was set up soon after the outbreak of war in the Balkans. It carried the populist trend a step further and sought to substitute the identity of the nation for the old Ottoman and Islamic identity, though the nation still was not labelled 'Turkish'. The CND was an unofficial organization founded by the Committee to encourage people to support the war effort. Later on money was collected by voluntary subscription to buy battleships for the fleet. This new sense of involvement of 'the man in the street' was sharply reflected in the popular demonstrations and indignations against Britain when the latter commandeered the two ships she had built for the Porte. The Committee had succeeded in making populism an essential element in Turkish political life.

Another facet of the political revolution was the brutalization of political life. Once politics ceased to be the sport of the ruling classes the rules were changed accordingly. Under Abdülhamid death sentences were the exception not the rule. Dissent was made impotent through isolation and dissenters in exile could always recant. The Liberals would have maintained these rules if they had come to power; in 1908 Kâmil sent *Mizancı* Murad into 'exile with pay'.[1]

The Unionists were men of a different stamp. To them politics was much more than a game and having seized power they meant to hold on to it. To do so they were willing to use all possible means, so that repression and violence became the order of the day. Nothing was sacred in the pursuit of power and those guilty of dissent must be prepared to pay with their lives. Yet the Unionist regime never became oppressive in the totalitarian sense. The Unionists were concerned only about their political position and so long as this was not directly threatened their attitude remained liberal.

The Committee [as one authority has put it] had no general objection to criticism; only to criticism of itself, and of its current actions. The discussion of the larger social, philosophic, and even—for the first time— religious issues was unimpeded, and the great debate about Turkey's future . . . was now engaged with renewed vigour and extended scope.[2]

The Young Turk Revolution is sometimes cited as the model for military intervention in politics, so common in our own day. Indeed, the term 'Young Turk' now forms a part of current journalese to describe a *coup d'état* of junior officers. Paradoxically the 1908 movement was primarily a political operation with only marginal military overtones. Military intervention—and then not by junior officers—took place in 1909 only after the civilians had proved their incapacity to maintain law and order. The senior officers, who set up a tutelary regime exercising control through martial law, were no more competent than the civilians to cope with the difficult situation. The catastrophic defeats in the Balkan wars prepared the ground for their own elimination and the rise of the junior officers.

Initially both the senior officers and the civilians were anxious to keep the junior officers out of politics. Bright young officers with

[1] See above, p. 26.   [2] B. Lewis, *Emergence*, 228.

charismatic appeal were posted away from Istanbul and isolated. Enver served as a military attaché in Berlin, Hafız Hakkı in Vienna, Ali Fethi in Paris, while Cemal was made *vali* of Adana and then moved to Baghdad. Only in late 1912 did the Committee call upon the junior officers to play an active role in politics. This was in preparation for the *coup* against Kâmil Paşa, and the initiative seems to have come from Talât. It is noteworthy that Enver, who became the protagonist of the *coup*, was in Libya and did not arrive in Istanbul until late in December.

After the destruction of Ottoman arms in the Balkans, the situation required a reorientation in the attitude of the military and the civilians towards each other. The result was the politicization of the army and the overt military involvement in politics. It was a partnership of equals and did not lead to the domination of the civilians by the soldier, not even in wartime. It was the establishment of an equilibrium which enabled the Committee to reorganize the army and prepare the country for World War I, in which Turkey performed surprisingly well.

Contemporary critics of the Committee who were sympathetic to the revolution, like Yusuf Akçura, pointed out that 'the real aim of the 1908 Revolution should be a social revolution rather than the mere restoration of the constitutional régime'. Ahmed Agayev (Ağaoğlu) charged that 'the Revolution has been . . . only military and political and confined to the educated classes. The people of different social classes are still living and thinking in their old ways.'[1] Both criticisms were valid in the years 1909 and 1910 when they were made. But they revealed the impatience of the critics and a lack of awareness of the fact that a social revolution could not precede the assumption of political power. Even after that it would not be automatic.

After their remarkably successful *coup d'état* in 1908, the Unionists had the alternative of either destroying the old institutions and sources of power and creating new ones; or maintaining the existing institutions and exploiting them on behalf of their movement. Lacking the will to follow the first course they naturally turned to the second. The Unionists were essentially pragmatic in outlook, little concerned with ideology. They attempted a revolution with—not against—the power of the state. Their

---

[1] Yusuf Akçura, *İçtihad* (Cairo, 1909), 9, and Ahmed Agayev, *Sırat-ı Müstakim*, no. 113 (Istanbul, 1910), quoted in Berkes, *Secularism*, 347–8.

political behaviour, seemingly inconsistent at times, was usually guided by prudent empiricism. Therefore, at first they supported the existing social order and zealously proclaimed their desire to save the state. This won for them the tacit support of the bureaucracy and the acquiescence of many, otherwise hostile, elements. By 1914 the Unionists had assumed complete political control and the stage was set for the social and economic revolution.

BIOGRAPHICAL APPENDIX

MOST of the personalities who figure in the text have not been sufficiently identified since they have been placed only in the context of the
six years under review. It is hoped that these brief sketches in the Appendix will diminish the confusion of names in the reader's mind and help
to place the personalities and the period in the broader perspective of
modern Turkish history. The names have been listed alphabetically.
The names in [ ] were adopted in 1934 according to pre-1934 usage
following the 'surname law'.

ABDÜLHAMID II (1842–1918). Ruled from September 1876 to April
1909. Succeeded his brother Murad V. Promulgated the Ottoman
Constitution on 23 December 1876, proroguing Parliament on 13 February 1878. Thereafter ruled autocratically for next thirty years. Forced
to restore constitution by Young Turks in July 1908, he tried to exploit
insurrection of April 1909 in order to regain his old power. As a result
deposed and removed to Salonika. Brought back to Istanbul in 1912,
there was a fear of demonstrations in his favour; fears proved unfounded.
Spent his last years in the Palace of Beylerbeyi, dying there on 10
February 1918.

HACI ÂDİL [ARDA] (1869–1935). Prominent Unionist, deputy, and
administrator. Trained as a lawyer he worked as a customs and excise
official in the Yemen (1889), Istanbul (1892–1904), and Salonika (1904)
where he joined the CUP. After the Revolution he was elected deputy for
Tekfurdaği (1908), Gümülcine (1912), and Bursa (1914). He was sent to
Edirne as *vali* in 1909 and 1915 and also served as minister in a number
of Cabinets. Member of the inner group in the Committee, he nevertheless followed an independent and moderate line, not joining any faction.

AHMED AGAYEV [AĞAOĞLU] (1869–1939), also known as Ağaoğlu
Ahmed. Journalist and Unionist politician. Turk from Azerbayjan,
educated in Tiflis, St. Petersburg, and Paris (1888) where he met Ahmed
Rıza and Dr. Nâzım and joined the CUP. Returned to Russia; taught law
and practised journalism. Came to Istanbul in 1908 after the Revolution
and joined Ministry of Education. Contributed articles to French,
Unionist daily, *Le Jeune Turc*. Founder-member with Yusuf Akçura of
Türk Yurdu (1911) and *Türk Ocağı* (1912). Taught history at *Darülfü-
nun* (1911–12). Member of General Assembly (*meclis-i umumî*) of CUP.
Deputy for Karahisarısahib (Afyon) in 1912 Parliament. Exponent of
Pan-Islamist, Pan-Turanist policies during war; went to Caucasus in
1917 to carry out propaganda. Arrested and exiled to Malta (1919).
Deputy in the Grand National Assembly under Mustafa Kemal [Atatürk].

YUSUF AKÇURA (1876–1935), also known as Akçuraoğlu Yusuf. Historian and Unionist politician, one of the nationalist idealogues and intellectuals of the CUP. Kazan Turk who came to Istanbul for his education and graduated from War College in 1896. Exiled to Libya for anti-Hamidian activities (1897), he escaped to Paris and completed studies in political science. Returned to Russia and became active in journalism. After the Revolution came to Istanbul and taught history at *Harb Akademisi* and *Darülfünun*. Edited nationalist journals like *Türk Yurdu* (1911) and *Türk Ocağı* (1912); founder-member of *Millî Meşrutiyet Fırkası* (National Constitutional Party) (1912)—deputy for Istanbul (1923) in Grand National Assembly; President of Turkish Historical Society (*Türk Tarih Kurumu*) (1931); and Professor of History at the newly established Ankara University (1933).

MEHMET CEMAL AZMİ (1866–1922). Unionist, deputy, and administrator. Graduated from *Mülkiye* in 1891. Before the Revolution director of the Salonika Law School and an important member of the local Unionist organization. Elected deputy for Preveze in 1908 he resigned in January 1909 and was appointed *vali* of Hudavendigâr (Bursa). Re-elected to Parliament as deputy for Çorum (1914) he resigned soon after, being appointed *vali* of Konya, one of the most important provinces, especially in wartime. Escaped to Europe (1918); assassinated by Armenians in Berlin (1922).

HÜSEYİN CAHİT [YALÇIN] (1875–1957). Man of letters and Unionist politician. Graduated from *Mülkiye* (1896) and became school-teacher, journalist, translator, and author. Joined the Committee after the Revolution, and was elected deputy for Istanbul in all three Parliaments. Founded and edited *Tanin*. Member of General Assembly, Vice-President of the Chamber of Deputies (1914–16) and President 1916–18. Very close to Talât in Unionist organization. Arrested by allies and deported to Malta (1919). Deputy in Grand National Assembly (V–IX Parliaments). Continued literary and journalistic activities until death.

MEHMED CAVİT (1875–1926). Academician, financier, and Unionist politician from Salonika. Son of a local merchant. Graduated from *Mülkiye* (1896); class-mate of Hüseyin Cahit, with whom he maintained a close relationship throughout life. Joined Agricultural Bank; Ministry of Education, and left government service (1902). Returned to Salonika, and joined CUP; taught political economy and wrote textbooks. After the Revolution, was elected deputy for Salonika (1908 and 1912) and Çanakkale (1914). Served as Minister of Finance and Public Works in a number of cabinets; also taught at *Mülkiye*. Member of General Assembly (1916–18). After dissolution of CUP (1918) kept out of politics. Hanged in 1926 for his role in a 'conspiracy' to assassinate Mustafa Kemal Paşa.

AHMED CEMAL (1872–1922). Soldier-statesman and notorious as the senior member of the so-called triumvirate of Enver, Talât, and Cemal. Sometimes known as *Büyük* Cemal. Graduated from War College (1895) and attached to III Army in Salonika. Joined CUP in 1906. After the

Revolution member of Central Committee (*merkez-i umumî*) (1908); military governor of Üsküdar (1909), promoted to rank of colonel. *Vali* of Adana (1909); Baghdad (1911); commander of Konya Reserves (1912); Balkan Wars (1912–13); Military Governor of Istanbul (1913). Served in cabinets as Minister of Public Works and later Marine. In 1914 sent to Syria to command IV Army. Resigned on 2 November 1918 and escaped abroad; assassinated in Tiflis by Armenians.

HALİD EFENDİZÂDE MEHMED CEMALEDDİN (1848–1917). *Şeyhülislâm*. Came from an old family of *ülema* going down to the sixteenth century; father was a *Kazasker*. Became *Şeyhülislâm* in 1891. After the Revolution hostile to the Unionists and allied to Kâmil Paşa and Liberals. *Şeyhülislâm* in Kâmil's cabinets (1908 and 1912), he fell from power in 1913 and left with Kâmil; for Cairo where he wrote his memoirs and died. Conservative and Pan-Islamist and therefore opposed to the nationalist policies of the CUP.

ALİ CENANİ BEY, Syrian notable and deputy. Came from an old and prominent landowning family and was one of the links between this class and the CUP. Represented Aleppo in the 1908 and 1912 Parliaments and Ayintab (Gaziantep) in 1912 Parliament. One of the Vice-Presidents of the Parliamentary Party of the CUP (1911). His son served as deputy for Gaziantep in IV Parliament of the Grand National Assembly.

HİRİSTO DALÇEF. One of the four or five Slav socialists in 1908 Parliament. Deputy for Serez in first Parliament. Not re-elected in 1912 because of his radicalism and independence of the CUP.

GAZİ İBRAHİM EDHEM PAŞA (1844–1909). Soldier and minister. Graduated from *Harbiye* (1864) and fought with distinction in Balkans (1876) and in Russo-Turkish War (1877–8). Received honorific of *Gazi* (conquerer in holy war) against Greeks (1896). One of the most respected generals in the Ottoman army. After the Revolution appointed to the Senate. Abdülhamid tried to use his high standing with the army by appointing him War Minister on 14 April 1909, thereby strengthening the regime set up by the rebels. Edhem Paşa resigned when *Hareket Ordusu* (Action Army) marched on Istanbul, and left for Egypt where he died.

EMRULLAH EFENDİ (1858–1914). Man of letters, deputy, and minister. Son of Ali Efendi, a merchant, he graduated from *Mülkiye* (1882) and joined bureaucracy. Forced to flee to Switzerland because of his anti-Hamidian activities; extradited by Swiss authorities. After the Revolution appointed director of *Galatasaray* and elected deputy for Kırkkilise in 1908 and 1912. He was Minister of Education in 1909 and 1911.

ENVER PAŞA (1881–1922). Soldier, statesman. Junior yet most famous member of the notorious Young Turk trio of Enver, Talât, and Cemal. Born in Istanbul, the son of a minor civil servant, he graduated in 1902 from *Harbiye* and posted to III Army. Joined CUP in Manastır (1906); rose to fame as one of the leaders of 1908 insurrection. After the Revolution member of Central Committee (1908); Military Attaché in Berlin (1909); Libya (1911); Balkans (1913). Promoted Brigadier-General and made Minister of War (1914). Unsuccessful commander in the field against Russians at Sarıkamış (1915). After the defeat in 1918 escaped abroad with Unionist leaders. Killed in Türkestan fighting the Bolsheviks. As a leader he commanded personal allegiance rather than the allegiance of an organized faction in CUP. Magnetic and charismatic personality combined with courage; but no organization.

ESAD PAŞA (b. 1862). Soldier. Originally from Epirus (Greece). Commander-in-Chief of III Army; replaced by Mahmud Şevket Paşa in 1908. Belonged to the old school of senior officers who believed that soldiers should stay out of politics. Anti-Unionist. Became famous for his role in the defence of Yanina during Balkan Wars, and later served with distinction at Gallipoli as commander of Arıburnu front. Minister of Marine for fifteen days in Salih Paşa's Cabinet of 1920.

HASAN FEHMİ (d. 1909). Anti-Unionist journalist and member of Liberal Union. Albanian by origin. Worked on the staff of Ahmed Rıza's *Meşveret* in Paris. After the Revolution edited the most outspoken anti-CUP paper, the *Serbestî*. Assassinated on Galata Bridge on 7 April 1909; this was the prelude to the insurrection of 13 April.

AVLONYALI MEHMED FERİD PAŞA (1851–1914). Grand Vezir. Born in Yanya, the son of Mustafa Nuri Paşa, a *mutasarrıf*. Joined bureaucracy (1867); *vali* of Konya (1898). Ardent conservative and loyal to Abdülhamid, he was Grand Vezir at the outbreak of the Revolution. His dismissal marked Sultan's first concession to the Young Turks. After the Revolution, *vali* of Aydın (1909). Unionists always viewed him with suspicion; his appointment to ministerial post regarded as a sign of anti-Committee activity (1912). Senator (1912). Left for Egypt after Unionist *coup* (1913) and died there.

DAMAD MEHMED FERİD PAŞA (1853–1923). Grand Vezir and Liberal politician. Joined Foreign Office and served in Paris, London, St. Petersburg, and Bombay. In 1886 married Abdülhamid's widowed sister Mediha, thereby becoming a *damad*. In 1888 appointed to Council of State and made minister. After the Revolution became one of the leaders of the Liberals and appointed to Senate. Chairman of Hürriyet ve İtilâf Fırkası ('Freedom and Accord' Party) (1911). After the war formed three cabinets in 1919 and took strong anti-nationalist line. Signed Treaty of Sèvres. Close to Sultan Mehmed VI. Left for Nice (1922) following the success of the Kemalists.

ALİ FETHİ [OKYAR] (1880–1943). Soldier, politician, and statesman. Joined CUP (1906); after the Revolution sent to Paris as Military Attaché; Member of General Assembly (1911); Libya (1911–12); signed agreement between Turkey and Bulgaria (1912). Minister to Sofia (1915). Deputy for Manastır (1912) and Istanbul (1914). After World War I active in Kemalist movement; close to Mustafa Kemal. Deputy in Grand National Assembly and Minister of Interior (1923); Prime Minister (1924–5); Ambassador to Paris (1925–30). Founded 'Free Party' (1930); Ambassador to London (1934). Deputy for Bolu and Minister of Justice (1939).

TEVFİK FİKRET (1867–1915). Poet and man of letters; prominent in *Servet-i Fünun* movement. Graduated from *Galatasaray* (1888) and joined secretariat of the Foreign Office. Taught at Robert College; active in movement against Abdülhamid. After the Revolution set up *Tanin* with Hüseyin Cahit and became director of *Galatasaray*. Disagreement with Unionists, probably on personal grounds. Joined Liberals, supporting them with his pen, though without much discernible effect.

HACI ALİ GÂLİB. Journalist and *âlim*. Unionist deputy for Karesi (Balıkesir) in all three Parliaments. Treasurer of Parliamentary Party of CUP (1911). Editor of a newspaper, *Ciddi*. Religious and chauvinistic deputy. Could not trace his later political career.

HABİB BEY (d. 1928). Soldier and deputy; known as *topçu* (gunner). One of the junior officers who joined Niyazi's insurrection. After the Revolution member of the Central Committee (1908); retired from army with rank of *Kolağası* (adjutant-major) and elected deputy for Bolu in 1908 and 1912. One of the nominal leaders of the Unionist dissidents in Parliament (1911). Arrested by allies and deported to Malta (1919).

BABANZÂDE İSMAİL HAKKI (1876–1913). Lecturer and journalist. Born in Baghdad; came from a family of Kurdish notables, the son of Zihni Paşa. Educated at *Galatasaray* and *Mülkiye*, where he later taught law. Wrote biography of Bismarck. After the Revolution elected deputy for Baghdad in 1908 and 1912. Minister of Education in Hakkı Paşa's Cabinet. Political editor of *Tanin*. Though prominent and influential in Unionist circles he was never part of the inner group.

HAFIZ HAKKI PAŞA (1879–1915). Soldier and important member of the CUP who came with Unionist delegation from Salonika in July 1908. Military Attaché to Vienna (1908) and active in the army. Rose to prominence in 1914 after military purge. Went to Berlin with Halil [MENTEŞE] in October 1914 to discuss Turkey's entry into war. Paşa with rank of general with command of III Army destroyed by Enver (1915). Died of typhus on 12 February 1915. Described by Liman von Sanders as 'beyond doubt one of the most prominent Turkish general staff officers who was considered an ambitious competitor of Enver'.

İBRAHİM HAKKI PAŞA (1863–1918). Grand Vezir, diplomat, and jurist. Began his career in bureaucracy and also as law lecturer. Capable and therefore rose very rapidly in both professions. After the Revolution, Minister of the Interior and Education for very brief terms (1908–9). Ambassador to Rome (1909–10). Grand Vezir (1910–11). Negotiated Anglo-Turkish Agreement concerning Persian Gulf (1913–14). Ambassador to Berlin (1915); negotiated Turco-German Treaty (1917). Senator (1917). Plenipotentiary at Brest-Litovsk (1918). Died in Berlin.

BEDROS HALAÇYAN (b. 1871). Armenian deputy and minister. Law graduate from Paris; began his career in the Ottoman Public Debt. After the Revolution he was elected deputy for Istanbul in all three elections; Minister of Public Works in Hakkı Paşa's Cabinet and in Said Paşa's 1912 ministry. Though influential in the CUP he was never part of the inner machinery. Followed an independent and moderate policy.

HALİL [MENTEŞE] (1874–1948). Unionist deputy and minister. Came from a landowing family of western Anatolia. Studied law in Istanbul and agriculture in Paris. Acquired a taste for political philosophy and studied Rousseau and Herbert Spencer; said to have been an admirer of French institutions and ideas. After the Revolution represented local constituency of Menteşe in all three Parliaments. Leader of the Parliamentary Party (1909 and 1912), member of the General Assembly and President of the Chamber of Deputies. Minister of Foreign Affairs (October 1915–February 1917). Throughout the decade he played an influential and moderating role in the Committee. Arrested and deported to Malta by allies (1919). Deputy for İzmir in Grand National Assembly (IV–VII Parliaments).

MEHMED SAİD HALİM PAŞA (1863–1921). Unionist Grand Vezir and diplomat, grandson of Mehmed Ali of Egypt, and member of the Egyptian ruling family. In 1888 appointed to Ottoman Council of State (*Şurayı Devlet*). Came back to Istanbul after Revolution; appointed to Senate. Sent to Europe by CUP during Libyan war to rally support for Turks. President of Council of State (1912). General Secretary of CUP (1913). Foreign Minister in Şevket Paşa's Cabinet, becoming Grand Vezir after latter's assassination. Resigned in February 1917 after the failure of Islamist policy of which he was one of the chief representatives. In 1919 arrested and exiled to Malta. Assassinated by Armenians in Rome (1921).

TAHİR HAYRETTİN. Leading anti-Unionist politician and Liberal deputy for Istanbul in the first Parliament. Son of the Ottoman and Tunisian Grand Vezir, Hayrettin Paşa. Came into prominence after defeating the Unionist candidate, Memduh Bey, in the Istanbul by-election of December 1911. Prior to this financed and edited anti-CUP papers like *Şehra*, *Tanzimat*, etc. Left Turkey following Şevket Paşa's assassination after which Unionists persecuted the opposition. Tahir Bey's brother *Damad* Salih Paşa was hanged for his role in assassination plot.

ÜRGÜPLÜ MUSTAFA HAYRİ (1867–1921). Unionist deputy and minister. Trained as an *âlim* but opted out and joined bureaucracy. After the Revolution served as member for Niğde, his home constituency, in all the Parliaments. Member of General Assembly (1908–17); Vice-President of Parliamentary Party (1910). Minister of Justice (1911), *Evkâf* (1911–12 and 1913–14). Appointed *Şeyhülislâm* in March 1914, resigning in May

1916. Appointed to Senate (1916). Arrested and deported to Malta (1919). Member of *ülema* by training, Hayri Bey was a liberal and modernist by inclination. Belonged to no Unionist faction; followed an independent and moderate line. With the growth of factionalism after 1914 he became isolated; repelled by the corruption and nepotism practised by certain members of the Committee.

HÜSEYİN HİLMİ PAŞA (1855–1923). Grand Vezir and diplomat. Joined Ottoman bureaucracy and saw service in all parts of the Empire. Acquired reputation of a liberal and efficient administrator, especially as Inspector-General of Rumelia (1903–8). Popular with Young Turks and after the Revolution became minister (Interior 1908–9; Justice 1912) and Grand Vezir (1909–10); not very successful. As ambassador to Vienna (1914–18) he was more successful. After armistice forbidden by Sultan's regime to return to Turkey because of past Unionist connections. Died in Vienna. Honest, hardworking, but colourless personality, better suited for peaceful times and not for chaotic period in which he had to work.

HÜSEYİN HÜSNÜ PAŞA (1852–1918). Divisional general of III Army in Salonika (1908). Commander of 'Action Army' which marched against rebels in April 1909 and camped at Çatalca. Strict disciplinarian and professional soldier who did not believe in mixing politics with military duty. Though he was not one of the senior officers removed in the 1914 purge, he was not given an active command during the war.

İPEKLİ HAFIZ İBRAHİM. One of the earliest members of CUP, joining in 1889, and prominent in local organization. After the Revolution member of Central Committee (1908) and deputy for İpek (Albania) in 1908 and 1912 Parliaments.

ÂRİF İSMET (d. 1911). Doctor and Unionist deputy for Biga in first Parliament. Vocal against Liberals in Parliament, İsmail Kemal in particular.

AHMED İZZET PAŞA (1864–1937). Soldier, War Minister, and Grand Vezir. Born in Manastır, graduated from *Harbiye* in 1884. Spent years 1891–4 in Germany, where he worked with Liman von Sanders. By 1908 he was Chief of Staff. Yemen (1910–11); Balkans (1912). Being a soldier of the old school he stayed out of politics. After Şevket Paşa's assassination Unionists needed respected and reputable general for War Ministry; post given to İzzet. Replaced in 1914 by Enver Paşa and appointed Senator. During armistice İzzet formed a ministry lasting twenty-five days (October–November 1918).

HÜSEYİN KADRİ (1870–1934). Member of the Central Committee of the CUP (1908). Deputy for Karesi (Balıkesir) in the 1912 and 1914 Parliaments.

MEHMED KÂMİL PAŞA (1832–1913). Grand Vezir and statesman. Born in Cyprus, educated locally and in Egypt at the military academy. Joined Ottoman civil service and worked in all parts of Empire: *vali* of Aleppo (1869); Kosova (1877); Minister of *Evkâf* (1880); Grand Vezir

(1885). Kâmil's Anglophilism led to this political eclipse after 1891; only British support saved him from exile and other punishments. This gave him reputation for independence and liberalism among Young Turks and made him popular with them. After the Revolution Kâmil's Anglophile policy and concession to European Powers as well as his alliance with Liberals brought him into conflict with CUP.

EMANUEL KARASU (d. 1934). Lawyer and Unionist deputy from Salonika. Sephardic Jew and Freemason, Grand Master of 'Macedonia Risorta' Lodge. Prominent in Salonika branch of CUP; provided movement with protection of Masonic lodges. After the Revolution, foreign observers, especially English, saw him as one of the leaders and 'evil' influences of CUP. Influential, but not as influential as people thought. Deputy for Salonika (1908 and 1912) and Istanbul (1914). During the war, one of the food controllers; amassed a huge fortune. Left for Italy (1919), took Italian citizenship, and settled in Trieste.

ALİ KEMAL (1867–1922). Lecturer, journalist, and Liberal politician. Exiled to Aleppo by Abdülhamid he fled to Europe in 1889. After the Revolution edited anti-CUP newspapers like İkdam and Peyam; taught at Mülkiye (1908–9). Stood for Parliament (1908 and 1909); defeated on both occasions. Exiled in 1913; returned after the war and was Minister of Education and Interior in Damad Ferid Paşa's Cabinets. Lynched by Kemalists for anti-nationalist activities.

İSMAİL KEMAL (1844–1920). Liberal deputy and Albanian nationalist. Came from a family of notables which had seen better days. Forced to flee to Europe because of liberal and nationalist tendencies (1900). In Brussels published journals called Albania and Le Salut de l'Albanie. After the Revolution deputy for Berat (1908) and leader if the Ahrar Fırkası (1909). Tried to assume control of April 1909 insurrection. Opted for independent Albania (1912) and led the liberal faction. Left behind memoirs which have made him famous in Europe.

MUSTAFA KEMAL [ATATÜRK] (1881–1938). Soldier, statesman, and first President of Turkish Republic. Graduated from General Staff Academy (1905). Sent to Syria; founded Vatan (Fatherland Society) (1906). Transferred to III Army (1907). Divisional staff officer in 'Action Army' (1909); Libya (1911–12); Balkans (1913); Military Attaché in Sofia (1913). Gallipoli (1915), Caucasus (1916), Syria (1917). Assumed command of national movement in Anatolia (1919).

ÖMER MANSUR PAŞA (1878–19). Unionist deputy and administrator. Son of Mansur Kâhya Paşa, a Turkish official in Bengazi (Libya). Mansur Paşa was deputy for Bengazi (1908 and 1912) and Vice-President of the Parliamentary Party (1911).

MEMDUH BEY. Unionist deputy and minister. Defeated in the famous Istanbul by-election of 1911 by Tahir Hayrettin, but elected deputy for Istanbul in 1912. Minister of Justice in Said Paşa's 1912 Cabinet.

ALİ HAYDAR MİDHAT (1872–c. 1946). Deputy; son of Midhat Paşa, whose biography he wrote. Spent much of his life abroad. Returned in 1908 and tried to enter Parliament as an independent. Defeated in 1908 and finally elected in 1914 as deputy for Divaniye (Iraq).

AZİZ ALİ MİSRİ (c. 1879–1959). Arab soldier and politician. Graduated from war college in 1904 and served in Macedonia where he joined CUP. After the Revolution remained in III Army and came with 'Action Army' in 1909. Joined Arab nationalist parties of Istanbul (1909). Fought in Yemen (1910); Libya (1911–12). Arrested in 1914 and expelled to Egypt. Joined Arab revolt (1916). In the 1940s and 1950s supported 'Free Officers' in Egypt and sent to Russia as Egyptian ambassador in 1954.

GAZİ AHMED MUHTAR PAŞA (1839–1918). Soldier, statesman, and Grand Vezir. Successful military and administrative career; given title of Gazi (1877) for role in Russo-Turkish war. High Commissioner in Egypt (1885–1906); said to have won confidence of Young Turks in exile and betrayed it to Abdülhamid. Deeply attached to Sultan; tutored Prince Yusuf İzzettin, heir-apparent after 1909. After the Revolution appointed Senator; became President of Senate in 1911. Made Grand Vezir (1912); again, as in April 1909 with Edhem Paşa, Liberals hoped to use an old and famous soldier to consolidate their power.

MAHMUD MUHTAR PAŞA (1867–1935). Soldier, minister, and diplomat, son of Gazi Ahmed Muhtar. After training in War Academy went to Germany. Appointed Commander of I Army (Istanbul) in 1908, he was a strict disciplinarian, dealing firmly with minor mutiny (October 1908). Forced to flee Istanbul (April 1909); appointed vali of Aydın (August 1909). Minister of Marine in father's 1912 Cabinet, and had command in Balkan War. Ambassador to Berlin (1913–15). Offered a command by Enver in 1914, refused and retired in 1915, moving to Switzerland. A man of progressive outlook, he tried to work with Unionists but unable to reconcile his social background with the changes.

ALİ MÜNİR [ÇAĞIL] (1874–196). Unionist deputy and administrator. Represented Çorum in three Parliaments; resigned on 25 May 1914 and took administrative post. Vice-President of Parliamentary Party (1911). Deputy for Çorum in Grand National Assembly (II–VIII Parliaments).

MEHMED MURAD (1853–1912). Journalist, historian, and Liberal politician, also known as Mizancı Murad and Dağıstanlı Murad. Born in Tiflis, educated in Russia. In Istanbul taught history at Mülkiye and worked for Dette publique. Fled to Cairo because of his revolutionary activities, and published anti-Hamidian paper, Mizan (Balance). Went to Paris (1896); became possibly principal leader of Young Turks in exile; president of Geneva branch. In 1897 'bought off' by Abdülhamid, returned to Istanbul and became a member of Şurayı Devlet. After 1908 supported Liberals and even allied with reactionary elements. Continued to publish Mizan which was suspended after 31 Mart Vak'ası.

ÖMER NACİ (1880–1916). Soldier, author, and Unionist deputy; active in *Servet-i Fünun* movement. Early member of CUP, forced to flee to Paris, the Caucasus, and Iran (1907), where he was arrested, imprisoned, and released after Revolution on Unionist representation. Very influential in Committee. Tripoli (1911), Balkans (1912). Deputy for Kırkkilise in second Parliament. Member of Central Committee (1910–12). Sent to negotiate with Armenian leaders (September 1914) concerning Turkey's entry in war. Died on Iran front.

YUNUS NADİ [ABALIOĞLU] (1880–1945). Journalist and deputy. Son of Abalızâde Hacı Halil Efendi of Muğla. Spent all his life in journalism. Joined CUP after Revolution and edited Unionist paper *Rumeli* (Salonika, 1910), *Tasvir-i Efkâr* (1914), *Yeni Gün* (1918), etc.; and most famous of all *Cumhuriyet* (1924). Elected deputy for Aydın in 1912 and 1914. Also served in first six Parliaments of the Turkish Republic.

MUSTAFA NÂİL BEY (1861–1926). Civil servant and lecturer. Born in Istanbul, graduated from *Mülkiye* (1884); entered government service working in secretariats of various ministries (External Affairs, Finance, and Education). Appointed president of Educational Council (1905). After the Revolution, Minister of Education in Hilmi Paşa's second Cabinet (May–December 1909); Finance Minister in Hakkı Paşa's Cabinet. Appointed to Senate (1911); hereafter appears to have opted out of public life! Hanged for complicity in anti-Kemal 'plot' (1926).

DR. NÂZIM (*c.* 1870–1926). Doctor, minister, and perhaps the most influential Unionist behind the scene. Also known as *Selânikli* Nâzım. One of the earliest members of Committee in Istanbul (1889). Joined *Tıbbiye* (medical school), completed studies in Paris, where he worked closely with Ahmed Rıza. In 1907 returned to Salonika on invitation of CUP: made fusion of Paris and Salonika branches of Committee. Carried out Unionist propaganda in Anatolia. After restoration of constitution, was content to continue working behind the scene; remained director of Salonika Municipal Hospital. Virtually a permanent member of Central Committee; Secretary-General until 1911. Only joined Cabinet as Minister of Education in 1918 (August–October). Hanged in 1926 for collusion in 'plot' to assassinate Mustafa Kemal Paşa.

HÜSEYİN NÂZIM PAŞA (1848–1913). After *Harbiye* completed military training at *St-Cyr* in France. Man of great personal courage and independence; virtually exiled to Baghdad by Abdülhamid. In 1908 given command of II Army at Edirne. Used by Liberals to weaken Committee's influence in army. Commander of Istanbul garrison (April 1909). Sent to Baghdad as *vali* after 1909 insurrection (April 1910–February 1911). Popular with Arabs; reformist. Minister of War (1912–13) after overthrow of CUP. Shot dead at *Babıâli* on 23 Jan. 1913.

AHMED NESİMİ [SAYMAN] (d. 1958). Deputy and minister. Also known as *Giritli* Ahmed Nesimi, being son of Saffetzâde and coming from a prominent Cretan family. Educated in Paris at École des Sciences

Politiques where he joined CUP. Became protégé of İbrahim Hakkı Paşa. Elected deputy in all three Parliaments, he was also a member of the General Assembly. Important in the inner councils of the CUP, he rose to prominence during war, first as Minister of Agriculture and then Foreign Affairs. Went to Brest-Litovsk (1918) as one of the plenipotentiasies. Arrested and deported to Malta (1919). Tried for collusion in İzmir 'plot' (1926); but released.

AHMED NİYAZİ (1873–1912). Soldier. Also known as *Kolağası* (adjutant-major) Niyazi. Rose to fame as the leader of insurrection culminating in the restoration of the constitution. Received publicity for a while; became known as *Kahraman-ı Hürriyet* and a battleship was to be named after him. Unionists had his memoirs 'ghosted' to give publicity to their own movement. Niyazi returned to military duties. Came with *Hareket Ordusu* (1909), fought in Libya and was assassinated in Albania.

DR. RIZA NUR (1879–1943). Liberal politician and minister. Graduate of *Tıbbiye*, trained as military surgeon. After the Revolution elected deputy for Sinop in the first Parliament. One of the leaders of *Ahrar*; escaped to Egypt after failure of April 1909 insurrection; arrested (1910) for planning *coup* against CUP. Exiled to Paris (1913) when Unionists came to power. Returned to Turkey during armistice and appointed Minister of Foreign Affairs (1922), Health (1923). Deputy for Sinop in Grand National Assembly (I–II). Banished from Turkey (1924) for anti-state activities; allowed to return in 1938, after Atatürk's death. Became a cultural Turkish nationalist; wrote a play *Ebulgazi Bahadur Han* (1925) in *Çağatay* Turkish; also edited *Revue de turcologie* and *Tanrı dağ*.

MUSTAFA RAHMİ [EVRANOS]. Unionist deputy and administrator. Came from a prominent landowning family of Rumelia; joined CUP in 1906 becoming an influential member in Talât's group. Elected deputy for Salonika in 1908 and 1912; *vali* of İzmir (1915). Became very powerful locally and virtually independent of Istanbul, disregarding Armenian policy and establishing good relations with nationals of enemy powers. Porte feared Rahmi might be in contact with western allies in Athens.

MARSHAL RECEP PAŞA (1842–1908). Soldier and War Minister. Man of great integrity and independent ideas; exiled to Libya by Abdülhamid. As commander of Ottoman forces in Libya (1903) agreed to carry out military operation against Istanbul along with Young Turks. Appointed War Minister in Kâmil's 1908 Cabinet, he died within a few days of coming to office.

MANYASİZÂDE REFİK (1853–1909). Lawyer, lecturer, deputy, and minister. One of Midhat Paşa's legal advisers; banished to Kavala after Midhat's exile. Taught law at Salonika Law School and joined CUP. In 1908 appointed Minister of Police without portfolio (August) and Minister of Justice (November). Elected deputy for Istanbul; died in March 1909.

MEHMED REŞAD EFENDİ (1844–1918). Sultan Mehmed V, son of

Abdülmecid. Succeeded Abdülhamid in April 1909. Having spent his life in seclusion and coming to the throne in old age, he was no match for the Young Turks. Fell under their control and was content to play role of figurehead.

MUSTAFA REŞİD PAŞA (1858 19). Diplomat and minister. Led mission to negotiate peace between Bulgaria and Serbia (1885). Minister at Bucharest (1893); Rome (1896); Hague (1897); Vienna (1908). Belonging to the old administrative élite he sided with Liberals and was scathing towards Unionists. Joined Cabinets of Ahmed Muhtar and Kâmil (1912) as Minister of Commerce and Agriculture. Leader of delegation to London Conference (1912–13). Foreign Minister in armistice cabinets (1918) and Ambassador to London (1920). Experienced diplomat and capable negotiator.

MEHMED RİFAT PAŞA (1860–1925). Son of Hasan Efendi, a merchant. Born in Istanbul; graduated from *Mülkiye* (1882) and entered Translation Bureau of Foreign Office. Consul-General Tiflis (1885) and thereafter, Athens, Berlin, and London. Ambassador to Athens (1897); London (1905–8). Returned to Istanbul after Revolution and elected deputy for Istanbul. Foreign Minister (1909–11). Ambassador to Paris (1911–14); succeeded Hakkı Paşa in Berlin (1918). Refused to enter cabinets of armistice period. Retired.

AHMED RIZA (1859–1950). Civil servant, 'professional revolutionary', deputy, and most famous of the Young Turks in exile. Director of Public Instruction in Bursa, he escaped to Paris in 1889. Published *Meşveret* (Consultation) and organized Young Turks abroad. Elected deputy for Istanbul (1908 and 1912) and President of the Chamber. Influential in early days of constitutional régime; but too sophisticated and cosmopolitan for his Unionist colleagues and the conservatism of the period. Relegated to Senate (1912) he became chief critic of Unionist policies. During armistice appealed to France for political and diplomatic support.

ALİ RIZA PAŞA (1859–1933). Soldier, minister, and Grand Vezir. Born in Istanbul, son of *Binbaşı* Tevfik. Graduated from *Harbiye* (1885); three years in Germany. Taught at *Harbiye* and worked as Staff Officer. *Vali* of Manastır (1897), Yemen. After the Revolution made Senator and Minister of War in Kâmil's 1908 Cabinet. Balkan Wars (1912). October 1919 replaced *Damad* Ferid Paşa as Grand Vezir, resigning in March 1920. Minister of Public Works and later Interior in Tevfik Paşa's Cabinet (1921). When Tevfik resigned (November 1922), Ali Rıza was pensioned off.

ÖMER RÜŞDÜ PAŞA (1843–1922). Soldier and War Minister. Born in Kütahya, graduated from *Harbiye* (1866); Russo-Turkish War (1877); Turco-Greek War (1896), given title of *Gazi*. Appointed War Minister in Said Paşa's 1908 Cabinet. Appointed to Senate.

PRINCE SABAHEDDİN. (1877–1948). Ideologue of the Liberals and leader of anti-Unionist groups. Son of *Damad* Mahmud Paşa (1855–1903), who escaped to Paris with sons Sabaheddin and Lütfullah (1899). On father's death Sabaheddin became leader of faction of Young Turks and formed *Teşebbüsü Şahsi ve Ademi Merkeziyet Cemiyeti* (the League for Private Initiative and Decentralization). Returned to Istanbul on 2 September 1908, bringing with him his father's bones. Never assumed overt leadership of Liberals but worked from behind the scene. Forced to leave Turkey (1913), he lived abroad for rest of his life.

EYÜB SABRİ [AKGÖL] (1876–1950). Soldier and Unionist politician. Junior officer (*kolağası*) in Ohri (1908), joined and became one of the leaders of the July insurrection. Elected member of Central Committee of CUP (1909), he held this position until dissolution of Committee (October 1918). In Republic, deputy in five Parliaments of Grand National Assembly.

MEHMED SADİK (1860–1940). Soldier and Liberal politician, also known as *Miralay* (Colonel) Sadık. Born in Istanbul, son of *Filibeli* Abdullah. Graduated from *Harbiye* (1882); stationed in Rumelia he became head of Manastır branch of CUP. At time of Revolution, an important military member of Committee. Became alienated probably because of conservatism; member of *Melâmî* order of dervishes. Formed *Hizb-i Cedid* (1910); united with 'Freedom and Accord' Party (1911). Left Turkey (1913); went to Egypt and Europe and intrigued with foreign powers (Britain, Greece, and France) against Porte (1914 ff.). Returned to Turkey after war but was not permitted to stay.

MEHMED SAID PAŞA (1838–1914). Grand Vezir. Born in Erzurum, joined local bureaucracy (1853). Came to Istanbul and rose to prominence under *Damad* Celâleddin Paşa in 1870s. Abdülhamid's First Secretary (1876). First Grand Vezirate (1879). Until Revolution career see-sawed in a manner customary in court politics. Became Grand Vezir on 22 July 1908 for seventh time. At first hostile to and out of favour with CUP, soon came to an understanding with them. Unionists were forced to rely upon such personalities to rule on their behalf.

AHMED SAMİM (1844–1910). Liberal journalist. Son of *Binbaşı* Tevfik; born in Perzerin (Albania). Editor of *İtilâf* and *Cidal* (1909), and *Sedayı Millet* (1909–10), a paper owned by Greek Yorgaki Molla Hrinos. Assassinated at *Bahçekapı* on 9 June 1910; probably part of Liberal campaign to arouse anti-Unionist reaction.

MEHMED SEYYİD (1866–1925). Law professor and Unionist deputy. Taught at *Darülfünun*. Deputy for İzmir in all three Parliaments. Vice-President of Parliamentary Party (1910); president (1911). Moderate Unionist, able to reconcile different factions in Committee. Resigned from Parliament (1916), appointed Senator. During armistice period founded *Teceddüd Fırkası* (New Party) with other moderate Unionists. Deputy in second Parliament of Grand National Assembly. Minister of Justice; advised Mustafa Kemal on legal aspects of secular Republic. On this subject he wrote *Hilâfet ve Hakimiyyet-i Millîye* (Istanbul, 1923) and *Hilâfetin Mahiyeti Şer'iyesi Hakkında Nutuk* (published speech from Grand National Assembly, 1924).

DR. BAHAEDDİN ŞAKİR (1877–1922). Doctor and one of the important members of inner group in CUP. Banished to Erzincan for revolutionary activity (1891), escaped to Egypt and Paris. Worked with Ahmed Rıza and established paper *Şurayı Ümmet*. After the Revolution never became deputy or minister; worked in inner organization. Member of Central Committee (1912–18); chief of political section of *Teşkilâtı Mahsusa* (1914). Escaped to Berlin after war. Baku conference (1920). Assassinated by Armenians (1922).

ABDURRAHMAN ŞEREF (1853–1925). Historian and minister. Born in Istanbul, son of Hasan Efendi. Educated at *Galatasaray* and taught at *Mülkiye*. Appointed to Senate after restoration of constitution. Minister of Education in Hilmi Paşa's first Cabinet and Said's 1911 Cabinet. His fame as historian rests on *Tarih-i Devlet-i Osmaniye*, 2 vols. (Istanbul, 1309 A.H.) and *Tarih Musahabeleri* (Istanbul, 1340 A.H.). Also taught at *Darülfünun*.

ŞERİF PAŞA (1865–1944). Diplomat and organizer of Liberal opposition abroad. Kurd by origin. Ottoman ambassador in Stockholm at time of Revolution, he seems to have hoped for high position under Young Turks. Hopes frustrated. Organized anti-Unionist movement in Paris called *İslâhatı Esasiyei Osmaniye Fırkası*; French name: Le Parti Radical Ottoman. Living in France, opposed to Turkey's entry into war. In 1918, at peace conference organized Kurdish Committee called '*Khoybur*' aiming at establishing a Kurdish state. Idea was to frustrate Armenian designs on Kurdish areas.

MAHMUD ŞEVKET PAŞA (1856–1913). Soldier, minister, and Grand Vezir. Born in Iraq, the son of Süleyman Bey, *mutasarrıf* of Basra. Graduated from *Harbiye* (1882); spent about nine years in Germany. *Vali* of Kosova at the time of the Revolution. Given command of III Army, became most powerful figure in Empire after crushing April 1909 insurrection. Never joined Committee; only tolerated it because of its patriotic ideology which coincided with his own sentiment.

MİDHAT ŞÜKRÜ [BLEDA] (1874–1957). Unionist politician and very high in inner councils of CUP. Accountant in local education department in Salonika. Founder-member of *Osmanlı Hürriyet Cemiyeti* (1906) which later became CUP. Forced to escape to Europe because of revolutionary activity; worked in Geneva branch of Committee. After the Revolution elected deputy for Serez (1908), Drama (1912), and Burdur (1916 by-election). Almost a permanent member of the Central Committee and *Kâtibi Umumî* (1917–18).

MEHMED TALÂT (1874–1921). Unionist deputy, minister, and Grand Vezir, and most important single member of Committee, giving it much of its character. Of humble origin and limited education, taught Turkish at Jewish school in Edirne and worked in post office. Said to be a *Bektaşi*; founder-member of *Osmanlı Hürriyet Cemiyeti* (1906). After the Revolution deputy for Edirne in all three Parliaments, Minister of the Interior in a number of Cabinets, and leader of the main faction in the Committee. Became Grand Vezir (1917), resigning in 1918 at dissolution of Committee. Escaped to Europe and was assassinated in Berlin on 16 March 1921. Said to be a shrewd politician, he was also a man possessing great charm and personal integrity.

SEYYİD TALİB. Arab nationalist deputy and Iraqi politician. Came from family of notables which provided the '*Naqib al-Ashraf*' of Basra. Related by marriage to family of Abu Huda al Seyyidi, one of the most influential men in *Yıldız* under Abdülhamid. After the Revolution represented Basra in Parliament (1908–14), and led Arab faction. His resignation on 3 June 1914 showed that CUP had failed to reach agreement with Arabs in Parliament. Played double game with British and Turks during war. Head of provisional Iraqi government after war.

AHMED TEVFİK PAŞA (1845–1936). Diplomat and Grand Vezir. Trained as soldier, resigned (1865) and joined Translation Bureau of Sublime Porte. Posted to Rome (1872), Vienna (1873), Athens (1875). Ambassador to Berlin (1885). Foreign Minister (1895), and again in Said's 1908 Cabinet. Deeply attached to Palace and hostile towards Unionists, appointed Grand Vezir on 14 April 1909. After insurrection, ambassador to London (1909–14). After the war formed two ministries in 1919. President of Senate (1920) and last Grand Vezir of the Ottoman Empire (November 1920).

ABDÜLHAMİD ZEHRAWİ (1871–1916). Arab nationalist deputy. Before the Revolution edited a secret anti-Hamidian paper in Homs. Escaped to Egypt and spent years 1902–8 there. Elected deputy for Hama (1908); deputy speaker of Chamber (1911). Prominent in Liberal Party. President of Arab Congress in Paris (1913); Senator (1913). Member of *ülema*; expert on Islamic law (*fikh*) and philosophy. Wanted to be appointed *Şeyhülislâm*. Hanged by Cemal Paşa (1916) along with other Arab notables for conspiring against Porte.

ZEKİ BEY. Difficult to identify with absolute certainty. Seems to have become a general and Paşa after 1914 military purges. Zeki Paşa was appointed adjutant to Kaiser in November 1914 and military representative at German headquarters during war. Accompanied İbrahim Hakkı to Brest-Litovsk (1918) as plenipotentiary. Close to Enver Paşa.

HALİD ZİYA [UŞAKLIGİL] (1866–1945). Leading author and Unionist. Came from prominent family, son of Hacı Halil. Edited *Nevruz* in İzmir and *Servet-i Fünun* (1896); worked in civil service and later in the tobacco *régie*. After the Revolution lectured at the university on aesthetics and foreign literature. Appointed First Secretary to Sultan (1909); wrote *Saray ve Ötesi*, 3 vols. (Istanbul, 1940–2), describing his experience. Diplomatic missions to Europe (1913–14). In the Republic took little part in nationalist literary developments, preferring to remain the old cosmopolitan.

MEHMED ZİYA [GÖKALP] (1875/6–1924). Nationalist ideologue, poet, philosopher, and sociologist. Born in Diyarbakır, came to Istanbul (1896) for further education and joined CUP. Imprisoned and banished to Diyarbakır for revolutionary activities (1897). After the Revolution went to 1909 Congress in Salonika as representative of local branch. Elected a member of Central Committee, a position he held until 1918. Very close to Talât. During decade, Ziya taught philosophy, wrote and edited periodicals, evolved and clarified ideas on ideology. Arrested and deported by allies to Malta (1919), had a cool reception from Kemalists on his return in 1921. Later reconciled with Kemalists, he was deputy for Diyarbakır in the second Parliament.

BIBLIOGRAPHY

A. UNPUBLISHED MATERIALS

(i) FOREIGN OFFICE ARCHIVES. Correspondence between The Foreign Office, London, and the British Embassy, Istanbul, at the Public Record Office (PRO), London.

1908—F.O.	371/540 ff.	
1909	/747 ff.	
1910	/991 ff.	
1911	/1228 ff.	
1912	/1481 ff.	
1913	/1757 ff.	
1914	/2137/79138 (contains Annual Report for 1913)	

(ii) EMBASSY AND CONSULAR ARCHIVES. Correspondence between the British Embassy, Istanbul, and British Consulates in the Ottoman Empire, and other miscellaneous correspondence, at PRO, London.

1908—F.O. 195/2280	(Constantinople)
/2281	(Dragomans)
/2290	(Military Attaché)
/2297 /2298	(From Salonica)
/2302	(Sublime Porte)
1909—F.O. 195/2315	(Constantinople)
/2316	(Dragomans)
/2322	(Memoranda)
/2323	(Military Attaché)
/2328–30	(From Salonica)
/2333	(Sublime Porte)
1910—F.O. 195/2335	(Adrianople)
/2345	(Constantinople–Crete)
/2346	(Dragomans, Military Attaché)
/2352	(Circulars to Consuls, Memoranda)
/2357–9	(From Salonica)
/2361	(Sublime Porte)
1911—F.O. 195/2364	(Adrianople)
/2374	(Constantinople)
/2381–2	(From Salonica)
/2384–5	(Sublime Porte)
/2386	(Trebizond, Dragomans, Military Attaché, Memoranda, Circulars to Consuls)

1912—F.O. 195/2387	Files 1–4	
	/2388	8–20
	/2389	24
	/2390	24
	/2391	25–40
	/2392	41–50
1913—F.O. 195/2448	(Balkan Wars Peace Negotiations)	
	/2451/340	(*Coup d'état*, January 1913)
	/423	(The Arabs and the CUP)
	/2452/928	(England and Turkey)
	/1299	(The Turkish Throne)
	/1574	(Kiamil Pasha)
	/5396	(Conversation with Jemal Bey, later Paşa)

(iii) PRIVATE PAPERS at PRO, London.

1. *Bertie Papers*, 1899–1919.

(Papers of Francis Leveson Bertie, first Viscount Bertie of Thame, 1844–1919, and ambassador at Paris, 1905–18.)
F.O. 800/72

2. *Grey Papers*, 1905–16.

(Papers of Edward Grey, third Baronet and Viscount Grey of Fallodon, 1862–1913. Foreign Secretary 1905–16.)
F.O. 800/78 1905–10 (General)
/79 1911–16 (General)
/91 1905–8 (Memoranda)
/92 1909–11 (Memoranda)
/93 1912–14 (Memoranda)

3. *Hardinge Papers*, 1906–11.

(Papers of Charles Hardinge, Baron Hardinge of Penshurst, 1858–1944, and Permanent Under-Secretary of State, F.O., 1906–10.)
F.O. 800/184

4. *Lowther Papers*, 1908–13.

(Papers of Gerard Augustus Lowther, ambassador at Istanbul, 1908–1913.)
F.O. 800/185A (Turkey)

5. *Vambery Papers*

F.O. 800/32 1895–1911

B. NEWSPAPERS

(i) TURKISH

İkdam (İstanbul). It also appeared as *Yeni İkdam* and *İktiham*.
Sabah (İstanbul).
Sedayi Millet (İstanbul).

184 BIBLIOGRAPHY

Serbesti (İstanbul).
Şurayi Ümmet (İstanbul).
Takvim-i Vekayi (İstanbul).
Tanin (İstanbul). It also appeared as *Yeni Tanin, Cenin, Senin, Renin*, and *Hak*.

(ii) OTHER LANGUAGES

The Levant Herald and Eastern Express (İstanbul).
Stamboul (İstanbul).
The Times (London).

C. MEMOIRS

(i) TURKISH

Abdülhamid. *İkinci Abdülhamid'in Hatıra Defteri*. İstanbul, 1960.

Cavit, Mehmet. 'Meşrutiyet Devrine ait Cavit Beyin Hatıraları', *Tanin*, 3 August 1943–22 December 1946.

Cemal Paşa. *Hatıralar*, ed. Behçet Cemal. İstanbul, 1959.

Cemalüddin Efendi. *Hatırat-ı Siyasiye*. İstanbul, 1920 (1336).

Cevat, Ali. *İkinci Meşrutiyetin İlânı ve Otuzbir Mart Hadisesi*, ed. F. R. Unat. Ankara, (1960).

Duru, Kâzım Nami. *İttihat ve Terakki Hatıralarım*. İstanbul, 1957.

—— *Arnavutluk ve Mekadonya Hatıralarım*. İstanbul, 1959.

Kuran, Ahmed Bedevi. *Harbiye Mektebinde Hürriyet Mücadelesi*. Istanbul, n.d.

Menteşe, Halil. 'Eski Meclisi Mebusan Reisi Halil Menteşenin Hatıraları', *Cumhuriyet*, 13 October–11 December 1946.

Midhat, Ali Haydar. *Hatıralarım, 1872–1946*. İstanbul, 1946.

Nadi, Yunus. *İhtilâl ve İnkılâb-ı Osmanî*. İstanbul, 1909 (1325). Extracts in *Cumhuriyet*, 31 March–21 April 1959.

Niyazi, Ahmed. *Hatırat-ı Niyazi*. İstanbul, 1910 (1326).

Rıza, Ahmed. 'İlk Meclisi Mebusan Reisi Ahmet Rıza Beyin Hatıraları', *Cumhuriyet*, 26 January–19 February 1950.

Tahsin Paşa. *Abdülhamid ve Yıldız Hatıraları*. İstanbul, 1931.

Talât Paşa. *Talât Paşanın Hatıraları*, ed. H. C. Yalçın, 2nd ed. İstanbul, 1958.

Tansu, Samih Nâfiz. *İki Devrin Perde Arkası*. İstanbul, 1964.

Türkgeldi, Ali Fuad. *Görüp İşittiklerim*, 2nd ed. Ankara, 1951.

Uşaklıgil, Halid Ziya. *Saray ve Ötesi*, 3 vols. İstanbul, 1940–1.

Yalçın, Hüseyin Cahit. 'Meşrutiyet Hatıraları, 1908–1918', *Fikir Hareketleri*, no. 71 ff., 28 February 1935.

(ii) OTHERS

Djemal Pasha, Ahmed. *Memories of a Turkish statesman, 1913–1919*. London, 1922.

Grey, Edward. *Twenty-five years, 1892–1916*. London, 1925.

Hardinge, Charles. *Old diplomacy*. London, 1947.

Kemal, İsmail. *The memoirs of İsmail Kemal Bey*, ed. Sommerville Story, London, 1920.

Pears, Sir Edwin. *Forty years in Constantinople*. London, 1916.

Ramsay, Sir W. M. *The revolution in Constantinople and Turkey. A diary*. London, 1909.

Ryan, Sir Andrew. *The last of the Dragomans*. London, 1951.

Sanders, Liman von. *Five years in Turkey*. Annapolis, 1927.

Sazonov, Serge. *Fateful years*. London, 1928.

Talaat Pasha. 'Posthumous memoirs of Talaat Pasha', *Current history*, v. New York, 1921.

Townshend, A. F. *A military consul in Turkey*. London, 1910.

Tugay, Emine Foat. *Three centuries*. London, 1963.

Vambery, Armin. 'Personal recollections of Abdul Hamid and his Court' *NC*, lxv (June 1909), 980–93; lxvi (July 1909), 69–88.

—— *The story of my struggles*. London, 1913.

Waugh, Sir Telford. *Turkey, yesterday, today and to-morrow*. London, 1930.

Whitman, Sidney. *Turkish memories*. London, 1914.

D. BOOKS AND ARTICLES
(i) TURKISH

A. A. A. (Abdülhak Adnan-Adıvar). 'İbrahim Hakkı Paşa', *İA*, v/11 (1951), 892–4.

Akyüz, Kenan. *Tevfik Fikret*. Ankara, 1947.

Amca, Hasan. *Doğmayan Hürriyet*. İstanbul, 1958.

Avni, Hüseyin. *Bir Yarım Müstemleke Oluş Tarihi*. İstanbul, 1932.

—— *1908 de Ecnebi Sermayesine Karşı İlk Kalkınmalar*. İstanbul, 1935.

Baysun, Cavid. 'Ahmed Muhtar Paşa', *İA*, viii (1959), 516–32.

Bayur, Hilmi Kâmil, *Sadrazam Kâmil Paşa — Siyasî Hayatı*. Ankara, 1954.

Bayur, Yusuf Hikmet. *Türk İnkilâbı Tarihi*, i, ii, pts. 1–2. İstanbul, 1940–3.

—— 'İkinci Meşrutiyet Devri Üzerinde Bazı Düşünceler', *Bell.* xxiii/90 (1959), 267–85.

Berkes, Niyazi. *Batıcılık, Ulusculuk ve Toplumsal Devrimler*. İstanbul, 1965.

Bleda, Mithat Şükrü. 'Bir Canlı Tarih Konuşuyor', *Resimli Tarih Mecmuası* (April, June, July 1953), 2196–74, 2392–7, and 2442–6 respectively.

Brockelmann, C. 'Bustani-Süleyman', *İA*, ii (1944), 284–5.

Çankaya, A. *Mülkiye Tarihi ve Mülkiyeliler*, 2 vols. Ankara, 1954.

Çapanoğlu, Münir Süleyman. *Türkiye'de Sosyalizm Hareketleri ve Sosyalist Hilmi.* İstanbul, 1964.

Danişmend, İsmail Hami. *İzahlı Osmanlı Tarihi Kronolojisi,* iv. İstanbul, 1961.

—— *31 Mart Vak'ası.* İstanbul, 1961.

Daver, Abidin. '31 Mart Vak'asının 42[inci] Yıldönümündeyiz', *Cumhuriyet,* 13 April 1951.

—— 'Hareket Ordusu Istanbula Nasıl Girmişti?', ibid., 24 April 1951.

Duru, Kâzım Nami. *Ziya Gökalp.* İstanbul, 1949.

Ergin, Osman. *Türkiye Maarif Tarihi,* 5 vols. İstanbul, 1939–43.

—— 'Babıâli', *Tarih Dünyası,* i/IX. 386–94.

Eroğlu, Lütfü. '31 Mart İsyanı', *AA,* lx (April 1949), 1716–19.

Gökbilgin, M. Tayyib. 'Babıâli', *İA,* ii (1942), 174–7.

—— 'Edirne', ibid. iv (1946), 107–27.

Göksel, Ali Nüzhet. *Ziya Gökalp,* 4th ed. İstanbul, 1963.

Gözübüyük, A. Şeref, and Kili, Suna. *Türk Anayasa Metinleri.* Ankara, 1957.

Günyol, Vedad. 'Matbuat: Türkler, pt. i — Türkiye', *İA,* vii (1956), 367–80.

Hamdi, Ali. 'Fedai Atıf Bey ve Şemsi Paşanın Katli', *Resimli Tarih Mecmuası,* lxv (May 1955), 3828–31.

İnal, Mahmud Kemal. *Osmanlı Devrinde Son Sadrıazamlar,* 14 pts. İstanbul, 1940–53.

İskit, Server. *Türkiyede Matbuat Rejimleri.* İstanbul, 1939.

—— *Türkiyede Matbuat İdareleri ve Politikaları.* İstanbul, 1943.

Kaplan, Mehmet. *Tevfik Fikret ve Şiiri.* İstanbul, 1946.

—— 'Halid Ziya', *İA,* v/I (1948), 143–7.

Karal, Enver Ziya. 'Mehmed V', ibid. vii (1956), 557–62.

Karpat, Kemal H. *Çağdaş Türk Edebiyatında Sosyal Konular.* İstanbul, 1962.

Kızıldoğan, Hüsrev, Sami. 'Vatan ve Hürriyet = İttihat ve Terakki', *Belleten,* i (1937), 619–25.

Koçu, Reşad Ekrem. *Osmanlı Muahedeleri ve Kapitülasyonlar.* İstanbul, 1934.

—— 'Türkiye'de Seçimin Tarihi, 1877–1950', *Tarih Dünyası,* i/V–VII (1950).

Kubalı, Hüseyin Nâil. 'Kanun-i Esasi: Türk Kanun-i Esasileri', *İA,* vi (1952), 168–75.

Külçe, Süleyman. *Firzovik Toplantısı ve Meşrutiyet.* İzmir, 1944.

—— *Türkiyede Masonluk.* İzmir, 1948.

Kuran, Ahmed Bedevi. *Osmanlı İmparatorluğunda İnkılâp Hareketleri ve Milli Mücadele.* İstanbul, 1959.

BIBLIOGRAPHY 187

Kuran, Ercüment. 'Said Paşa', *İA*, x (1964), 82–6.

Mardin, Şerif Ârif. *Jön Türklerin Siyasî Fikirleri, 1895–1908*. Ankara, 1964.

Nur, Rıza. *Hürriyet ve İtilâf Nasıl Doğdu ve Nasıl Öldü?* İstanbul, 1918.

Okandan, Recai G. *Amme Hukukumuzun Ana Hatları*, 4th ed. İstanbul, 1959.

Ongunsu, A. H. 'Abdülhamid II', *İA*, i (1943), 76–8.

Pakalın, Mehmed Zeki. *Son Sadrıazamlar ve Başvekiler* (vol. v deals with Mehmed Said Paşa). İstanbul, 1948.

Ragıp, Mustafa. *İttihat ve Terakki Tarihinde Esrar Perdesi.* İstanbul, 1934.

—— 'Meşrutiyet Devrinde İntihap Mücadeleleri', *Akşam*, 18 March 1943.

—— 'İntihabatta Parti İhtirası', ibid., 25 March 1943.

Reşad, Dr. Nihad. 'İttihad ve Terakkinin Muhaliflerle Temasları', *Cumhuriyet*, 22 November 1946.

Sabahattin, Prens. *Türkiye Nasıl Kurtarılabilir?* İstanbul, 1965.

Sadiq, Mohammad. 'Türkiye'de İkinci Meşrutiyet Devrinde Fikir Cereyanları' (unpublished Ph.D., Ankara University, 1964).

Sayman, Ferit H. 'Türkiye'de Sendika Hürriyeti', *Sosyal Hukuk ve İktisat Mecmuası*, i (September 1948).

Soysal, Mümtaz. *Dış Politika ve Parlamento*. Ankara, 1964.

Sülker, Kemal. *Türkiyede Sendikacılık.* İstanbul, 1955,

Sussheim, K. 'Arnavutluk', *İA*, i (1942), 573–92.

Şapolyo, Enver Behnan. *Ziya Gökalp, İttihat ve Terakki ve Meşrutiyet Tarihi.* İstanbul, 1943.

Şehsuvaroğlu, Dr. Bedii N. 'İkinci Meşrutiyet ve Âtıf Bey', *Belleten*, xxiii (1959), 307–32.

Şehsuvaroğlu, Haluk. 'Bir Hatıratın Son Sayfaları', *Akşam*, 1 March 1950.

—— 'Ahmet Rıza ve Muarızları', ibid., 14 January 1950.

—— '31 Mart Vak'ası', *Cumhuriyet*, 11 May 1951.

Tugay, Asaf. *İbret*, 2 vols. İstanbul, 1962.

Tunaya, Tarık Zafer. 'Jön Türk ve Sosyal İnkılâp Lideri Sabahaddin', *Sosyal, Hukuk ve İktisat Mecmuası*, iii (November 1948), 119–26.

—— '31 Mart Vaka'sı', *Vatan*, 10 March 1949.

—— 'Türkiyede İlk İrtica Partisi İttihadı Muhammedi Fırkası', ibid., 16 March 1949.

—— '41 Yıl Sonra Hürriyetin İlânı', ibid., 23 July 1949.

—— İkinci Meşrutiyet', ibid., 23 July 1950.

—— *Türkiye'de Siyasî Partiler (1859–1952).* İstanbul, 1952.

—— *Türkiye'nin Siyasî Hayatında Batılılaşma Hareketleri.* İstanbul, 1960.

—— *İslâmcılık Cereyanı.* İstanbul, 1962.

Turhan, Mümtaz. *Kültür Değişmeleri*, 1st ed. İstanbul, 1959.

188 BIBLIOGRAPHY

Tütengil, Cavit Orhan. *Prens Sabahattin.* İstanbul, 1954.

Uzunçarşılı, İsmail Hakkı. 'Gazi Ahmet Muhtar Paşaya Dair', *Resimli Tarih Mecmuası*, 1 (August 1954), 3273–5.

——'II Abdülhamid Devrinde Kâmil Paşa', *Belleten*, xix/73 (1955), 203–18.

——'1908 Yılında İkinci Meşrutiyetin ne Suretle İlân Edildiğine dair Vesikalar', ibid. xx/77 (1956), 103–74.

Yalçın, Hüseyin Cahit. *Talât Paşa.* İstanbul, 1943.

——'Edirnenin İşgali ve Kurtuluşu', *Tanin*, 26 March 1944.

——'Bizde Türkçülük', ibid., 18 May 1944.

——'Turancılık Hareketi', ibid., 19 May 1944.

(ii) OTHERS

Abbott, G. F. *Turkey in transition.* London, 1909.

—— *The holy war in Tripoli.* London, 1912.

——'Peace?', *NC*, lxxiii (1913), 41–52.

Ahmad, Feroz. 'Great Britain's relations with the Young Turks, 1908-1914', *MES*, ii/iv (July 1966), 302–29.

—— Articles on Hüseyin Hilmi and İbrahim Hakkı, in *EI²*.

Allen, W. E. D. *The Turks in Europe.* London, 1919.

Aristarchi, G. *Législation ottomane*, v. Istanbul, 1878.

Askew, W. C. *Europe and Italy's acquisition of Libya.* Durham, North Carolina, 1942.

Barclay, Sir Thomas. *The Turco-Italian war and its problems.* London, 1912.

Benaroya, Abraham. 'A note on "The Socialist Federation of Saloniki"', *Jewish Social Studies*, ii (1949), 69–72.

Bennett, E. N. 'Press censors and war correspondents: Some experiences in Turkey', *NC*, lxxiii (1913), 28–40.

Bérard, É. V. *La Révolution turque.* Paris, 1909.

—— *La Mort de Stamboul.* Paris, 1913.

Berkes, Niyazi. *Turkish nationalism and western civilization: Selected Essays of Ziya Gökalp.* London, 1959.

——'Historical background of Turkish secularism', in *Islam and the West*, ed. Richard N. Frye. The Hague, 1957, 41–68.

—— *The development of secularism in Turkey.* Montreal, 1964.

Bilinski, A. Rustem Bey de. 'The Turkish army', *CR*, xcii (September 1907), 403–9.

——'The Turkish revolution', ibid. lxiv (September 1908), 253–72.

Biliotti, Adrien, and Sedad, Ahmed. *Législation ottomane depuis le rétablissement de la Constitution 24 Djemazi-ul-Ahir 1326-10 juillet 1326.* Paris, 1912.

Birge, J. K. *A guide to Turkish area study*. Washington, 1949.

Blaisdell, A. C. *European financial control in the Ottoman empire*. New York. 1929.

Bouvat, L. 'La guerre balkanique dans la presse ottomane', *RMM*, xxi (1912), 222–37.

Butterfield, Herbert. 'Sir Edward Grey in July 1914', Irish Conference of Historians, *Historical Studies*, v (London, 1965), 1–25.

Buxton, Charles R. *Turkey in revolution*. London, 1909.

Buxton, Noel. 'The Young Turks', *NC*, lxv (1909), 16–24.

—— 'Young Turkey after two years', ibid. lxix (1911), 417–32.

Cachia, A. J. *Libya under the second Ottoman occupation (1835–1911)*. Tripoli, 1945.

Chapman, Mary K. *Great Britain and the Baghdad railway, 1888–1914*. Massachusetts, 1948.

Charlton, Hon. Mrs. Zeeneb. 'Six Osmanli patriots', *NC*, lxxiv (1913), 1220–9.

A. L. C. (A. le Chatalier). 'La Contre-Révolution', *RMM*, vii (1909), 451–69.

Conker, Orhan, and Witmeur, Émile. *Redressement économique et industrialisation de la nouvelle Turquie*. Paris, 1937.

Conwell-Evans, T. P. *Foreign policy from a back bench, 1904–1918* (a study based on the papers of Lord Noel-Buxton). London, 1932.

Cunningham, Allan. "Dragomania": The Dragomans of the British Embassy in Turkey', *St. Antony's papers*, no. 11, *MEA*, no. 2 (London, 1961), 81–100.

—— 'The wrong horse?—A study of Anglo-Turkish relations before the First World War', ibid., no. 17, *MEA*, no. 4 (Oxford, 1965), 56–76.

David, Wade Dewood. *European diplomacy in the Near Eastern question 1906–1909*. Illinois, 1940.

Davison, Roderic H. 'Turkish attitudes concerning Christian–Muslim equality in the nineteenth century', *American Historical Review*, lix (1953–4), 844–64.

—— *Reform in the Ottoman empire, 1856–1876*. Princeton, New Jersey, 1963.

Denais, Joseph. *La Turquie nouvelle et l'Ancien Régime*. Paris, 1909.

De Novo, J. A. *American interests and policies in the Middle East, 1900–1939*. Minnesota, 1963.

Deny, Jean. 'Zia Goek Alp', *RMM*, lxi (1925), 1–41.

—— 'Abd al-Hamid II', *EI²*.

—— 'Ahmad Wafik Pasha (Ahmet Vefik Paşa)', ibid.

Devereux, Robert. *The first Ottoman constitutional period: A study of the Midhat constitution and parliament*. Baltimore, 1963.

Dillon, E. J. 'The unforeseen happens as usual', *CR*, xciv (1908), 364–84.

Dillon, E. J. 'The reforming Turk', *QR*, ccx (1909), 231–53.

—— 'A clue to the Turkish tangle', *CR*, xcv (1909), 743–56.

Diplomatist (George Young). *Nationalism and war in the Near East.* London, 1915.

Dugdale. E. T. S. *German diplomatic documents, 1871–1914,* iii–iv. London, 1930–1.

Earle, E. M. *Turkey, the great powers and the Baghdad railway.* London, 1923.

Edib, Halide (Adıvar). *Memoirs of Halide Edib.* London, 1926.

—— *Turkey faces west.* New Haven, 1930.

—— *Conflict of east and west in Turkey,* 3rd ed. Lahore, 1963.

Emin, Ahmed. *The development of modern Turkey as measured by its press.* New York, 1914.

Fehmi, Yusuf. *La Révolution ottomane, 1908–1910.* Paris, 1911.

—— *Considérations sur la Turquie vaincue.* Paris, 1913.

Feis, Herbert. *Europe, the world's banker, 1870–1914.* New Haven, 1930.

Fesch, Paul. *Les Jeunes Turcs.* Paris, 1909.

Franco, Gad. *Développements constitutionnels en Turquie.* Constantinople, 1925.

Frey, Fredrick W. *The Turkish political élite.* M.I.T., 1965

Fua, Albert. *Le Comité Union et Progrès contre la Constitution.* Paris, 1912.

Gooch, G., P. and Temperley, H. *British documents on the origins of the war, 1898–1914,* v. ix/1. London, 1928 and 1933.

Gordon, Leland James. *American relations with Turkey, 1830–1930, an economic interpretation.* Philadelphia, 1932.

Graves, Philip P. *Briton and Turk.* London, 1941.

Gwinner, Arthur von. 'The Baghdad railway and the quest of British co-operation', *NC*, lxv (1909), 1083–94.

Halil Halid (Bey). 'The origin of the revolt in Turkey', ibid. lxv (1909), 755–60.

Halpern, Manfred. *The politics of social change in the Middle East and North Africa.* Princeton, 1963.

Hamilton, Angus. 'Turkey: The old regime and the new', *FR*, lxxxiv (1908), 369–82.

Hammann, Otto. *The world policy of Germany, 1890–1912.* London, 1927.

Haupt, G. 'Le début du mouvement socialiste en Turquie', *Mouvement social,* xlv (1963), 121–37.

Helmreich, E. C. *Diplomacy of the Balkan wars, 1912–1913.* Massachusetts, 1938.

Herbert, Captain von. 'Kiamil Pasha and the succession in Turkey', *FR*, lxxxiv (1908), 419–29.

Hertslet, Sir Edward. *The map of Europe by treaty,* iv. London, 1891.

Heyd, Uriel. *Foundation of Turkish nationalism*. London, 1958.

Howard, Harry N. *The partition of Turkey, a diplomatic history, 1913–1923*. Norman University of Oklahoma Press, 1931.

Hurewitz, J. C. *Diplomacy in the Near and Middle East, 1535–1914*, i. Princeton, New Jersey, 1956.

Jackh, Ernest. *The rising crescent*. New York, 1944.

Karpat, Kemal H. *Turkey's politics: The transition to a multi-party system*. Princeton, New Jersey, 1959.

Kazancıgil, O. R. *Le Prince M. Sabaheddine: ses idées, sa carrière*. Paris, 1948.

Key, Kerim K. 'The origins of Turkish political parties', *World Affairs Interpreter* (April 1955), 49–60.

Knight, Edward Fredrick. *The awakening of Turkey*. London, 1909.

Langer, William L. 'Russia, the Straits question and the origins of the Balkan league', *Political Science Quarterly*, xliii (1928), 321–63.

Lee, Dwight, E. 'The origins of Pan-Islamism', *American Historical Review* (1942), 278–87.

Lewis, Bernard. 'History-writing and national revival in Turkey', *MEA*, iv (1953), 218–27.

—— 'The impact of the French revolution on Turkey', *Journal of World History* (1953), 105–25.

—— 'Turkey: Westernization', in Gustave E. von Grunebaum (ed.), *Unity and variety in Muslim civilization*. Chicago, 1955, 311–31.

—— 'Bab-i Mashikhat', *EI²*.

—— 'Başvekil and Başvekalet Arşivi', ibid.

—— 'Dustur (Turkey)', ibid.

—— 'Düyûn-i 'Umumiyye', ibid.

—— *The emergence of modern Turkey*. Oxford University Press, 3rd ed., 1965.

Lewis, G. L. *Turkey*, 2nd ed. London, 1959.

McCullagh, Francis. 'The Constantinople mutiny of April 13th', *FR*, lxxxvi (1909), 58–69.

MacDonald, John. *Turkey and the eastern question*. London, 1912.

Mandelstam, Andrei Nikolaevich. *Le Sort de l'Empire ottoman*. Lausanne, 1917.

Mardin, Şerif. *The genesis of young Ottoman thought*. Princeton, 1962.

—— 'Libertarian movements in the Ottoman empire 1878–1895', *MEJ*, xiv (1962), 169–82.

Margoliouth, D. S. 'Constantinople at the declaration of the constitution', *FR*, lxxxiv (1908), 563–70.

—— *The fall of Abd-ul-Hamid*. London, 1910.

Mears, E. G., and others. *Modern Turkey*. New York, 1924.

Midhat, Ali Haider. *The life of Midhat Pasha*. London, 1903.

Miller, W. *The Ottoman empire and its successors*. Cambridge, 1923.

Ministère des Affaires Étrangères. *Documents diplomatiques français* (*1871–1914*), 2nd series (1901–14), xi, xiv (1950–6); 3rd series (1911–14), i–vi (Paris, 1931–3).

Moukhtar Pacha, Mahmoud. *Mon Commandement au cours de la campagne des Balkans de 1912*. Paris–Nancy, 1913.

—— *La Turquie, l'Allemagne et l'Europe depuis le Traité de Berlin*. Paris, 1924.

Nicolaidès, N. *Une Année de constitution: 11/24 juillet 1908–11/24 juillet 1909*. Bruxelles, 1909.

Nuri, Subhi. *Le Régime représentatif en Turquie*. Paris, 1914.

Ostrorog, Léon. *Pour la réforme de la justice ottomane*. Paris, 1912.

——*The Turkish problem* (English trans., Winifred Stephens). London, 1919.

Ozanne, J. W. 'The Balkan fiasco', *NC*, lxxiv (1913), 295–300.

Pears, Sir Edwin. 'Christians and Islam in Turkey', ibid. lxxiii (1913), 278–91.

—— *Life of Abdul Hamid*. London, 1917.

Pilcher, George. 'In the Chatalja lines during the November battle', *NC*, lxxiii, (1913), 624–43.

Pinon, René. *L'Europe et la Jeune Turquie*, 2nd ed. Paris, 1911.

Presland, John. *Deedes Bey*. London, 1942.

Ramsaur, E. E. 'The Bektashi dervishes and the Young Turks', *Moslem World*, xxxii (1942), 7–14.

—— *The Young Turks: Prelude to the revolution of 1908*, Princeton, 1957.

Rankin, Reginald. *The inner history of the Balkan war*. London, 1914.

Rodkey, F. S. 'Ottoman concern about western economic penetration in the Levant, 1849–1856', *Journal of Modern History*, xxx (1956), 348–53.

Rouvière, Franck. *Essai sur l'évolution des idées constitutionnelles en Turquie*. Montpellier, 1910.

Rustow, D. A. 'The Near East', in G. A. Almond and J. S. Coleman (eds.), *The politics of developing areas*. Princeton, New Jersey, 1960.

—— Articles on Djam'iyya (section on Turkey), Djavid Bey, Enwer Pasha, and *Damad* Ferid Pasha, in *EI²*.

Sadiq, Mohammad. 'Religion and politics in Turkey, 1908–18', *Bulletin of the Institute of Islamic Studies*. Aligarh University, nos. 8–9, 1964–5 (not seen).

Sarrou, H. M. A. *La Jeune Turquie et la révolution*. Paris–Nancy, 1912.

Smith, Elaine D. *Turkey: Origins of the Kemalist movement, 1919–1923*. Washington, D.C., 1959.

Sousa, Nasim. *The capitulary régime of Turkey, its history, origin and nature.* Baltimore, 1933.

Starr, Joshua. 'The Socialist Federation of Saloniki', *Jewish Social Studies*, vii (1945), 323–6.

Stavrianos, L. S. 'The Balkan committee', *The Queen's Quarterly*, xlviii (1941), 258–67.

Storrs, Ronald. *Orientations.* London, 1937.

Strupp, Dr. Karl. *Ausgewählte diplomatische Aktenstücke zur orientalischen Frage.* Gotha, 1916.

Temperley, Harold. 'British policy towards parliamentary rule and constitutionalism in Turkey (1830–1914)', *CHJ*, iv (1932–4), 156–91.

Thaden, Edward C. *Russia and the Balkan alliance of 1912.* University Park, Pa., 1965.

Toynbee, A. J. *Turkey: A past and a future.* New York, 1917.

—— 'The Islamic world since the peace settlement', in *Survey of international affairs*, i (1925).

Tunaya, T. Z. 'Elections in Turkish history', *MEA*, v (1954), 116–19.

Upward, Allen. *The east end of Europe.* London, 1908.

Viator. 'The Turkish revolution', *FR*, lxxxiv (1908), 353–68.

Ward, Sir A. W., and Gooch, G. P. (eds.) *The Cambridge history of British foreign policy, 1783–1919*, iii, *1866–1919*. Cambridge, 1923.

Ward, R. E., and Rustow, D. A. (eds.). *Political modernization in Japan and Turkey.* Princeton, New Jersey, 1964.

Washburn, George. *Fifty years in Constantinople and recollections of Robert College.* New York, 1909.

Whitehouse, J. Howard. 'Bulgaria and Servia in war: The revelation of nationality', *NC*, lxxiii (1913), 19–27.

Woods, H. Charles. 'The situation in Albania and in Macedonia', *FR*, xci (1912), 912–25.

—— 'The internal situation in Turkey and the effect of the war upon it', ibid. xci (1912), 334–46.

'X.' 'Les courants politiques dans la Turquie contemporaine', *RMM*, xxi (1912), 158–221.

—— 'Les rapports du mouvement politique et du mouvement social dans l'Empire ottoman', ibid. xxii (1913), 165–78.

—— 'Doctrines et programmes des partis politiques ottomans', ibid. xxii (1913), 151–64.

—— 'Le Panislamisme et le Panturquisme', ibid. xxii (1913), 179–220.

Zeine, Zeine N. *Arab-Turkish relations and the emergence of Arab nationalism.* Beirut, 1958.

INDEX

(*Note.* Since this book deals with the period before 1934, when the Turks adopted surnames, persons listed in this index have been placed under the last component of the personal name. The surname of those who lived to adopt one is given in square brackets. Turkish titles following the name Ağa, Bey, Efendi, Hanim, or Paşa are not taken into account.)

PRINTED IN GREAT BRITAIN
AT THE UNIVERSITY PRESS, OXFORD
BY VIVIAN RIDLER
PRINTER TO THE UNIVERSITY